Theorizing Sexual Violence

Routledge Research in Gender and Society

Theorizing Sexual Violence

Edited by Renée J. Heberle
and Victoria Grace

Routledge
Taylor & Francis Group
New York   London

First published 2009
by Routledge
711 Third Avenue, New York, NY 10017

Simultaneously published in the UK
by Routledge
2 Park Square, Milton Park, Abingdon, Oxon OX14 4RN

Routledge is an imprint of the Taylor & Francis Group, an informa business

First issued in paperback 2011

© 2009 Taylor & Francis

Typeset in Sabon by IBT Global.

Library of Congress Cataloging in Publication Data

Theorizing sexual violence / edited by Renée J. Heberle and Victoria Grace.
   p. cm. — (Routledge research in gender and society ; 21)
  Includes bibliographical references and index.
  1. Sex crimes. 2. Women — Crimes against. 3. Abused women. 4. Rape.
  5. Sex offenders. I. Heberle, Renée J. II. Grace, Victoria.
  HV6556.T48 2009
  364.15'3 — dc22
  2009003756

ISBN13: 978-0-415-89853-9 (pbk)
ISBN13: 978-0-415-96133-2 (hbk)
ISBN13: 978-0-203-87487-5 (ebk)

Theorizing Sexual Violence

Edited by Renée J. Heberle
and Victoria Grace

Routledge
Taylor & Francis Group
New York   London

First published 2009
by Routledge
711 Third Avenue, New York, NY 10017

Simultaneously published in the UK
by Routledge
2 Park Square, Milton Park, Abingdon, Oxon OX14 4RN

Routledge is an imprint of the Taylor & Francis Group, an informa business
First issued in paperback 2011

© 2009 Taylor & Francis

Typeset in Sabon by IBT Global.

Library of Congress Cataloging in Publication Data
Theorizing sexual violence / edited by Renée J. Heberle and Victoria Grace.
   p. cm. — (Routledge research in gender and society ; 21)
Includes bibliographical references and index.
1. Sex crimes. 2. Women—Crimes against. 3. Abused women. 4. Rape.
5. Sex offenders. I. Heberle, Renée J. II. Grace, Victoria.
HV6556.T48 2009
364.15'3—dc22
2009003756

ISBN13: 978-0-415-89853-9 (pbk)
ISBN13: 978-0-415-96133-2 (hbk)
ISBN13: 978-0-203-87487-5 (ebk)

Contents

Foreword

Joanna Bourke

Sexual violence is heavily researched but undertheorized, declare Renée J. Heberle and Victoria Grace in their introduction to this volume: now is the time for philosophers, historians, sociologists, and political scientists to critique the silences within their own disciplines. The work of critique is urgent. In the mass media and even in some academic circles, sexual torture is being positioned as natural and universal. From prehistoric times to the present, violent men are presented as though they were a constant feature of society. In *A Natural History of Rape: Biological Bases of Forced Sex* (2000), evolutionary psychologists Randy Thornhill and Craig Palmer argued that rape could be seen as a biological imperative.[1] However, as Ann J. Cahill correctly states in this volume, there are "many biological possibilities that are not political realities." Sexual violence is fundamentally situated in historical time and geographical space, and is permeated through and through with humdrum practices, everyday knowledges. Feminist practice and history were founded on habits of critique, both outwards and inwards: therein lies its ability not only to *imagine* a world without sexual violence, but also to *recreate* our world.

For many theorists in this book, the first step involves a reinterrogation of the masculine. Although sexed bodies are both vulnerable and vindictive, there is no "gender equivalence" in sexual violence. Men act in sexually aggressive ways much more frequently than women. Yet, in contemporary theory, the male subject generally appears in cartoonish simplicity, either as all powerful guardians of the phallic imaginary or else as pathetic creatures, emasculated by their own pursuit of power. But, as a number of the chapters in this volume suggest, sexual aggressors are not patriarchy's storm troopers, but its inadequate spawn. As opposed to those theorists assuming the power of the male sex organ, the authors in this volume suggest it is a deeply flawed instrument of power and one with none of the resilience of, for instance, the fist. As Nicola Gavey reminds us in this volume, male genitalia are vulnerable. In talking about weapons of torture, Elaine Scarry refers to the way in which "in converting the other person's pain into his own power, the torturer experiences the entire occurrence exclusively from the nonvulnerable end of the weapon." However, in those forms of sexual abuse involving the penis, the perpetrator's attention begins to "slip down the weapon toward the vulnerable end," contesting its power.[2] This makes penile rape a highly unstable form of torture, both as performance (erectile dysfunction is common, affecting around one-third of all rapes) and as strategy (exposing the brutal force beneath patriarchy's caress).

As I argue in *Rape: A History from the 1860s to the Present* (2007), sexually aggressive men in modern western society actually enervate male power regimes. They corrode the category 'man' and its (imaginary) phallic edifice. In the modern period, compulsory heterosexuality, marriage vows, and the gendered division of labor have been particularly effective ways of controlling women. Although fear of rape has enabled men to assume the mantle of benevolent protectors while further confining 'their' womenfolk to domestic and other purportedly safe spheres, fear is a particularly blunt instrument of domination. The actions of men on the streets, intimidating, harassing and assaulting women, jeopardize the bastion of mature masculinity. Domesticated rapists (husband-rapists, for instance) subvert and threaten masculine governance, in part because they incite female resistance by exposing the brutal force beneath patriarchy's caress.

Further, following this shift in focus to the perpetrator, it is striking to observe how, since the 1980s in particular, the languages of psychological trauma have been co-opted by perpetrators of violence. Indeed, the invention of posttraumatic stress disorder in the 1980s was precisely a mechanism that allowed individuals who had tortured and raped Vietnamese women and men to be portrayed (and to portray themselves) as victims. The diagnosis of posttraumatic stress disorder was given to servicemen who had suffered the 'trauma' of raping and slaughtering other individuals. More recently, in the so-called War on Terror, psychological suffering is routinely used to explain the actions of female and male perpetrators. The *U. S. News and World Report* even blamed the Abu Ghraib torture on "the lack of a reliable local brothel where male soldiers are able to unwind. Experts have long appreciated the fact that sexual activity can often be a way of relieving the anxiety of war."[3] In the words of the popular talk show host Rush Limbaugh speaking about the perpetrators of the Abu Ghraib abuses on CBS News, "You know, these people are being fired at every day . . . you ever heard of emotional release? You of heard [sic] of need to blow some steam off?"[4] Acts of violence become indistinguishable from responses to (perceived or imagined) violence: acts are collapsed into responses. The harm of violence is situated not so much in the tortured bodies of the victims but in the injury done to the military as an institution—as an attack on codes of honor, group cohesion, and military readiness. The victims disappear from history.

This trauma trope—that is, the insistence on victim-status as rationalization (in advance of inflicting pain) and justification (after inflicting pain)—effectively frames the rape itself as a psychological event for the perpetrator while simultaneously erasing the specific corporeal and psychological identity of the victim. She becomes little more than an undifferentiated body-in-pain, the porous body of the sexually tortured. The universalizing of suffering removes the specifics of an individual's history and erases all agentic possibilities. It exchanges the dynamic pursuit of critique for the torpid realm of moral edification.

These universalistic assumptions about sexual violence arise, primarily, out of essentialist notions of the body and its doings. However, there is nothing natural or constant about the body and its sexualization. There is no authentic sexuality free from construction. Anthropological and historical work has long shown that parts of the body labeled and experienced as "sexual" change over time and vary dramatically over geographical space. In other words, the body is sexed through discursive practices. Certain body parts or practices *become* sexual through classification and regulation. Linguistic practices give meaning to bodies. Nevertheless, as I argue in *Rape: A History from the 1860s to the Present*, this sexed being is not merely a blank slate onto which narratives of violence are inscribed. Human subjects *choose* their "coming into being" from a range of discursive practices circulating within their historical time and place. Their choices don't simply "represent" their experience; they *constitute* it. As the philosopher Ann J. Cahill (whose work is also included in this volume) expressed it in her insightful book, *Rethinking Rape*:

> That the embodied subject is understood . . . as constructed by her or his social, historical, and political situation does not necessarily imply that such a subject is wholly and relentlessly determined by the situation. The fact that forces of power act on bodies and affect their literal shape and habits does not indicate that those forces act identically or with equal force on every single body. . . . [I]ndividual subjects . . . respond to the play of forces in radically different ways. . . . the body on which political and social forces act [are not] an inert surface.[5]

The sexed body "acts as an active and sometimes resistant factor," both in processes of subjection (the rape victims Cahill discusses) and those of subjugation (the perpetrators I scrutinize).

If we need to resist universal and essentialist assumptions about sexuality and the body, so too we must resist universalizing the act of sexual assault or rape itself. Obviously, legal definitions of sexual violence vary dramatically, by time period and by national and regional jurisdiction. Even within classificatory boundaries, there are striking differences in legal practice. Thus, in the United States, African Americans, impoverished male adolescents, and male immigrants have been most frequently stigmatized while white professionals and middle-class husbands have been let off the hook. This point is particularly salient when extended globally. International law against rape and torture is only applied to peoples and nations who are categorized as standing outside Anglo-European conceptions of civilization. As legal philosopher Costas Douzinas explained in *Human*

Rights and Empire (2007), the "promotion of morality and the defence of sovereignty . . . served two separate agendas of the great powers: the need to legitimize the new world order through its commitment to rights, without exposing the victorious states to scrutiny and criticism about their own flagrant violations."[6] It is linked to a colonial ideology of the *mission civilisatrice* and, as such, is highly racialized. So, rape as weapon of war and as a technology of dehumanization is effortlessly applied to Bosnia and Rwanda (both dubbed primitive, warring nations), but commentators remain reluctant to draw similar conclusions about reports of the behavior of American and British troops in Iraq and Afghanistan, even after digital culture has provided us with a proliferation of abusive images.

Wartime also provides theorists of sexual violence with particularly sharp illustrations of the problematic concept of "consent" in constructing the female subject. In wartimes, when food, shelter, and life itself depends upon sexual congress, the liberal emphasis on free and informed consent in deciding issues of rape is exposed as a sham. Even in peacetime, definitions of sexual abuse that are predicated on a male-who-acts and a female-who-reacts (through uttering a "no" or "yes") constructs female sexuality as reactive in contrast to an active male sexuality. Theoretically, it is important to note that the notion of consent and its inverse—the notion of "force"—have a history that can, and must, be interrogated.

As a number of theorists in this volume insist, it is dangerous to rely too much on the dichotomy of power versus passivity. There is no consent that is not constrained. Furthermore, as I have argued in a different context, positioning women as either "victim" or "survivor" can be another way of insisting that they have to take responsibility for healing themselves. Politics and material inequalities can be jettisoned; exchanged for speech-acts, or the redemptive potential of confessional speech. Feminist theorist Carine M. Mardorossian has convincingly elaborated this point in "Toward a New Feminist Theory of Rape" (2002). In contrast to second-wave feminism in which the victims showed that they were "more than the sum of their traumatic experiences that they had the ability to act and organize even as they were dealing with the psychic effects of rape," Mardorossian argues that in more recent years victims are represented "as irremediably and unidirectionally shaped by the traumatic experience of rape and hence incapable of dealing with anything but their own inner turmoil." Rape speaks to a woman's "inner self" as opposed to a "criminal act." Indeed, "real victims" (the traumatized) are increasingly distinguished from "angry feminists" (cognitively furious but portrayed as pathological).[7] Even *potential* victims are expected to act in order to prevent their own traumatization. The result is a negative feminist politics that leaves women no room for anything save the paradox of purchasing freedom by investing in the last generation of deadbolt locks.

This positioning of women in passive roles is theoretically dangerous for other reasons as well: it not only advances the notion that women are morally superior to men, it also refuses to admit that women can also be perpetrators of sexual violence. By sorting perpetrators and victims into positions of hierarchy, we are tricked into endorsing some abuse. Although it is undoubtedly true that, in adulthood, women are significantly more likely to be subjected to sexual violence than adult men, for certain groups of humans (most notably children or adults in prisons) the gap is not so startling. Not only the female body, but the male body too, is vulnerable.

The essayists in *Theorizing Sexual Violence* remain committed to a feminism that celebrates sexual pleasure while remaining committed to the fundamental struggle of critique. Power is always contested. Social practice occurs through choices made by subjects within time and place. As Michel Foucault put it in *The History of Sexuality*, "freedom lies in our capacity to discover the historical links between certain modes of self-understanding and modes of domination, and to resist the ways in which we have already been classified and identified by dominant discourses."[8] The role of theory is precisely to demystify dominant discourses and the category of the universal—revealing the fundamental undecidability of the human in the material world. The theoretical analyses in this volume provide us with new languages for rebelliousness and new practices in forging a world without sexual violence.

Joanna Bourke
Professor of History, Birkbeck College, University of London
Author of *Rape: A History from the 1860s to the Present*, Virago

NOTES

1. Randy Thornhill and Craig Palmer, *A Natural History of Rape: Biological Bases of Sexual Coercion* (Cambridge, MA: MIT Press, 2000).
2. Elaine Scarry, *The Body in Pain. The Making and Unmaking of the World* (New York: Oxford University Press, 1985), 59.
3. Marianne Szegedy-Maszak, "Sources of Sadism." *U. S. News and World Report* 136.18, May 24, 2004: 30.
4. "Rush: MPs Just 'Blowing Off Steam,'" CBS News, May 2, 2004, http://www.cbsnews.com/stories/2004/05/06/opinion/meyer/main616021.shtml. Also see Jack Hitt, "The Diddly Award," *Mother Jones* September/October 2004, http://www.motherjones.com/news/feature/2004/09–401.html.
5. Ann Cahill, *Rethinking Rape* (Ithaca, NY: Cornell University Press, 2001), 101–102.
6. Costas Douzinas, *Human Rights and Empire. The Political Philosophy of Cosmopolitanism* (Abington, Oxfordshire, UK: Routledge-Cavendish, 2007), 28.
7. Carine M. Mardorossian, "Toward a New Feminist Theory of Rape," *Signs: Journal of Women in Culture and Society* 27.3 (Spring 2002): 743–775.
8. Michel Foucault, *The History of Sexuality, Volume 1: An Introduction*, trans. Robert Hurley (London: Penguin, 1990).

Introduction

Theorizing Sexual Violence: Subjectivity and Politics in Late Modernity

Renée J. Heberle and Victoria Grace

The 'problem' of sexual violence, in the myriad forms it takes, has been alternatively normalized and challenged through various public responses and narratives. Since the feminist movement in the West began to bring sexual violence to the forefront of political struggle, the heightened visibility of the issue has encouraged a plethora of institutionalized responses and analytical approaches. Legal reform movements have been exposing how law excludes and/or obscures this particular form of violence as such. Cultural codes of approval and implicit social agreements to remain silent about sexual violence have been disrupted by feminist protest and consciousness-raising.[1] The national movements have turned international with nongovernmental organizations and international law taking up sexual violence as an actionable offense against human rights which has been brought before international tribunals as itself a war crime.[2] The ongoing struggle to create a progressive public/political understanding of and response to sexual violence aiming to ultimately bring it to an end is now global in reach even while differentiated historical contexts sustain very particular regimes of truth about the phenomenon and its impact.

Sexual violence has been forced onto the agendas of reluctant public institutions, national and international, over the last four decades. Since the first speak outs against rape and sexual assault were organized and protests were organized against pornography, since the Duluth, Minnesota Project to coordinate community efforts against domestic violence was founded in 1975,[3] and as the assertion that sexual harassment was a violation of civil rights saw some success in the courts,[4] literature on the many forms of sexual violence has proliferated. This literature includes studies of victims, of perpetrators, of advocates, of professionals in the field, of the phenomenon itself, of how the criminal and civil court systems might approach it and why they fail. Psychology, criminology, and sociology have figured prominently as the appropriate disciplines to study the phenomenon in terms of its causes and effects, to evaluate treatment, and/or discover new and undeveloped strategies for confronting the issue in communities.

Backlash responses such as those provided by Christina Hoff Summers and Katie Roiphe[5] are popular for their identification of feminism as the problem to be solved in adjudicating sexual violence. In this way of thinking, antiviolence feminists are renamed as 'victim' feminists because they identify women as always already potentially victimized as they think about the relationship between gender identity and sexual violence. Our response to this kind of criticism of the work of radical feminists such as Catherine MacKinnon and those who have struggled to render sexual violence a public/political matter rather than a personal/pathological issue is clearly not to agree that feminism is the problem to be solved. Rather we think feminism is the most productive site of inquiry wherein the kind of self-reflexive critique is likely to take place that can force various societies to look at themselves through the lens of the commonplace status of sexual violence and rethink assumptions about gendered and sexed existence.

The authors in this volume assume that to rethink sexual violence we have to rethink the terms on which we become sexed and gendered subjects, but also on which we think about representation and remedy. The authors in this volume gesture toward this without claiming any final conclusions about what gendered and sexed relationships might look like if sexual violence were no longer a possibility.

The authors presume that we have to politicize the problem as we think about solutions. The problem of sexual violence in itself is not self-evident in its essence; it does not have an essence once we begin to look closely at the attendant issues through multiple lenses; there is no singular form that sexual violence can be reduced to even as we seek to make it visible as an unjust and damaging action.

While funding remains inadequate and state organized responses chauvinistic in their cautionary tales of the threat to women and children, and while the issue remains in the shadows of national domestic political agendas, there has, nonetheless, been built an edifice of legal strategies, educative approaches, and service oriented institutions over the last fifty years, now further supported by national legislation in many countries. Several countries have institutionalized responses to sexual violence; for example, the passage of the Violence Against Women Act in the United States in 1995 after several years of failure (it was first proposed in 1990) was considered by some to be a profound accomplishment.[6] None of this should be trivialized in terms of the impact on the lives of those threatened and harmed by sexual violence. Indeed, recognition of the accomplishments of feminists and women's advocates locally and globally is in itself of political value, given contemporary narratives of the death of feminism, or the myth that we live in a postfeminist era, or the complaint that Western feminism is imposing values and norms on 'other' societies when issues about gender and sexual violence are addressed. In fact, indigenous feminist and women's movements have globalized the reach of antiviolence advocacy.[7]

However, the concern driving this volume is that levels of sexual violence have not diminished, that institutionalized responses too often result in obscuring the dynamics of sexual difference that perpetuate sexualized violences, and that feminist approaches to the phenomenon have not yet taken up the possibilities of contemporary critical theorizing about gender and sexuality that could open the field to new insight about its own successes and challenges. The thinking that informs this volume is that strategies for confronting and remedying the harms of sexual violence are never 'innocent' or clean of the historical contexts and power relationships in which they emerge and should not be immune to feminist scrutiny and critique. The strength of feminism resides in its self-reflexive habits of critique. This can appear paralyzing, but can also offer new insight into why sexual violence has not diminished. In spite of the persistent efforts by feminists and advocates, legal reforms, and cultural/educative efforts, sexual violence remains with us as an ongoing crisis informing and shaping our gendered lives.

We wish to highlight the multiplicity and mutability of experiences recognized as significant in fighting back against sexual violence. We are more or less persuaded that sustaining the tropes of victimization and innocence on the part of those attacked, abused, prostituted, and raped, and asserting the monstrous nature of perpetrators will not sustain a politics that will bring that to an end.

This volume aspires to contribute to theory that reinvigorates critical understandings of sexual violence, has a concern for research grounded in action, and takes up the relationship between sex, sexuality, violence, and gender identity. We are interested in bearing witness to a plurality of approaches that resist the normative assumptions about male and female identity, and masculine and feminine subjectivity, that perpetuate sexualized forms of violence.

Taking sexual violence in the form of rape, assault, hetero-psychological/physical abuse, and coercion as a point of departure, the authors take up questions about the relationship between sex, sexuality, and violence in order to better understand the terms on which women's sexual suffering is perpetuated, thereby undermining their capacity for personhood and autonomy. We perceive that while sexual violence as a phenomenon is heavily researched, it remains undertheorized. As noted above, the bulk of research currently lies within the fields of psychology, criminology, and sociology. This research is invaluable, informed by and indebted to feminism. It does not, however, ask the same kinds of questions we encouraged our authors to ask in the call for papers for this volume.

We asked them to consider difficult questions about whether some responses to the phenomenon of sexual violence perpetuate the status quo of gendered identity formations. The behavioral research on sexual violence from medical, psychological, and criminological perspectives does not move beyond a dominance/submission model with its attendant assumptions about the fixed subjectivity of men and women. This volume takes up antiessentialist views of gender identity, of subjectivity and agency, of rationality and consent, many of which have been developed by queer theorists, as they study the dynamics and consequences of sexual violence. For the most part the authors assume that the deconstruction of naturalized binaries, the proliferation of sites identified as political, and antiessentialist approaches to identity and subjectivity are progressive, if not entirely unproblematic, moves within feminism. The authors take up the insights of postmodern critique with the common goal of theorizing and acting effectively against the bodily and psychic suffering perpetuated by the rigid rituals of gendered and sexed life.

The authors in this volume take theorizing about sexual violence into some unexplored territory, given that they are critical of the dominance/submission model for interpreting sexual violence. They explore strategies for subverting the dualistic terrain of masculine/feminine identification, structured in terms of identity/difference, which make sexual violence so likely. They inquire as to how we might politicize sexual violence without reducing that politics to the mediation or adjudication of claims of victimization. Some of the authors pose empirical questions as their point of departure for responding to these inquiries. Others explore somewhat unexpected theoretical resources to interpret the relationship between violence, specifically sexual, or sexualized violence, and gendered subjectivity.

The authors in this volume take into account the heterogeneous quality of sexual violences and how they are experienced and interpreted in significantly different ways. If there is an underlying assumption it is that sexual difference in itself is constituted at least in part by sexualized forms of violence and that sexual difference in itself is mutable across experiences of race, class, ethnic, and other identity formations. Further, we think the terms on which sexual difference is constructed in any historical context or cultural space will be significantly altered, even radically changed if we actually were to see an end to sexual violence. So, while the terms on which sexual difference is constructed and inform sexual violence is the primary focus of this volume, and while some focus on normative practices and forms of masculinity and femininity (Western, white, bourgeois) in terms of how these perpetuate sexual violence, others take into account how sexual violence and responses to sexual violence perpetuate 'othering' dynamics.

Instances of sexual violence are unique, infinitely contingent on personal history, and social, political, and historical conditions of possibility. That said, there are discourses and narratives that shape the conditions in which sexual violence becomes more or less likely. For the purpose of her historical research, Joanna Bourke[8] takes the act of sexual violence to have occurred when a person claims that an act or experience is one of sexual violence. This apparently simple claim avoids metaphysical conundrums related to metadefinitions of 'sexual violence'. It also serves to turn the focus onto the perpetrator without any imperative to inscribe a perpetrator/victim binary. There are certainly dangers in this approach, as Bourke carefully acknowledges, but we share her view that feminist scholarship needs to develop this focus on the act of sexual violence.

To theorize is, then, in part to critique the very descriptions or constructions of the incidences of sexual violence that perpetuate the terms on which it thrives. We take gendered violence to refer to instances when gender identity is implicated in acts of violence, and 'sexual' violence to those when violence is sexual or sexualized. Furthermore, when sexual arousal is involved in an act of violation there is a violence done *to* sex itself, to pleasure and desire.

Feminist knowledge projects can be traversed by ambivalence and a certain wariness related to the desire that animates and sustains them. This tension may reflect the simultaneous desire for an understanding that can act in socially transformative ways, to bear witness to real change, and yet for a mindfulness of the criticality a feminist epistemology will insist upon vis-à-vis the avoidance of any master discourses that attempt to 'say what is.' To rage against sexual violence, gendered violence, compels the question 'why'—why is this happening to her, why does this happen to women (or to me, or why it is that this could happen to me)? Asking *why we ask why* is fundamental to a feminist ethics of knowing. The 'why' appears obvious in the face of the harm, trauma, and injustice of acts of sexual violence. However, we argue that to call into question the animating dynamics and desires of the questions themselves, to focus on our own desire within our knowledge projects, brings a crucial reflexivity to theoretical, textual practices that otherwise risk reiterating the very structure of violence they supposedly oppose. An aim for this volume is to bring this critical reflexivity to bear on theorizing sexual violence.

In formulating our intent for this volume, the editors want to move feminist understandings of sexual violence forward in ways that will foreshadow possibilities for real changes in the aggressivity accompanying social relations of gender. And yet at the same time we take up the critical work of feminist theory. Our knowledge project here is not to 'say what is' (in the naïve presumption that this will then lead to prescribing action for change), but rather engage in a process of critique of those discourses that construct 'what is', to name and symbolize that which is excluded from those discourses. Such an epistemology aims to envision and create a feminist discourse that mobilizes meanings that have been barred; the very act of their exclusion, their sociocultural inaccessibility to symbolization, has sustained the violences that are the object of our critique.

THE ESSAYS

Taken as a whole, this volume effects a critical engagement with the way subjectivity and politics traverse and co-construct each other in our contemporary era of 'late modernity.' Ann Cahill's chapter seeks a reconsideration of the work that the concept of objectification achieves for feminist theorizing around gender relations, in relation to sexual violence. To appeal to concerns about objectification suggests the diminution or erasure of the subjectivity of the woman who is violated, and the corollary that this is a source of harm. Cahill claims that this binary of subject and object is not only problematic in and of itself, but it is also in a sense inaccurate. On the contrary, the feminine must be a *subject* for the masculine violator; it is precisely her subjectivity that is actively enlisted in this violation, even as 'object.' Without her subjectivity, his violation is meaningless. He needs her to be a subject, to be subjected. Furthermore, Cahill argues that to be a sexual subject 'necessarily and appropriately entails a degree of passivity and objectification.' Objectification, in the sense of being a 'thing-for-sex,' does not in and of itself account for the harm of sexual violence; it does not negate the sexual subject. Cahill suggests an alternative construct, one she calls 'derivatization,' to characterize the relation she theorizes to be at the heart of sexual violence. In this figuration, the subjectivity of the viola- tor entirely appropriates the otherness of the victim. He 'projects his own desires, and nothing but those desires' onto the woman to the point that her ability to be anything other than the construct of his desire is obliter- ated: 'the victim is turned into a derivative of the will of the assailant' as her otherness is annihilated, incapacitated.

Cahill considers the implications of this shift in conceptualization for the legal framing of sexual violence. In particular she highlights the ques- tion of the presence or absence of consent, which continues to constitute feminine sexual desire as acquiescent within a heteronormative sexuality. The absurdity of the assumed contractual nature of sexual relations is evident in current changes to the New Zealand sexual violence legislation being considered by the judicial system, whereby alleged offenders who wish to claim that sex with their 'victims' was consensual, would have to prove in court what measures they took to gain consent. Cahill asks how the theory of consent would be entirely recast through seeking evidence of how the woman's desire actively shaped the interaction with another sexual subject.

While Cahill references psychoanalytic theory, particularly Irigaray's, to elaborate her ideas, Victoria Grace engages psychoanalytic theory to confront the question of how gendered violence might be considered to be sacrificial, and what this means for feminist theorizing of sexual violence. How can the masculine subject (and why is it the masculine subject?) be a subject of violence, of violence that is gendered, of gendered violence that is specifically sexual? To explore these questions, Grace works through a series of theoretical points. With reference to Rene Girard, Martha Reineke, and Julia Kristeva, sacrifice is shown to shape the formation of subjectivity in late modernity through the negation or expulsion of that which threatens the boundary of the embodied subject. The masculine subject, positioned in a potentially sacrificial relation to the feminine, sustains his boundar- ies through violence when threatened with engulfment. This violence is sustained through a kind of shoring up of the subject's sense of itself; when the inevitably alienated subject is confronted with his incompleteness, his misrecognition of his embodied mastery, 'death' is kept at bay by whatever means necessary.

To understand the 'sexual' in sexual violence, how sexual arousal is implicated in the very act of violating an other, the psychoanalytic notion of the fantasy must be addressed. If the fantasy—so fundamental to sexual desire and possibly infused with violence and abjection—is confused with reality, sexual violence is even more readily precipitated. Grace argues that the role of a sacrificial logic is central to understanding how sexual violence is enacted when, in Lacanian terms, the subject is understood to be structured differentially as masculine or feminine. As such gendered subjects have a different relation to *jouissance,* and therefore a different ethical task to redirect the anguish of the inevitable split at the heart of subjectivity.

Can this ethical task at the heart of gendered responses to the death-drive and *jouissance* be in any way related to the current feminist interest in the political work that might be done through the recognition of the inevitable 'vulnerability' of the body? Following the line of argument developed by Grace, such a focus would appear to depart from the fundamental ambivalence at the heart of any psychoanalytic theorizing: vulnerability is always already something else besides. Ann Murphy takes up this question of the 'ethics of vulnerability.' She outlines the current feminist claim for an ethics that appeals to recognition of one's own vulnerability as the basis for acknowledgement of the vulnerability of others. Murphy claims that this ethic is flawed in a number of ways, and these flaws point to the political failings of such an ethic. Firstly, it is abundantly apparent that vulnerability can lead to retributive violence; in this connection Murphy insists that the realization of one's own vulnerability provides absolutely no guarantee that this will motivate the respect of such vulnerability by potentially violent others. Secondly, from the perspective of ethics, "there is no normative or prescriptive force to be mined from these experiences"; in other words, to claim an inherent vulnerability does not in and of itself issue any particular ethical stance or political position to be taken up in relation to that vulnerability on the part of others. And thirdly, this is risky for women, and more risky for some women than for others. Murphy is concerned that an appeal to an ethics of vulnerability not only abstracts sexual violence from the political 'reality' of experience, but it furthermore obscures the fact that some violences against some women (and indeed some vulnerabilities) are visible while others remain invisible. Murphy discusses women as agents of violence to further develop the problems with this identification of women and vulnerability. These differentiations complicate any idea that women are unified in their vulnerability, and this complication speaks to her title of 'reality check.'

Murphy takes Judith Butler's recent work as an example of a feminist ethics that appeals to the recognition of vulnerability, and discusses it in relation to Catherine MacKinnon to bring into relief the stakes of "mining this motif in the service of ethics." Is a recognition of vulnerability a new ethic, a new feminist discourse? Murphy alerts us to the problems inherent in the assumptions of such a claim and points to the suspicion among feminists as to what such a theory or ethic could achieve in terms of concrete political, efficacy.

An enduring feminist aim is, without doubt, the redress and amelioration of women's vulnerability to violence in various forms. Murphy references the rhetoric of 'wholeness' and integrity as an active motif in feminist discourse on recovery from rape or sexual assault. In a sense this rhetoric crystallizes the precariousness of any "return to vulnerability" in feminist theory, as it detours us from the inherent ambiguity of embodied vulnerability, and at the same time points to its political risk. Melanie Boyd takes up the question of this ambiguity in its raw immediacy through literature whose protagonists complicate this entire conundrum. The damage of incest is her topic. Boyd discusses multiple disruptions to the political tropes that have conventionally anchored the politics of father–daughter incest: *helplessness* (attesting to the child's innocence); *damage* (identifying incest as wrong and harmful); and *recovery* (redressing personal victimhood through a survivor discourse of transformation and healing).

Through an in-depth discussion of two novels—Saphire's *Push* and Kathryn Harrison's *The Kiss*—Boyd unravels these tropes to expose a reflection on incest that refuses the 'healing' they presume. Such a refusal to 'heal' is shown to be a refusal to reject or overcome the formative role that the agonies of incest played in their lives; a refusal to rewrite their histories in redemptive terms, but rather to fully recognise the way they used damage to constitute their subjectivities. Particularly in the case of *The Kiss,* we see how father–daughter incest is played out in the wider dynamics of family relationships. Without a rhetoric of helpless victimhood, the politics of testimony loses its potency. Through Boyd's chapter on refiguring the damage of incest, the inherent vulnerability of bodies is indeed recognised, but this recognition cannot be deployed towards a foreclosure of father–daughter incest. On the contrary, this recognition strengthens the daughter's resolve to write incest into her history.

Boyd's chapter searches testimonial literature for critical ways of rethinking the relationship between violence and subjectivity. Nicola Gavey's chapter also explores questions of violence and subjectivity. She explores archival materials of the feminist movements and activism in the United States in the 1960s and 1970s in order to bring back to the table the militant, aggressive, responses by feminists to the various forms sexual violence takes, from catcalls on the street to rape. Since the early 1980s and the appropriation of feminist activism against sexual violence and rape by mainstream social service and educational institutions, an emphasis on legal reform and cautionary strategies directed at women and children have become the norm. Upon reviewing the archival materials, Gavey's chapter points to a number of possible reasons for the shifts from the militant and physically aggressive reactions advocated by early second-wave feminist activism to a more cautionary and reformist approach. One of the most significant may be that the very definition of rape and sexual violence has changed from being assumed to be about stranger rape and street harassment to the acknowledgement of the reality that the vast majority of violence happens between people who know each other as acquaintances or as intimates. This necessarily complicates possible responses to sexual violence. Self-defense strategies, particularly by women who are battered, may well lead to their arrest and charges being brought against them. Physical resistance may escalate the dangers of injury and/or the risk of death.

Gavey's purpose, however, is to reclaim and remember possibilities articulated by feminists that will challenge the rigidity of gender roles and heterosexist norms that frame or 'build the scaffolding' for rape. Feminists can find resources in our own histories as we critically interrogate the mainstream approaches that explain rape in terms of miscommunication or individual pathologies. One could argue that the persistence and ubiquity of 'dating' violence and 'domestic' violence and child sexual abuse calls ever more urgently for the reevaluation of how gender roles and cultural norms that shape sexual difference inform the likelihood of sexual violence. What Sharon Marcus called the "rape script"[9] is not anomalous but embedded in how gender identity is constituted. That said, what Gavey calls 'physical feminism' raises its own questions about how to prevent those who are attacked in intimate or familial settings from themselves being arrested or targeted as the perpetrator. Physical feminism could ultimately transform sensibilities about masculinity and femininity, deconstructing the terms on which we map aggressivity and passivity onto these identity formations, but it is not without severe risk.

The ever-shifting expectations of the feminine with respect to sexuality complicate efforts to combat sexual violence. Gavey points specifically to the dangers of contemporary, highly commercialized, versions of sexualized femininity. Becoming an object of sexual attention is celebrated as empowering. Interpreting the manner that popular culture constructs our sensibilities about our lives as sexual beings is a complex project, but it can be argued that while sexual demands and forms of sexual expression are now more often made or represented by women, they are still about representing the feminine figure as supplicant to the masculine figure for affirmation and fulfilment. They perpetuate the feminine as the passive figure, albeit, one seeking more actively, even aggressively, for the man who will make her whole.

Gavey's work encourages a reconfiguration of how the masculine and the feminine is understood in relationship to aggression and threat. The culture of sex, of victimization and aggressivity, is not static. It is dynamic and taking note of historical shifts is important as feminism attempts to sustain a critical and even confrontational approach to mainstream norms that govern our sensibilities about masculinity and femininity.

Renée J. Heberle's chapter explores how mainstream norms of liberal political culture and subjectivity inform the possibilities for sexual violence. Feminist political theorists have argued that the private/public split so crucial to the terms on which liberalism thrives obscures violence against women. Carole Pateman, for example, explains sexual violence in part by arguing that male dominance is written into the social contract while female submission is dictated by the sexual contract as that which governs 'private' norms and relations. Heberle argues that a Nietzschean reading of the terms of the social contract may offer more insight into the dynamics that inform the possibilities for sexual violence under the terms of a liberal social contract. Rather than take liberalism at its word as a story of the rational individual coming into agreement with his fellows in the name of protecting and defending themselves and properties (including women), a Nietzschean reading of liberalism against the grain suggests that it is informed by a dynamic of anxiety, reactive identity formations, and 'ressentiment.' Heberle argues that the social contract is best read in light of a masochistic sensibility. It is as a potential victim of the betrayal of trust, of crime, of uncertainty, that masculine figures enter into contracts. In considering the self-willed submission to authority that the contractual relation implies, Heberle suggests, along with Cahill and Grace, that masculinity is not so self-assured as some feminist arguments may claim in its relationship to that which is 'other,' that which threatens, that which must be punished as a means to sustain a sense of self. This exploration of masculinity under the terms of the liberal social contract identifies sexual violence not as the action of self-assured, dominant individuals, but as a reaction to the threat of self-dissolution. Thus, the more rigidly gender identity in relation to political subjectivity is asserted and sustained, the more likely it is to be informed by reactive forms of violence. Heberle brings the paradoxes of liberal 'freedom' as self-willed submission to the authority of the state to bear on thinking about sexual violence.

While Heberle theorizes liberal individualism as the effect of anxiety about sustaining a coherent sense of self under conditions of freedom, Meghana Nayak studies the responses of the US military complex to the persistent and ubiquitous presence of sexual violence within its ranks and as committed against civilians by its members. She suggests this effort is complicit in shoring up the legitimacy project of the military as the defender of democracy.

As a theorist of democratic transitions and as a critic of mainstream democracy theory, Nayak wishes to call into question how it is that ostensibly democratic societies, or the institutions created to defend the terms on which democracies can survive, sustain not only high levels of sexual violence, but have not successfully created effective strategies to stop that violence. Nayak studies the emergence of the recognition within the military and Congress that sexual violence is an issue they had to publicly address. Their legitimacy has, at least in some small part, come to rest on not appearing to allow such violence in the ranks, on the bases, or against those civilians among whom military actors live. Attention must be paid by military authorities as the legitimacy of the military as an institution is at stake as these problems become public knowledge. However, as Nayak's argument suggests, the project of militarism is inseparable from masculinist norms and perspectives. Those norms of aggressivity, the defense of 'honor,' and the all important differentiation from that which might be identified as 'feminine,' will not sustain an environment free of sexual violence. They require sexual violence as part and parcel of militarist principles. Despite the romantic notion that 'honor' and 'real men' do not hurt women or 'others,' this is not the grounds on which militarist institutions sustain solidarity, presence, even a sense of mission. Those are sustained on the basis of inherently masculinist principles which necessarily exclude the voices of those who suffer its effects, the critics that may challenge its core values, or those who understand that that culture and relationships of power create the terms on which sexual violence is possible, not individualized pathologies or private conflicts.

The concluding chapter by Elizabeth Philipose takes up the internationalization of the struggle against sexual violence. Feminists have been successful in rendering sexual violence subject to international norms of justice in war. Women's rights are slowly, but surely, being recognized as human rights in the context of international law. Yet in the process of prosecuting war crimes of rape and sexual abuse in the international tribunals assigned in Yugoslavia and Rwanda, neocolonial patterns of European dominance of people of color are affirmed. Philipose's chapter shows us that international legal forums for justice are contaminated by neocolonial relationships of dominance and reproduce imperial assumptions about the irrational, ethnicized Other who needs help regulating and/or rationalizing their use of force in warfare. Philipose is careful to point out that she is not advocating cultural relativism but instead, the exposure of how some peoples are considered more prone to 'spectacular' forms of sexualized violence than others simply because the violence of those who make the rules of international law is not marked, recorded or held up to the same level of scrutiny.

Legal forums are particularly likely to represent sexual violence in unidimensional ways, requiring victims whose status as such is irrefutable and perpetrators whose status as pathological deviants can be asserted without challenge by adjudicators of justice. But most importantly, international law requires that there be a standard of militarist behavior that is governed by laws. It is when we look closely at the implementation of these laws that we can see the complexity of the project of drawing lines once and for all between legitimate and illegitimate forms of violence and between what is properly left to the jurisdiction of domestic and or military tribunals and what should be subject to international scrutiny. If laws are written by the winners of war, the international laws of remediation will not hold the winners to account for the violences committed on the way to victory. The effort to hold perpetrators of sexual violence in war accountable in the way that any other war criminal would be held accountable is limited as long as only the losers in international conflict are prosecuted. The racial and ethnic dynamics of the trials and the ways the 'otherness' of the accused contributes to neocolonial relationships of power must be taken into account.

* * *

Metatheories about the sexual suffering of women or about the dominance of men are not adequate to capture the nuances and shifting meanings and dynamics of sexual violence. The assertion of foundational principles, such as "men rape because they can," do not help us understand why some men do not rape or how it is that women experience and respond to violence in their everyday lives. Naturalizing rape as the inevitable outcome of being gendered male or female does not help us know how shifts in gender and sexed identity norms may change the terms on which sexual violence is 'known' to a population, how cultures make sense of it, or why the recognition of it as a crime is not an adequate remedy. The embeddedness of sexual violence in daily life contrasts with the spectacularization and sentimentalization of particular incidents which drive popular consciousness and interpretations of what sexual violence is about.

Taking seriously the contemporary insights of postmodern feminist and queer theory about gender identity and sexuality requires a rethinking of how we theorize sexual violence. The traditional typology of feminist theories, liberal, socialist, radical, cultural, or multicultural, will not exhaust the possibilities of how to think about sexual violence. Indeed, they each have serious consequences and limits on our imagined possibilities for ending it. This volume focuses on theorizing the phenomenon of sexualized violence in itself and the discursive and material means by which it is perpetuated in spite of formalistic changes in the legal system and some increase in social attention. We believe that until gender and sexed identity is radically reconfigured, until the political terms of this precariously achieved subjectivity is confronted, sexual violence will remain a ubiquitous and damaging part of life for men and women. It is toward the ends of theorizing relationships between that reconfiguration and sexual violence that we put together this volume.

NOTES

1. See, for an example of essays about "rape culture," Emily Buchwald, Pamela R. Fletcher, and Martha Roth, eds., *Transforming A Rape Culture* (Minneapolis, MN: Milkweed Press, 1993).
2. See Elizabeth Philipose's chapter in this volume. Also see Sally Engle Merry, *Human Rights and Gender Violence: Translating International Law into Local Justice* (Chicago, IL: University of Chicago Press, 2005); Catharine MacKinnon, *Are Women Human? And Other International Dialogues*

(Cambridge, MA: Belknap/Harvard University Press, 2006); Elizabeth Philipose, "The Laws of War and Human Rights," *Hypatia* 11, 4 (1996): 46–62.

3. Melanie F. Shepard and Ellen L. Pence, *Coordinating Community Responses to Domestic Violence: Lessons from Duluth and Beyond* (Thousand Oaks, CA: Sage Press, 1999); Susan Schechter, *Women and Male Violence: the Visions and Struggles of the Battered Women's Movement* (Boston: South End Press, 1982).

4. Catharine MacKinnon, "Sexual Harassment: Its First Decade in Court," in *Feminism Unmodified* (Cambridge, MA: Harvard University Press, 1987), 103–116.

5. Christina Hoff-Sommers, *Who Stole Feminism?: How Women Betrayed Women* (New York: Simon and Schuster, 1995); Katie Roiphe, The Morning After: Sex, Fear, and Feminism on Campus (Boston: Little Brown, 1993).

6. We should not forget that VAWA was a part of the vast extension of the reach of the policing powers of the state in the United States during the "war on crime" in the 1980s and 1990s and indeed passed as part of an omnibus crime bill; its passage was thus tagged as a crime-fighting measure.

7. See Nevedita Menon, "Sexual Violence: Recovering the Body," in *Recovering Subversion: Feminist Politics Beyond the Law* (Urbana, IL: University of Illinois Press, 2004), XX–XX, for an excellent discussion and critique of feminist strategies in India. Also see Ruth A. Miller, *The Limits of Bodily Integrity: Abortion, Adultery, and Rape Legislation in Comparative Perspective* (Burlington, VT: Ashgate Press, 2007), for a comparative analysis of legislation related to reproduction and rape in France, Turkey, Italy, and, in historical perspective, the Ottoman Empire. The chapters in this volume echo the critical impulses in these two interpretive treatments of feminist strategies, political culture, and national legislation.

8. Joanna Bourke, *Rape: A History from 1860 to the Present Day* (London: Virago Press, 2007).

9. Sharon Marcus, "Fighting Bodies, Fighting Words: A Theory and Politics of Rape Prevention," in *Feminists Theorize the Political*, ed. Judith Butler and Joan Scott (New York: Routledge, 1993), 389–403.

1 Sexual Violence and Objectification

Ann J. Cahill

Amidst all the cultural noise about ours being a 'postfeminist' age—a time when women have, allegedly, achieved such social and political equality so as to make feminism obsolete and unnecessary—the rates of sexual violence against women serve as a palpable reminder of women's continued oppression.[1] In an earlier work, I called for a retheorizing of this entrenched social phenomenon and argued that utilizing some conceptual tools developed by continental feminism would result in a more comprehensive, nuanced understanding.[2] Specifically, I claimed that the approaches of Susan Brownmiller and Catharine MacKinnon, two of the most recognized feminist thinkers on this subject, were both flawed in their incomplete appreciation of embodied subjectivity and the complex ways in which bodies, power, individuals, and social discourses interact.

Here I continue my thinking on sexual violence, with a particular eye toward the role the concept of objectification has played in our understanding of it. This piece is part of a larger exploration—and critique—of the notion of objectification that I am currently developing. In short, that critique will claim that the philosophical baggage associated with objectification has become overly cumbersome, weighted down as it is with various kinds of assumptions that most contemporary feminist theorists would find untenable, and that it should be abandoned. In its place, I will offer a new concept, 'derivatization,' which, I argue, characterizes the social phenomenon often associated with the objectification of women, but without those questionable assumptions. As feminists have generally defined 'objectification' as 'treating a person as an object,' I suggest defining 'derivatization' as 'treating a person as a derivative,' where the ethical principle being violated is not that persons are not things (a principle that denies the materiality of human existence) but rather that persons should not be reduced to other person's desires, wishes, or projects. In short, I understand derivatization as a violation of a distinctly Irigarian ethics of (sexual) difference. To derivatize is to portray, render, understand, or approach a subject solely as the reflection, projection, or expression of another subject's being, desires, fears, etc. The derivatized subject becomes reducible in all relevant ways to the derivatizing subject's existence—no other elements of her[3] being or subjectivity are perceived to be relevant. Indeed, it is most likely that aspects of her subjectivity that do not reflect directly the derivatizer's subjectivity won't be perceived at all, and may in fact be suppressed or even disallowed.

The derivatized subject is not quite a nonperson. She may express desires, emotions, and preferences; she may articulate consent or the lack thereof (especially when the lack of consent only heightens the erotic nature of the encounter); she may even play a role of alleged dominance in relation to the derivatizer. One may understand a dominatrix, for example, as a derivatized woman; despite the explicit power differential between the dominatrix and the submissive, still the overall dynamic exists for the satisfaction of the submissive; the being and behavior of the dominatrix is ultimately reducible to the needs and desires of the submissive. There are few if any ways, then, in which the derivatized subject functions in ways similar to inanimate objects. The derivatized subject inhabits a particular kind of subjectivity—a subjectivity that is stunted, or muted, as I shall argue below, but a subjectivity nonetheless.

The questions at the center of this particular chapter, then, are the following: how has objectification been deployed in feminist understandings of sexual violence, and to what degree does it succeed or fail in illuminating that phenomenon? And: can derivatization function more effectively? Before exploring those questions, however, I should briefly define some terms. For the purposes of this discussion, I will often use the terms 'sexual violence' and 'rape' interchangeably. The definition of the latter term has been of particular interest to philosophers and legal theorists,[4] and in many ways the difficulty of arriving at a consensus definition of the term speaks to the murky intertwining of sexuality and violence that marks the current construction of heterosexuality. After all, if coercion is understood as a defining element of rape, what are we to do with all the myriad ways in which women are, in Adrienne Rich's famous analysis,[5] compelled to become, be, and act heterosexual? Moreover, the term 'sexual violence' is usually understood to be somewhat broader than 'rape,' which almost always indicates bodily penetration of some sort. Sexual violence, on the other hand, could describe forms of molestation that do not include penetration, or even (again, depending on one's definition) violence that does not include physical contact, such as verbal harassment.

For the purposes of this discussion, I am concerned with all forms of sexual violence, although for the most part I am assuming an element of physical contact. Rape shows up as a particular form of sexual violence, one that is, perhaps, more readily recognized as the act of violence that it is than are some other forms of sexual violence. In speaking of sexual violence, I am referring to situations wherein one or more persons impose a sexual interaction upon another unwilling person.

Of course, the social and political meanings and dynamics of sexual violence are heavily dependent upon their context. The ways in which a particular culture defines and organizes a host of institutions—gender, sexuality, familial relations, property law, and ethnic identity, just to name a few—shape individual experiences of rape as well as community responses to them.[6] Although I suspect that derivatization could potentially illuminate the ethical harms in rape in a variety of historical and social contexts, my analysis below is generally limited to the phenomenon of sexual violence as currently experienced and constructed by contemporary Western society. Thus I am understanding sexual violence as a phenomenon that occurs mostly, but not exclusively, between individuals acquainted with each other; that is imposed disproportionately against women; that serves as a force that shapes the topography of virtually all women's lives; that inspires social (and legal) reactions that range from horror to outright tolerance; and that represents a significant trauma to victims, with negative psychological and physiological effects that can persist for considerable lengths of time.

Finally, I will regularly refer to assailants as male, and victims as female. This level of generalization is not entirely empirically accurate—boys and men are vulnerable to sexual violence, and girls and women are capable of enacting sexual violence. Moreover, transgendered persons, who may not fit neatly into either category, can be found on either side of the equation. However, that members of all sexes are theoretical candidates for either role does not justify treating the phenomenon as a sex- or gender-neutral one. The vast majority of sexual violence is perpetrated by men, and the vast majority of the victims are women. To ignore this disproportionality (which, of course, I do not view as natural or biologically necessary) is to misunderstand the phenomenon at the outset.[7]

THE OBJECTIFICATION OF THE VICTIM OF SEXUAL VIOLENCE

What do feminists mean when they say that victims of sexual violence are (sexually) objectified? There are (at least) two ways to understand this claim. One could argue that the assailant views his victim as a mere thing, a being who is either not human or less than human. Thus defined, the victim becomes a justifiable target for violence and harm, since she is not accorded the moral status of a full human person. In this way, the objectification that occurs within the phenomenon of rape is directly linked to other forms of objectification:

> In stark contrast to the old perspective on rape and rapists, the feminist analysis located the cause of rape in the culture in which it is embedded. As the myriad manifestations of a misogynist and patriarchal culture were articulated, it became increasingly clear that rape could be reasonably defined as a concrete acting out of culturally normative beliefs and images. The objectification of women in culture-wide images, such as in advertising, the denigration of women in pornography, and

the institutional oppression of women as it is encoded in the legal system were all documented as examples of cultural norms that directly and inexorably lead to rape. In this new context, rapists were seen not as pathological deviants from societal norms but, rather, as normal men who act out in individual dramas what their surrounding culture perpetrates institutionally.[8]

From this perspective, a rape victim is a thing to be used according to the rapist's wishes with no regard for her own well-being, safety, or subjectivity: in fact, because she is less than human, such factors barely if at all register in the calculus of choice. Her well-being simply doesn't matter because, from the perspective of the objectifying assailant, it almost literally doesn't exist. In particular, her body is constructed as pure materiality, uninhabited by human consciousness or worth: the victim becomes a 'thing object,' morally similar to other inanimate entities—at least those that are ownable, and can be broken without grave consequences.

Alternatively (and historically, somewhat more problematic in feminist theory), the rape victim could be seen as a *sex object*. This status differs somewhat from the objectification described above in that it is explicitly and clearly sexualized; thus, the victim is not only seen as a thing, but as a thing-for-sex. In this sense, the victim may be understood to be sexually appealing to the assailant—perhaps even so much that, from the perspective of the assailant and often that of society in general, she bears the blame of her own victimization. When feminists understand the rape victim as sex object, of course, they do not imply that it is the victim's sexuality that is the cause of the violence. Rather, they claim that the construction of heterosexuality in contemporary Western culture demands that sexuality and dominance are so deeply intertwined as to be inseparable, such that to be a sex object, to be on the receiving end of a sexualizing, male gaze, always comes with the threat of violence.

It is interesting to note that both kinds of objectification can be understood as causes *and* effects of sexual violence. To be a 'thing object' and to be a sex object, in some horrifically a priori sense, makes one *eligible* for sexual violence: such a being is in the category of 'rapeable,' whether consciously or unconsciously. The specific act of sexual violence can also be understood as transforming that eligibility into actuality: by raping a person, an assailant not only recognizes her as a 'thing object' and/or sex object, but actually transforms her into such. Sharon Marcus emphasizes this point when she argues that:

Social structures *inscribe* on men's and women's embodied selves and psyches the misogynist inequalities which enable rape to occur. These generalized inequalities are not simply prescribed by a totalized oppressive language, nor fully inscribed before the rape occurs—rape itself is one of the specific techniques which continually scripts these inequalities anew . . . Masculine power and feminine powerlessness neither simply precede nor cause rape; rather, rape is one of culture's many modes of feminizing women.[9]

The woman's inferior status as 'thing object' and/or sex object is reified, incarnated, made real through bodily, sexual violence.[10]

These two approaches to objectification and sexual violence can, in general terms, be mapped on to the two contrasting theoretical models about rape that I mentioned above. Theorists such as Susan Brownmiller argued famously that sexual violence was primarily about power and violence, not sexuality.[11] To ask questions concerning sexual appeal in relation to sexual violence—to question whether, for example, the victim was sexually appealing to the assailant, or whether the assailant was sexually aroused by the encounter—was to miss the point entirely (and, perhaps more relevantly, was to risk blaming the victim for inciting the violent behavior in the first place). Sexuality was at most a means of effecting violence and expressing power, and the specificity of that means was considered to be fairly irrelevant, both in the motivation of the assailant (i.e., he wasn't primarily seeking a sexual partner, but rather a person to dominate) and the experience of the victim. For Brownmiller, what mattered in both the experience and the phenomenon of sexual violence was the expression of power, the domination of one person over another, the cruelty and violence forced upon the victim. In divorcing power from sexuality, this approach can be understood as constructing the victim of sexual violence as an object, a thing, but not necessarily or significantly a sexualized thing. Sexual violence here becomes equated with other forms of nonsexual violence, and in fact at least one philosopher recommended a legal definition of rape that removed the role of sex and sexuality entirely.[12]

On the other hand, the approach of thinkers such as Catharine MacKinnon placed sexual violence very much on the continuum of dominant heterosexual behaviors and norms, even claiming that rape was merely the logical extension of a culture that eroticized domination and submission:

> What is it about women's experience that produces a distinctive perspective on social reality? How is an angle of vision and an interpretive hermeneutics of social life created in the group women? What happens to women to give them a particular interest in social arrangements, something to have a consciousness *of*? How are the qualities we know as male and female socially created and enforced on an everyday level? Sexual objectification of women—first in the world, then in the head, first in visual appropriation, then in forced sex, finally in sexual murder—provides answers.[13]

The rape victim, as someone who is totally overwhelmed and defined by the imposition of sexual violence, is the sex object par excellence, and it is her very abjection that is so sexually appealing. Hence the ubiquitous images of rape in pornography produced for heterosexual men: the woman who is dominated is sexual precisely because of that domination, and sexiness becomes necessarily intertwined with submission, weakness, and victimization. From this perspective, rape is not only sexual, but the hallmark of an inherently unequal and oppressive sexual system, a system that, like virtually all oppressive regimes, communicates its values through propaganda and demands that the oppressed class adopt and perpetuate their own abject status. Hence MacKinnon's rather infamous indictment of pornography:

> Pornography is a means through which sexuality is socially constructed, a site of construction, a domain of exercise. It constructs women as things for sexual use and constructs its consumers to desperately want women to desperately want possession and cruelty and dehumanization. Inequality itself, subjection itself, hierarchy itself, objectification itself, with self-determination ecstatically relinquished, is the apparent content of women's sexual desire and desirability.[14]

As I argued in my earlier work, I find both approaches to sexual violence—the one that considers it to be primarily about power rather than sex, and the one that considers it to be not only primarily but in fact paradigmatically about sex—to be significantly limited, particularly insofar as they misunderstand the complex relationships among the body, self, and society. While Brownmiller addresses rape as a political problem, she grounds it in biology, claiming that rape happens because it is a biological possibility. Yet there are many biological possibilities that are not political realities: the fact that certain bodies *can* do certain things does not explain *why* they do them, nor does it sufficiently account for the fact *that* they do them. Moreover, Brownmiller's removal of sexuality from the phenomenon of sexual violence seems to imply that being raped is generally identical to being assaulted in a nonsexual way—an implication that contradicts many women's lived experiences. In general, Brownmiller fails to understand the body and sexuality as social and political artifacts; she also assumes a sex/violence distinction that is untenable.

MacKinnon, on the other hand, has an unsophisticated understanding of the capacities of power, seeing them as total and unrelenting. A notion of power that brings with it the possibility of resistance is both more convincing and of greater explanatory strength, because women and their experiences of rape (including their various ways of resisting rape, both individually and collectively) cannot be understood as solely defined and limited by patriarchy.

In one regard, at least, MacKinnon's position may appear to be more congruent with my analysis than this critique would imply: "if women are socially defined such that female sexuality cannot be lived or spoken or felt or even somatically sensed apart from its enforced definition, so that it is its own lack, then there is no such thing as a woman as such; there are only walking embodiments of men's projected needs."[15] The difference between MacKinnon's position and my own is subtle, but crucial. As I understand her arguments, MacKinnon claims that the patriarchal construction of feminine sexuality literally creates women with certain desires, expectations, orientations; that patriarchy makes women women; that all that constitutes femininity/femaleness is reducible to masculinity/maleness. The radical scope of MacKinnon's theory, as many of her critics have pointed out,[16] makes resistance theoretically difficult, if not impossible. At the very least, women cannot resist *qua* women. In my view, as elaborated next, it is not the case that women are by definition derivatives, but rather that they are (often, not always, and in a myriad of ways) derivatized. In other words, from my view (and that of Irigaray), the category of 'woman' (as unstable and multiple as it is) exists beyond patriarchal definitions of femininity and womanliness. Finally, MacKinnon's approach to rape also seems contrary to female lived experience, insofar as it collapses a distinction—that between sexual violence and other sexual experiences—that many women experience as at least sometimes clear.

Indeed, despite the deep divisions between these two approaches, both fail at similar points: they do not sufficiently account for the relevance of the body and the complex role of intersubjectivity with regard to sexual violence. They remain committed to traditionally modern dichotomies (such as self/society and mind/body)—an ultimately fatal commitment, and one that also underlies the role that objectification, sometimes implicitly, plays in their thought. As a facet of these theories, objectification is similarly inadequate, and does not sufficiently clarify the ethical and philosophical meanings inherent in sexual violence.

Let us take first the notion that the victim of sexual violence is nothing but an object, a thing, to the assailant. One difficulty here is that the assumption that the victim of sexual violence is treated as a thing, a nonperson, ignores the fact that the subjectivity, the personhood, of the victim is crucial to the meaning of the act of rape. If the victim were truly stripped of all subjectivity, if she really appeared to the assailant to be nothing more than a thing, an inanimate object devoid of feelings or sensations, then the experience of forcibly imposing his body and will upon her would have relatively little appeal. One might as well rape a blow-up doll, a choice that would come with significantly fewer risks. But the victim is never just an object to the assailant; her pain and anguish are not only recognized, but in fact actively sought, and they must be the kind of pain and anguish which a human person experiences. In order to establish his own dominance, the assailant must have a real person to dominate; she may be seen as a lesser person than he, as a kind of person who is deserving of this treatment, but she remains a kind of person: she cannot be a mere object. If the rapist seeks to obliterate the subjectivity of the victim, his actions always belie that desire. For he needs her, he needs a victim, in order to become and be a victimizer.

To put this point somewhat differently: to commit an act of sexual violence is to attempt to harm another being, to effect anguish and suffering. In order to impose this kind of harm, the victim must be harmable. The blow-up doll cannot be violated, cannot experience the agony of sexual violence. An assailant may attempt to fulfill a rape fantasy by imagining that the blow-up doll is a real person, but that act of imagination does not a rape make. Only an embodied subject, with a certain level of sentience and consciousness, who has the possibility of sexual (inter)subjectivity, can be harmed by the imposition of an unwanted sexual encounter.[17]

The work of Jessica Benjamin is particularly helpful in understanding the complexity of this dynamic. From her psychoanalytic perspective, domination involves an inherently paradoxical logic, one that at once involves the seeking of and destruction of recognition. In attempting to utterly overwhelm his victim, the dominator risks turning the victim into someone who is not worth dominating, or, more precisely, whose domination is meaningless: "The master's denial of the other's subjectivity leaves him faced with isolation as the only alternative to being engulfed by the dehumanized other. In either case, the master is actually alone, because the person he is with is no person at all."[18] Elsewhere, Benjamin writes:

> The effect we have on something or someone is a way of confirming our reality. If our acts have no effect on the other, or if the other refuses to recognize our act, we feel ourselves to be powerless. But if we act in such a way so that the other person is completely negated, there is no one there to recognize us. Therefore it is necessary that, when we affect an other, she or he not simply dissolve under the impact of our actions. The other must simultaneously maintain her or his integrity, as well as be affected.[19]

For Benjamin, the distinction between erotic sexuality and domination is not the presence or absence of what she calls "destruction" (and which I understand to be the recognition of the otherness of the other, the negation of the other as "not me"), but rather, whether the other "survives":

> This dynamic of destruction and survival is the central pattern of erotic union. In erotic union, the other receives and recognizes the subject's acts including his acts of destruction. Eros is certainly not free of all that we associate with aggression, assertion, mastery, and domination. But what makes sexuality erotic is the survival of the other with and despite destruction. What distinguishes Eros from perversion is not freedom from fantasies of power and surrender, for Eros does not purge sexual fantasy—it plays with it. The idea of destruction reminds us that the element of aggression is necessary in erotic life; it is the element of *survival*, the difference the other can make, which distinguishes erotic union, which plays with the fantasy of domination, from real domination.[20]

In erotic union, in other words, the other *remains* other, and is not subsumed or overwhelmed by the self: it is active and can, in Benjamin's terms, "make a difference." Acts of domination are attempts to deny such intersubjectivity, to place the dominator in the place of the only self, to say to the victim: you cannot make any difference, I am totally in charge. But intersubjectivity is not so easily thrown off, as Hegel knew. The master needs the slave to be a master, and so the object can never be utterly objectified.

This is not to say that all acts of rape involve conscious recognition of the victim of the rapist *qua* rapist. So-called date rape drugs, for example, work in such a way as to ensure the victim's lack of consciousness. She usually has no memory of the assault, and experiences it not directly, but retroactively, often reconstructing what must have happened from physical evidence (and by the time she does realize what has happened, the drugs have almost always passed through her system and are undetectable). Here, one could say, the assailant does not have the experience of dominating a person: at the moment of the assault, she has virtually no self-awareness, and one could even argue that she does not experience the rape itself (although obviously to realize that one has been raped is deeply harmful, and the physical/emotional/psychological harms can linger for a significant amount of time). The assailant has chemically eradicated the subjectivity of the victim and commits the assault on a being incapable of recognition.

Yet even here, I would argue, the victim still inhabits a significantly different position from other kinds of objects, particularly because the assailant has had to take active, conscious steps to overcome her subjectivity. The intentional purchasing of the drug, the surreptitious spiking of the drink, the witnessing of the incapacitating effects of the drug, the removal of the victim to a private place when she is incapable of making choices, these are all part of the assault, and they only make sense if the victim is another person, an identifiable subject. When an assailant rapes an incapacitated woman, he is not raping an inanimate object, but rather an embodied subject whose vulnerability he has exploited and whose agency he has forcibly overcome. That his control has extended thus far is part of the sexual charge that he experiences.

To say that the victim of sexual violence is constructed as a mere thing is, then, to fail to recognize the peculiar intersubjectivity that is in play in this phenomenon. One cannot rape an inanimate object; nor does rape turn a victim into an inanimate object. She remains, painfully, an embodied being, vulnerable to harm, yes, but a subject nevertheless.

And what of the approach that understands the rape victim as sex object? There are several difficulties with this model, not the least of which is that it seems uncomfortably close to dominant, and lasting, tendencies to blame the victim. To understand the victim as sexually appealing is dangerously close to inquiring about her dress, her previous sexual choices, her motivations and so forth, all ways in which patriarchal society has sought to shift a significant portion of the blame for sexual violence from the assailant to the victim. Yet, as I argued in my earlier work, a focus on sexuality need not entail victim culpability. Such equivocation is only possible under a particular construction of heterosexuality, one which posits women as tempting, threatening seductresses and men as sexual machines that cannot be controlled, even by themselves. Recognizing and rejecting this construction creates the space for acknowledging the role of sexuality (as an intrinsically intersubjective phenomenon) within the phenomenon of sexual violence; a role that may even be central, but which in no way abrogates the moral responsibility of the assailant.

The more salient difficulty of this approach is its assumption that to be a sex object is necessarily degrading and violent. Yet sexual objectification—being perceived as sexually appealing by another person, having one's material being appreciated aesthetically, viscerally, as desirable—can be a vital element of a robust, healthy subjectivity. Even to be seen as a thing-for-sex loses its sting, as long as human subjectivity is understood as involving both 'thingness,' (that is, materiality) and sexuality. To be a sexual, embodied human being is to be a material entity capable of engaging sexually with other sexual, embodied human beings, and this engagement can (perhaps should!) include sexualizing gazes.[21]

What is at stake here is a model of sexuality that inevitably entails an active agent—someone 'doing' something—and a passive recipient—someone who is 'done to.' These roles are not only persistently gendered, but also hierarchized: it is better to be the subject than the object, better to do than be done to. Doing enhances subjectivity; being done to is inherently degrading, and only inferior beings would consent to such a thing. This is a model deeply ingrained in Western metaphysics, and similarly deeply implicated in patterns of sexual inequality. In contrast to this model, I seek to approach sexual interactions—even those that are marked by violence and other forms of unethical behavior—as dynamic engagements between differentiated beings. Although that which differentiates beings is not limited to the body, bodily differences are clearly crucial here: it matters that the interaction is bodily, that the experience is an incarnate one. In other words, human sexual beings are objects: they are things (material entities) and they are the receivers of touch, gazes, and attention. Taken together, these two points demonstrate the connection between intersubjectivity and the necessity—even desirability—of objectification. Human sexual beings are always already both subject and object; or, more to the point, their very sexual subjectivity involves being a sexual object for another subject, such that subjectivity and objectification become ultimately enmeshed and intertwined. Moving in this direction would cast passivity, for example, in a very different way:

> Passivity is by no means inherently antithetical to sexual desire or pleasure—quite the contrary, if the level of stimulation is appropriate and can be contained. And one might likewise ask why subjectivity

should not be allied with passivity—or for that matter, with being adored and admired, the subject/object of someone else's narcissism, their partner in a mutual identificatory love. Can't passivity be enjoyed without relinquishing all claim to activity, without becoming simply the active lover's object, being rather a subject who owns the pleasure of each position?[22]

I would take an even stronger position than Benjamin here, and argue that to be a sexual subject necessarily and appropriately entails a degree of passivity and objectification. To be sexual, one must be seen as a thing-for-sex.

Of course, this is not to argue that it is *always* enhancing to be seen as a thing-for-sex. There are situations and contexts within which such gazing can be deeply inappropriate and harmful. My point, however, is that one cannot depend solely on objectification—or the presence of a sexualizing gaze—to name a situation or phenomenon ethically improper. If sexual violence often[23] involves constructing the victim as a sex object, as a thing-for-sex, this does not yet explain its harms or its ethical wrongness. To frame sexual violence in this way is to risk vilifying virtually all sexuality; it is also to fail to name the particularity of rape and sexual violence as distinct from other sexual experiences.

Whether the objectification associated with sexual violence is understood as 'thing objectification' or sex objectification, it seems to miss the mark. The victim of sexual violence is not a mere thing, and if she is the object of a sexualizing gaze, or perceived as a thing-for-sex, this does not account for the harm done to her. Both approaches seem incapable of understanding humans as intersubjective, embodied beings; in the first case, by misunderstanding the ways in which even assailants and their victims remain subjectively interdependent, and in the second, by presuming that any identification with or as a sexualized, material body is inherently debasing. If derivatization is to provide a more successful and productive model of sexual violence, it must avoid precisely these pitfalls.

SEXUAL VIOLENCE AS DERIVATIZATION

In my earlier work, I argued that understanding the phenomenon of rape demanded an understanding of embodied intersubjectivity, that is, the ways in which human subjects are constituted by their materiality and their relationships with other human subjects. To approach rape as an embodied experience is to accept that it is an experience that occurs between sexually specific subjects, one that marks the bodies involved in particular ways and one that is differentiated according to the specific bodies involved. To understand it as intersubjective is to accept that the experience constructs the agency and subjectivity of the individuals involved.

Such intersubjectivity, of course, does not amount to equality or symmetry. Indeed, what is at stake in an example of rape is the attempt on the part of one subject (the assailant) to overwhelm the subjectivity of the other (the victim) in a particularly sexualized way. He imposes his will upon her, imposes his body upon her, imposes his sexuality on her, obliterating her ability to speak or enforce her own will, prohibiting her from living her bodily, ontological autonomy. He projects upon her being the reflection of his own desires, and nothing but those desires: she who must become what he wants (a rape victim), is incapable of being anything other than that. The (temporary) totality of the obscuring of her subjectivity speaks to the utter foolishness of any mind/body distinction with regard to the experience. She is attacked as an embodied subject, as a whole entity, with particular focus on her sexual being.

I would argue that sexual violence is an example par excellence of derivatization. The victim is turned into a derivative of the will of the assailant: "violence is the outer perimeter of the less dramatic tendency of the subject to force the other to either be or want what it wants, to assimilate the other to itself or make it a threat. It is the extension of reducing difference to sameness, the inability to recognize the other without dissolving her/his otherness."[24] The ethical wrongs of this action cannot be found in the fact that she is a thing-for-sex, since situations where being a thing-for-sex is deeply affirming are easily imaginable. The problem is that the ability to control, define, and force the sexual encounter lies only with him. To be a thing-for-sex can be delightful if one's own sexuality is fully present in the interaction, if the exchange is in some fundamental way reciprocal, if one's own sexual desire is a lively and recognized element in the encounter. To be a thing-for-sex in a situation where one's own sexuality is dismissed, ignored, and violated is an affront to one's ontologically distinct sexual being, and constitutes a great harm against one's well-being and health.

If the victim of sexual violence may be perceived as a sex object for the assailant, that description cannot sufficiently account for the destruction of her own sexual autonomy. In *Rethinking Rape*, I suggested that the sexuality of an act of rape may be so asymmetrical as to justify saying that the assailant had 'had sex' with the victim, but the victim had not 'had sex' with the assailant. Derivatization helps us to understand this apparent paradox. Because the assailant derivatizes the victim, and, importantly, the victim's sexuality, the sexual exchange becomes a one-way interaction, that is to say, not a sexual exchange at all. I argue that the subjectivity of the victim remains, however paradoxically, present in the dynamic of sexual violence. However, her own, ontologically distinct sexuality is not allowed to be expressed or explored. The experience is intersubjective, but not sexually so. Only one person is really 'having sex'; the other person is having sex imposed upon them.

The derivatized victim is not a thing, not a nonperson. Just as dominant images of women in contemporary media show women expressing emotions and desires that only human subjects can, so the derivatized victim experiences and expresses pain, fear, and horror that are unique to the human subject (or at least are recognized and experienced as uniquely human). She is a limited, harmed, injured person, one whose ontologically necessary vulnerability has been exploited by a harmful other, but she does not become inanimate or nonhuman. Yes, her subjectivity is (temporarily) eclipsed, but in some ways that is the point: she must have a subjectivity that can be eclipsed, she must occupy the role of 'person' or 'subject' in order for her assailant to feel the thrill of violence. Moreover, as I have sometimes parenthetically indicated, and as long as the assault does not result in her death, the obliteration of her subjectivity is limited in time. Although the effects of sexual violence can linger for years, a victim does not remain *entirely* defined by her victimization for long. She remains, after all, an intersubjective being, and therefore other experiences (some of which, hopefully, involve healing) occur that affect her in different ways.

POTENTIAL LEGAL RAMIFICATIONS

In her critique of English and Australian rape law—a critique, it seems to me, that would apply as well to US law—Ngaire Naffine notes that "sex still takes the form of a sexual subject (a sexual initiator) who proposes sex to a sexual object (from whom consent is extracted). It is rape when the deal goes wrong."[25] This model confers upon the assailant a Cartesian independence, purchased at the cost of the victim's ontological distinctness:

> In the law of rape, the woman remains a vessel, that which contains his separate, self-contained, enclosed heterosexuality. She is not and cannot be herself an autonomous subject because then she would encroach upon his sexual subjectivity. For if she were herself a desiring, volitional subject, with separate, different, distinctive sexual desires, she too would have the right to set the terms of heterosexuality and so deny to him the right to have uncurtailed, autonomous heterosexuality—which depends on no-one but himself. She would have the right to determine what he alone must determine to be autonomous. It follows that to establish his sexual autonomy, to retain his Cartesian unity of self, he must erase hers. His desires must be extrapolated to hers. And so she remains a mystery to the law and to him. We are told that her desires are difficult to discern, that she does not really know what she wants. She is his desires or nothing. Always he remains the one who initiates the transaction for the possession of the container of his heterosexuality. Never does he negotiate with a separate, different, distinctive being with her own set of desires.[26]

The legal framing of sexual violence, in other words, reiterates the very derivatization of the assault itself. In insisting on the question of "did she consent?" the law persists in framing (hetero)sexuality in terms of male desire and female acquiescence, and remains conceptually incapable of constructing—and therefore *hearing*—women as beings whose identity and sexuality exist beyond the parameters of hegemonic masculinity.

What would it mean for the law to recognize women as "desiring, volitional subjects, with separate, different, distinctive sexual desires"? For one, the law would need to adopt a hermeneutics of suspicion toward heterosexuality that it currently lacks. Irigaray is often accused of heteronormativity;[27] nevertheless, I believe a more careful analysis demonstrates that her analysis actually constitutes a serious challenge to heterosexuality as currently understood. The radicalness of the difference Irigaray posits functions in such a way as to insist upon women's ontological, and therefore sexual, distinction from men: female sexuality (and morphology!) cannot be understood as 'matching' or 'completing' the male counterparts. Nothing about the sexes indicates that they *must* be with each other, and their being-with does not amount to constituting an integral whole. Irigaray claims that it is the difference itself that is foundational; everything about the ways in which differently sexed individuals interact is contingent (and therefore falls under the realm of the ethical). If Irigaray is right about sexual difference, then there is nothing natural, given, or necessary about heterosexuality, either as an institution or a practice.

Consent theory assumes both the naturalness of heterosexuality and its hierarchical nature by assuming that men propose and women acquiesce. Somehow—and not being, strictly speaking, a legal theorist, I am not clear as to how this could be effected—the law must move beyond the theory of consent in favor of a theory of desire, desire that is grounded in and framed by an explicit, persistent recognition of women as women, not as wives, daughters, or would-be lovers of men. Drucilla Cornell (while wary of the role that law would play in such a quest) points in this direction when she claims that "the right to the imaginary domain takes us beyond hierarchical definitions of self, whether given by class, caste, race, or gender. The freedom to create ourselves as sexed being, as feeling and reasoning persons, lies at the heart of the ideal that is the imaginary domain. Without it, we will not be able to share life's glories."[28] Women's sexuality must be understood as central to their ontologically distinct being, and therefore as central to their civil rights. It must also be understood as a facet of their identity that is not limited by or to their particular interactions with men (or with women, for that matter). The question should not be: did she consent? But: how was her desire, or lack thereof, heard and respected? Was there space for her sexual agency? Was she, as a sexual subject, an active participant in the interaction, shaping it with her particular desires in an interaction with another sexual subject? Or, to be even more Irigarian about it: were there two, here? Or only one?

Objectification—again, understood as treating a human person either as a material entity or as the recipient of a sexualizing gaze—does not necessarily violate the Irigarian principle of wonder. One person may view another as sexually appealing, as physically attractive, even as a thing-for-sex, without reducing the other to a projection or mirror of her/his own identity. Wonder is possible, if unlikely in a patriarchal society, and can—should!—include the body as its focus of attention. Rape does not turn women into things: it forcibly reduces their sexual being to that of another, thereby eclipsing their ontological distinctiveness. The two become one, and the one is the rapist.

An analysis of sexual violence as derivatizing is grounded in a model of the person that holds materiality and sexual specificity as central; thus, the sexuality and violence that constitute rape and other forms of sexual violence are conceptualized not as opposed to each other, but as deeply intertwined elements of a single phenomenon. And a crucial component of the physical/psychological aspect of the harms of rape is illuminated: that it subsumes the subjectivity of one person, who is worthy of ontological distinctness, under that of another. That it does so with physical violence, through sexuality, accounts for its profound harms, the depth of its destabilizing effects on the victim's health and psyche, and the crucial role it plays in a society committed to perpetuating male domination.

NOTES

1. The US Bureau of Justice reports that in 2005, 176,540 women in the United States experienced sexual assault; in the same year, 15,130 men were similarly victimized. However, it is worth noting that the rate of sexual assault, like other violent crimes, has undergone a significant reduction since 1993. See Shannan M. Catalano, "Criminal Victimization, 2005," Bureau of Justice Statistics Bulletin (September 2006), http://www.ojp.usdoj.gov/bjs/abstract/cv05.htm.
2. Ann J. Cahill, *Rethinking Rape* (Ithaca, NY: Cornell University Press, 2001).
3. As I will argue in a forthcoming work, women are far more likely to be sexually derivatized than men, although it is possible that men are derivatized more frequently in nonsexual ways.
4. Cahill, op.cit., 10–12.
5. Adrienne Rich, "Compulsory Heterosexuality and Lesbian Existence," in *Blood, Bread, and Poetry: Selected Prose 1979–1985* (New York: W.W. Norton, 1986), 23–75.
6. In considering the culturally specific nature of the phenomenon of sexual violence, it is worth remembering, as Christine Helliwell notes, that there are cultures where the phenomenon of rape is literally unthinkable, and so does not exist. Interestingly, in her discussion of the Gerai community of Southwest Kalimantan, Indonesia (which, as far as Helliwell could discern, was free from sexual violence), Helliwell cites the lack of the subject/object distinction, so central to Western culture, as partially accountable for the absence of rape and its literal incomprehensibility. See Christine Helliwell, "'It's Only a Penis': Rape, Feminism, and Difference," *Signs* 25 (2000): 789–816.
7. Of course, the gendered nature of the phenomenon of sexual violence goes well beyond the established gender identities of the persons involved. Rape

is both a gendered phenomenon—in that it is an act disproportionately committed by men upon women—and, as I mention below, a gendering phenomenon, one that constitutes gendered identities; therefore, its implication in a network of gender meanings is a complicated one.

8. David Lisak, "Sexual Aggression, Masculinity, and Fathers," *Signs* 16 (1991): 238–262.

9. Sharon Marcus, "Fighting Bodies, Fighting Words: A Theory and Politics of Rape Prevention," in *Feminists Theorize the Political*, eds. Judith Butler and Joan W. Scott (New York: Routledge, 1992), 385–403, p. 391.

10. Several theorists have described rape as a gendering/sexing act. Monique Plaza claimed that "it is *social sexing* which underlies rape" (29). See Monique Plaza, "Our Damages and Their Compensation: Rape: The Will Not to Know of Michel Foucault," *Feminist Issues* 1 (1981): 25–35. Helliwell goes even further: " . . . we must begin to explore the ways rape itself *produces* such experiences of masculinity and femininity and so inscribes sexual difference onto our bodies" (italics in the original; op.cit., 812)—in other words, these thinkers claim that the phenomenon of rape does not so much hierarchize already sexed bodies as much as it serves to manufacture sexual difference itself. Given my Irigarian inclinations, I am wary of positing sexual difference as the result of sexual violence; as my earlier work indicates, I understand the phenomenon of sexual violence as a failure to recognize sexual difference rather than a construction of it. Nevertheless, rape does reproduce gendered roles/behaviors/identities that are congruent with patriarchal society, and to this extent I agree with the theorists mentioned here.

11. Susan Brownmiller, *Against Our Will: Men, Women and Rape* (New York: Penguin, 1975).

12. Michael Davis, "Setting Penalties: What Does Rape Deserve?" *Law and Philosophy* 3 (1984): 61–110.

13. Catharine MacKinnon, "Sexuality, Pornography, and Method: 'Pleasure Under Patriarchy,'" *Ethics* 99 (1989): 314–346, 315.

14. Ibid., 327.

15. Catharine MacKinnon, *Toward a Feminist Theory of the State* (Cambridge, MA: Harvard University Press, 1989), 119.

16. See, for example, Drucilla Cornell, *At the Heart of Freedom: Feminism, Sex, and Equality* (Princeton, NJ: Princeton University Press, 1998); Carol Smart, *Feminism and the Power of Law* (New York: Routledge, 1989); Robin L. West, "The Difference in Women's Hedonic Lives: A Phenomenological Critique of Feminist Legal Theory," in *At the Boundaries of Law: Feminism and Legal Theory*, eds. Martha Albertson Fineman and Nancy Sweet Thomadsen (New York: Routledge, 1991), 115–134.

17. The case of the inanimate object is clear: a blow-up doll cannot be raped. But my references to embodied subjects and consciousness beg the question of other animate beings. Can humans rape nonhuman animals? And, does rape occur among nonhuman animals? This is a complex set of questions. To take up the former would entail an extensive analysis of the ethics of interspecies interactions with particular attention to sexuality, beginning with the question whether any sexual relations with nonhuman animals could be understood as ethical (if one were to ground sexual ethics solely on consent theory, for example, it would seem that virtually all sexual interactions with nonhuman animals would take the form of rape). To take up the latter would demand an exploration of the social organizations of different types of nonhuman animals, the role that sexuality played in their cultures, and the capacity for different kinds of harms. Such questions are beyond the scope of the

current discussion. However, it is interesting to note that the ethical valuing, or lack of same, of nonhuman animals has often paralleled the devaluing of women. And if some thinkers have noted the similarity between the objectification of women and that of nonhuman animals, I would argue that it might be more accurate to claim that both have been similarly derivatized.

18. Jessica Benjamin, *The Bonds of Love* (New York: Pantheon Books, 1988), 65.
19. In her fascinating analysis of "The Story of O," Benjamin focuses on the master's need for the slave's recognition, noting that if the slave is utterly objectified, she cannot perform this service, and thus must always be kept on the brink of subjectivity (ibid., 157–158). In a literal way, I am not so certain that a rapist demands the recognition of the victim in order to fulfill his desire to rape; it seems to me that there is a subtle, but perhaps relevant, distinction between a Hegelian recognition and a victim's expressions of pain and fear. Even if the assailant does not demand recognition, however, he demands the victim's subjectivity, and it is this need that I am concerned with here. See Jessica Benjamin, "The Bonds of Love: Rational Violence and Erotic Domination," *Feminist Studies* 6 (1980): 144–174, 151.
20. Benjamin 1988, op.cit, 74–75.
21. In some ways, this point echoes elements of the debates between (in Amy Allen's terms) the "antipornography feminists" and the "feminist sex radicals." Like Allen, I find the terms of these debates to be inherently problematic; she writes: "the point that [antipornography feminists] are too willing to *mirror* the view of women that they see in pornography in their own theories is well-taken," but "[The sex radical feminists] focus so much on women's empowerment and ability to resist domination that they tend to presuppose too rosy a picture of the possibilities for resistance and subversion of male domination through the consumption of pornography" (516, 518). Too often, it seems to me, these debates fail to take up the project of describing a positive model of sexual ethics; the feminist sex radicals seem to assume that sex per se is empowering, while the antiporn feminists risk defining virtually all (hetero)sex as damaging to women. The challenge is to articulate clearly the kinds of sexual interactions that enhance, rather than diminish, the subjectivity of those involved. See Amy Allen, "Pornography and Power," *Journal of Social Philosophy* 32 (2001): 512–531.
22. Ibid., 75.
23. But not always: there are certainly examples of sexual violence where the assailant would deny that he was sexually attracted to the victim. Yet I would argue that sexuality itself is always in play in sexual violence: if the assailant is not attracted to the victim, he is sexually aroused by the possibility of domination itself, or (say, in the context of war) by the possibility of bonding with other men, or harming one's enemy. The social and political meanings of rape are diverse and plentiful, but they always include a sexual element.
24. Benjamin 1998, op,cit., 86.
25. Ngaire Naffine, "Possession: Erotic Love in the Law of Rape," *The Modern Law Review* 57(1994): 10–37, 26.
26. Ibid., 33.
27. Elizabeth Grosz, "The Hetero and the Homo: The Sexual Ethics of Luce Irigaray," in *Engaging with Irigaray: Feminist Philosophy and Modern European Thought*, eds. Carolyn Burke, Naomi Schor, and Margaret Whitford (New York: Columbia University Press, 1994), 335–350.
28. Cornell, 1998, op,cit., p. ix.

2 Gendered Violence and Sacrificial Logics
Psychoanalytic Reflections

Victoria Grace

Nietzsche claimed, in the late nineteenth century, that violence must be understood as a way of responding to pain, particularly the pain of anguish, torment, loss.[1] The quest for the person tormented becomes to know the cause of the pain, as if by knowing (or imagining one knows) the cause of the pain, some relief can be obtained by unleashing anger and venom against that target (or a proxy target if necessary). I suffer—it must be someone's fault. He made the point that to react with anger and violence against the perceived cause of pain acts like a kind of narcotic whereby the expression of an excess of emotion deadens the pain, even if only temporarily. Further, we seek to impute meaning and purpose to our suffering. Nietzsche observes that the force and desire motivating the question: "to what purpose do I suffer?" reveals that it is not suffering that is the problem, but senseless suffering. To have a purpose, a reason, a cause, an explanation, is to make suffering possible to endure.[2] Nietzsche is of course critical of this desire for a reason or cause. In his view, the person(s) deemed guilty of causing pain can never be understood as an agent whose conscious *intention* is the 'cause' of his or her deeds; thus the 'cause' presents an endlessly receding horizon.

If women, or those embodying something of the order of the 'feminine,' are the imagined source of a torment for the 'masculine' that unleashes sexualized violence, it behooves feminists in their theoretical critique to imagine something other than an explanation of violence that reciprocates with rage against the masculine as the perceived cause of violence against the feminine, or indeed that displaces violence elsewhere. Critical reflexivity of the kind offered in this chapter reworks feminist desire away from a certain *ressentiment* that might focus attention on the superficial 'causes' of sexual violence, and towards analysis of the psychological, social, political, discursive, and significatory processes that might implicate violence in the very way in which subjectivity is constituted.

My aim in this chapter is to engage specific analyses of violence and the formation of subjectivity in the (post)modern West in a way that pursues a critical reflexivity. I wish to pursue the theorization of sexual violence in a way that does not seek a master discourse of assumed explanatory power, but which stays a course of ongoing critique, opening onto further questions. Nietzsche's reflections provide a starting point for considering the way the constitution of subjectivity is implicated in the possibility of violence. When the subject-in-pain experiences a catharsis through enacting a violent retaliation against the perceived cause of his or her pain, a sacrificial process is invoked. René Girard's theorization of sacrifice views such processes as fundamental to the formation of culture, which, he argues, is founded on the structuring of violence to control the violence resulting from mimetic desire. Regardless of whether Girard's universalism is accepted, through his theoretical exploration sacrificial processes become central to understanding violence. It is only with feminist and psychoanalytic theory, however, that it is possible to consider how gender becomes implicated in this structuring of violence, and how desire conditions the 'sexual' in specifically sexual violence. Girard's theory of the sacrificial has been engaged by Julia Kristeva as central to her endeavour to understand sexual difference, violence and subjectivity in a way that she, with others, argues is of crucial importance to feminist theorizing of gendered violence. After discussion of Girard's argument regarding violence, sacrifice, and the sacred, I discuss Kristeva's critique relying on the analysis offered by Martha Reineke,[3] with additional reference to that of Patricia Elliot.[4] In the second section of this chapter, I augment the substantive, political and ethical insights connecting violence, subjectivity, and gender through consideration of desire and the Lacanian subject to focus on specifically sexual violence. Subjects, structured as masculine or feminine, have a differential relation to *jouissance*,[5] and therefore a different ethical task to redirect the anguish, or suffering, contingent on the inevitable split at the heart of subjectivity.

Intimations of psychosocial transformations that are both political and ethical make critical psychoanalytic theorization of the social at the heart of subjectivity important to a feminist politics for understanding sexual violence. In this chapter I hope to foreground the significance of the work of Kristeva and other Lacanian theorists in this field. Firstly, I discuss Girard's theorization of violence and sacrifice to introduce the significance of sacrificial processes to the more general topic of violence.

VIOLENCE AND SACRIFICE

> Desire clings to violence and stalks it like a shadow because violence
> is the signifier of the cherished being, the signifier of divinity.[6]

The very nature of Girard's theoretical work mirrors or reflects the content of his key argument. He takes one very important idea and extrapolates its implications into every nook and cranny of intellectual endeavour. As the founding murder is argued to explain so much, so does Girard's theoretical impulse render it universally explanatory. In a kind of breathtaking theoretical imperialism, insight into the dynamics of human violence and the sacrificial in terms of mimetic desire explains, according to Girard, the origins of culture, language, religion, the sacred, desire, myth, time, psychosis, psychopathology, and ritual; it explains the functioning of power, exploitation, sexuality, homosexuality, heterosexuality, sadism, masochism, difference, hypnosis, shamanism, all aspects of memory; it reveals the truth of Shakespeare's theatre, the literature of Proust and of Dostoyevsky; Nietzsche had it wrong, as did Freud, Marx, Lacan; there is no such thing as the unconscious, Girard's theorization is capable of reconciling Charot, Bernheim, Janet, and Freud. Skepticism regarding the way Girard's analysis takes confident strides across the pages of history and prehistory on civilizations and archaic through to modern cultures must not detract from the significance of his key theoretical insight. I will briefly summarize my reading of mimetic desire and sacrifice, and then elaborate its various facets with reference to Girard's rendition before turning to the significance of the sacrificial for Kristeva, as analyzed by Reineke.

In Girard's analysis, at the core of human being there is a propensity to mimetic desire. Human beings imitate one another. Desire is quite simply imitative, in that we desire what the other desires. Desire does not transpire from within, but is mimetic. Where two desires converge on the same object, conflict ensues. The multiplication of these desires across a social group means that violence resulting from mimesis can escalate to involve the entire social group leading to what Girard calls a sacrificial crisis. At a critical point the dynamics of a pattern of all against all within a group flips to that of all against one. A sacrificial victim is sought (any sign of 'difference' will act as a satisfactory proxy), and collectively murdered. The resulting catharsis reinstates a pacific state within the group. These processes have been historically encapsulated in myths that mask their very functioning. The sacrificial victim is then a scapegoat, perceived to carry the origin of the violence. While mimetic violence escalates within the social group, differences between individuals are progressively reduced until the antagonists effectively mirror each other in a relationship of doubles. Restoration of differences, individuation, will be achieved through the sacrificial annihilation of a (different) other. Sacrifice thus becomes a mechanism to control violence inherent in the human condition. The murdered victim, once sacrificed, becomes valorized by the community, as the source of peace and restoration of differentiation. He or she becomes the communal focus of a sacralization. This process represents the founding of religion, the sacrificed victim becoming valued as sacred and worshipped or appeased as such. Ritual processes have developed to reenact the sacrificial murder, and myth has emerged to simultaneously erase the evidence.

The term 'sacrifice' has the same Latin root as sacred, and its earliest meanings related to the performance of priestly functions or sacred rites. The development of the concept of sacrifice in English from its meaning purely as a religious procedure to reflect a more profound sense of what such a procedure entails occurred as late as the sixteenth century. The transferred sense of the act of giving up one thing for another is first found in Shakespeare's *Romeo and Juliet* in 1592.[7] The force of Girard's analysis lies in this latter meaning, and the processes that have obscured the role of sacrifice in human culture, and arguably continue to do so.

According to Girard, the reciprocal, imitative nature of violence means that it invariably becomes caught in a vicious circle of vengeance and reprisals that sustain it indefinitely. The notion that even a slight outbreak of violence can lead to an exponential escalation through a kind of contagion has been studied and documented in literally thousands of myths and legends.[8] "Once a community enters the circle, it is unable to extricate itself."[9] The only way this extrication can happen is to identify a surrogate cause of the disastrous contagion of violence. In the destruction of a surrogate victim, Girard argues, not only does the community *believe* that it is ridding itself of its ills but it effectively *is*, because surrogate victimage precisely does break the circle and provides a reprieve from the emulative process that grips the collective imagination.

For Girard, desire must be formulated in the first instance as desire without object.[10] Desire as a mimetic process means that the individual will take another as his or her model, as the other whose desire he or she imitates. In this way the object under dispute in the rivalry is secondary, or derivative; desire is first of all activated by imitating the other who is desiring. While there is sufficient (social) distance between the model and the 'disciple,' imitative processes do not create conflict. However, when the distance between them closes, when the model and the 'disciple' become more and more alike specifically through the mimetic process, the disciple becomes a rival and this in turn leads to conflict. When there is no longer any way to differentiate the two from one another, this is what Girard calls the relationship of doubles; they are potentially locked into a reciprocal violence.[11]

Girard's research plots the elaboration of religion throughout the ages as the primary mechanism to control violence grounded in mimetic desire through the sacrificial process; the control of violence through violence; the murder that underpins the sacred; the destruction of a victim for the sake of the continuation of the community or group. While this process is undoubtedly attenuated through the more rigorous utilization of legal frameworks in the post-Christian era, it is this phenomenon of a sacrificial economy that is important to Reineke in her analysis of Kristeva, women and violence. A sacrificial economy is one in which the loss of differences, the threat of the loss of that which secures the subject in his or her individuality are offset, or defended against, through the annihilation of that which is seen as bearing the marks of difference and the threat of engulfment. Before moving on to consider how sacrifice might be considered important to theorizing gendered violence, it is useful to review how Girard views mimetic desire and sacrificial processes in the world of the late twentieth century West in which he wrote.

As Western modernity has less and less recourse to the sacred (although this is debatable) the control of violence is mediated more explicitly through legal frameworks and practices of 'criminal justice.' The revolution of the Christian message was to insist that the victim is innocent; to see that the victim does not embody the sources of violence within the community; that the victimization of a surrogate is a delusionary mechanism. As Girard argues, the intent of the imploring Christ figure was to draw attention to the fundamental problem of mimetic desire and break the circular contagion of reciprocal violence in its vengeance through a transformation of ethical responsibility and action. Christ was intent on exposing the founding murder as that original cultural formation involving the killing of an innocent scapegoat. Instead of responding to this plea to make this break, the institution of Christianity in part negated this message; it worshipped Christ precisely as a sacrificial victim (who would function to take away their sins), continued to ignore and erase the founding murder through mythologizing the crucifixion, and enabled mimetic desire to proceed apace, constrained through the ritualized religious mechanism as well as the law. The law insists that we must identify the guilty perpetrator, shift our rage and reprisal to he or she who is *really* the cause of our pain, and protect the innocent from being burdened with a guilt that is not theirs.

At the time of writing *Things Hidden Since the Foundation of the World* (1978), Girard was of the view that today the spirit of competition "gets increasingly inflamed." With no fixed points of reference (such as the place occupied by virtue of one's birth), "everything rests upon comparisons that are necessarily unstable and insecure."[12] If this was the case in the late 1970s, then the first decade of the twenty-first century surely attests to an intensification of this very phenomenon. The mediatized obsession with competitive game shows and entertainer shows on television for example (in whatever cultural context of mediatized consumption) is reaching a state of utter delirium; the saturation of images of (the imaginary mimetic desire for/to be) the celebrity attests to an intensification of Girard's observation. He wrote in 1978:

> As he sees that everything around him (sic) consists of *images, imitation,* and *admiration* (*image* and *imitate* derive from the same Latin root), he passionately desires the admiration of others. He wishes for all mimetic desires to be polarized around himself, and he lives through the inevitable lack of certainty—the mimetic character of what develops—with a tragic intensity.[13]

The desire for "all mimetic desires to be polarised around himself" is the desire to be the model, to *be* or embody the very image of desiring that others want to imitate. From this vantage point, even a very slight sign either of approval or rejection, esteem or criticism, can reverberate through the psyche as an extreme of ecstasy or abject humiliation (something Girard relates to the prevalence of "manic-depression").

The significance of sacrificial processes in the constellation of violence within and between human communities is brought into clear relief through Girard's analysis. What is missing from his account, however, is the way that gendered subjectivity articulates this violence along differential axes. In the following section I turn to consider Reineke's discussion of the work of Kristeva, with its focus on the role of the "sacrificial economy" in gendered violence, how it is constituted and how the very construction of subjectivity and sexual difference are implicated in this violence.

THE FEMININE AS VICTIM IN THE SACRIFICIAL ECONOMY

> I do not believe it is possible for a rational system, based on the data of consciousness, to respond to the evil and horror that exists in the world.[14]

In this statement, Kristeva invokes the necessity of psychoanalytic concepts and understandings for, importantly, the *response* to "evil and horror." Where Girard relies on religious and legal responses, on the conscious recognition of the surrogate victim and repudiation of cycles of violence, Kristeva insists that we need to fully engage unconscious processes animating our desires. Martha Reineke's reading of selected works by Kristeva, which is influenced by Patricia Elliot's reading[15] as well as those of Cleo Kearns[16] and Kelly Oliver,[17] foregrounds the sacrificial aspects of Kristeva's writings that are, so Reineke argues, critical for an understanding of gender and violence. Reineke claims that without the notion of an economy of violence shaped by sacrifice, and the precision such an analysis entails, "feminists cannot hope to come to terms with the intractable nature of violence."[18] Kristeva, as a psychoanalytic "theorist of sacrifice," shows how patterns of substitutionary violence are linked with societal patterns of sexual differentiation. Through this critical understanding, not only can the contours of the sacrificial contract grounding sexual difference in such an economy of violence be brought more clearly into view, but also ways can be sought to challenge and transform investments in sacrificial relations, to suggest what is at stake in advocating that a nonsacrificial ethic should flourish. In this section I will outline the central strands of Kristeva's theorization, to argue that sexual violence can be understood as a symptom of a deeper violence in the very constitution of the gendered subject.

In psychoanalytic terms, the subject is not the 'self,' not the conscious individual, not the ego. Following Lacan, the notion of the subject in this chapter is not the subject of the statement 'I . . . ,' but rather has no presence, does not appear, in what is said. The subject, in part, is constituted as the very split that is the inevitable accompaniment of acquiring language as a symbolising system; the subject is split between its conscious and unconscious divide. Lacan distinguishes three orders of the real, the imaginary, and the symbolic. The order of the real is not representable, its ineffability is extradiscursive; it is only through our imaginary and significatory practices that we construct 'reality.' Signifiers are not representative of elements of the real. Following Saussure, it is understood that they do not obtain their meaning through some kind of attachment to that which is (apparently) signified. The meaning they acquire is constituted through their relation to other signifiers, through their linkages. The imaginary in Lacan's vocabulary is that register in which the human infant first constitutes its sense of itself as a bounded, unified individual. Prior to this, the experience is one of bodily fragmentation, with the baby, then infant, experiencing a multitude of chaotic sensations that have no basis in any sense of a bounded self, separate from world or separate from others. Lacan's "mirror stage" marks the emergence of this sense of 'self' through recognizing an image in a mirror; an image that others interpellate as the totality of the child, reinforcing the spatial demarcation or bounding of where he or she begins and ends. This image is of the order of the imaginary, and furthermore, it is a misrecognition. The unified, idealized image of the infant appearing in the mirror, and to others, as 'me,' is constituted through the process of signifying, entering into the symbolic order; as Reineke outlines, "the human subject establishes itself *at the site* of that image."[19] There are two points fundamental to a Lacanian notion of the subject at this juncture: one is the fundamental split and alienation that accompanies this imaginary constitution, and the second is that the subject is not the *result* of that split, but rather *is* (at least in part) that split.[20]

The very logic of the signifying act means the signifier stands in place of, replaces, that which is assumed to be signified. The presence of the signifier in its guise of representation marks the absence of that which is assumed to be signified, that which is designated, or apparently (the apparent, the visual, the image, the imaginary) called into being. Thus meaning is present through the imaginary, through the relation of signifiers; it is a social construct embedded in social relationships, largely independently from the real. As Fink interprets Lacan, Lacan refers to this paradoxical or ambivalent construct as the "barred subject": the signifier stands in "for the subject who has now vanished."[21] In this way, the "barred subject" is effected in this split between the conscious (ego of the order of the imaginary) and the unconscious (the linkages, or chain, of signifiers) that comes from elsewhere as the discourse of the Other (the Other referring to that which is constituted as not the child, not me).[22] In alienation the subject is barred from *being*, from having a place, and instead the symbolic order is 'it,' relegating the subject to what Fink refers to as a "mere placeholder;" the symbolic order that enables the subject to constitute itself in the imaginary.

Thus, the subject can be conceptualized as that split between two forms of otherness: to quote Fink, "the ego as other, and the unconscious as the Other's discourse."[23]

Against this Lacanian background, the fragility of human subjectivity grounded in negativity comes into focus, and this is central to the way Reineke develops her engagement with Kristeva as a theorist of the sacrificial. The "Law of the Symbolic Order" must be abided by for the subject to secure this fragile position as 'subject.' As Reineke writes, this Law is "a Law of absence for the subject," noting that its "self-possessed status is essentially a façade."[24] The double irony in this securing is that, although unacknowledged, it is fully reliant on the Other for that very mirroring and for its significatory investments.

This constitution of the subject is of course not innocent of the accomplishment of sexual difference, rather, it is profoundly implicated in it. Reineke claims that Kristeva's understanding of the way subjects take up positions in relation to sexual difference very much follows Lacan's theorization. Being placed within the symbolic order is to be placed as gendered. This placement is structured in relation to what is commonly called the "master signifier." I will discuss this further in a later section, at this point what is important is to note that firstly there are only two places available for this structuring (masculine and feminine), and secondly, the master signifier is the phallus (at least in our context of Western modernity), which functions *as* that point of division. It ensues that the two sexed positions are structured in terms of one of two possibilities in relation to the master signifier. The dualism of sexual difference is thus a product of positioning within language; sexed subjectivity is integral to the founding alienation that is at stake in becoming a subject of language.

Reineke claims that Kristeva departs from Lacan in placing an emphasis on the nature and implications of the transition to the sociosymbolic order. Where Lacan describes a point of entry (albeit gradual) into the symbolic (and departure from the heterogeneity that precedes it), Kristeva focuses on the ambivalences surrounding this transition, and the constant boundary work that needs to occur throughout his or her life, for the subject to maintain its place. The term *semiotic*[25] is used by Kristeva to invoke the bodily experience that the pre-Oedipal infant has of the "mother body" or "the maternal matrix." Importantly, the maternal matrix is not a person, is not an actual mother who is subsequently nameable, is not an object to or for a subject; the maternal space is precisely not an ontological entity or phenomenon identifiable within the significatory practices of the symbolic order. Kristeva "associates the semiotic with the infant's perception of the world through the rhythms, melodies, and gestures of the maternal body."[26] Becoming a subject of/to the sociosymbolic order, however, does not mean a completed departure from the semiotic. The legacy of the semiotic continues, not in a nostalgic sense, but as an ongoing reminder to the subject of that which undermines any (mis)recognition of its place and status. The legacy of the semiotic is not uncomplicatedly that of an idyllic 'before,' it also is marked by the *abject*.

With reference to Kristeva's *Powers of Horror: An Essay on Abjection*, Elliot characterizes abjection as a kind of "revolt of being," as "an ejection of whatever threatens one with nonbeing, ambiguity, or of whatever forces upon one the experience of lack or loss."[27] Abjection alludes to the inbetween, neither one nor the other, crossing borders, obscuring boundaries, not respecting the rules and positions required by the symbolic order. As a "mechanism of subjectivity," abjection not only reminds the subject of his or her inevitable "living at a loss" (because of the fundamental alienation, estrangement or split, which is the price of becoming a subject of language), but this reminder is attached to the (abject) marks of the maternal matrix. In the context of discussing the dynamics of ejection, the abject, as this reminder, induces nausea, associated as it is with the bodily debris of blood, vomit, and other fluids of the pre-objectal experience:

> [A]s the subject emerges out of undifferentiated existence, it becomes aware of fragmentation and disunity. Its awareness is marked not by language, but by bodily refuse: blood, excrement, and vomit. Suggested to the emerging subject by this refuse are borders and the violation of these borders.[28]

The abject (typifying the unconscious), by definition is ejected, rejected; it is to be violently overcome in the identity-securing efforts of the subject. The child is urged to contain that which is of itself within its (imaginary) boundaries, and to expel whatever might threaten that effort.

That the abject appears to be inevitably inscribed into the feminine is a consequence of how that feminine is socially constructed in the symbolic order. As Elliot observes, Kristeva's analysis of sexual difference is based on a difference that "rests on the sacrifice of the feminine."[29] Before going on to consider the work of this sacrificial process and its implications for sexual violence, I need firstly to discuss the notion of *death-work*. Are we faced with an inevitable, intractable violence at the heart of the constitution of gendered subjectivity, one that will erupt in the psychosociopolitical domain of gender and sexual relations? Kristeva's response to this is that, although it is likely (and indeed prevalent), it is not structurally inevitable. The critical question is *how* the inevitable negativity that is definitional of being human, is engaged; *how* is a practice of absence undertaken?

The term *death-work* is preferred by Reineke (to Kristeva's *death-drive*) because of the way it alludes more directly to both the *labor* involved (a labor of the unconscious) and the sociocultural domains within which this 'work' is enacted. The founding estrangement and sense of lack at the heart of subjectivity moves the subject towards a desire for a plenitude or fullness of being: an absolute state that is associated with an infinity of time and space, in other words with that which is not mortal. Death is defended against and rejected within an economy of signification, yet at the same time desired and embraced as *jouissance*—as that which cannot be captured by this economy, and which constantly challenges it—as it makes creation, newness, pleasure, communion possible. How subjects approach this paradoxical imperative, how they do their death-work, raises the question of whether we live within the terms of a sacrificial economy, or reject these terms in the sense of move beyond and outside of them. Reineke is clear about it: "Although all subjects live at a loss, not all death-work is sacrificial."[30] Before discussing how death-work might not be sacrificial, I will turn to the question of how Reineke understands the sacrificial process in this context of death-work, and how she considers that substitutionary violence reflects a sacrificial logic and practice that is gendered.

The contemporary vernacular notion of sacrifice not only conveys a meaning of that which is given up, lost or destroyed for the sake of conserving something else. Following the earlier discussion on the work of Girard, the notion of sacrifice importantly implicates the body of the victim in its process. Ritual often replaces the actual body, even though the actual body is symbolically intended; the ritual is impossible without it. Death-work involves securing boundaries of the subject as a subject of language, against the threat of boundary-failure, a threat that is summoned by negativity. To engage this death-work through bodily violence is to substitute the "murder of soma"[31] for the original violence that language imposed: the substitution (and hence absence) of embodied experience of the semiotic for the presence of the signifier. As Reineke states:

> According to Kristeva, sacrifice puts an end to the vicissitudes of the semiotic by focusing, confining, and translating forces of negativity— the jouissance and rejection in death-work that makes human society possible—onto the body of a victim.[32]

This sacrifice is caught up irrevocably in (impossible yet compulsive) attempts to master the 'thetic,' to 'be' the subject whose place within the symbolic economy enables him or her to signify fully in the positive, having overcome all negativity; the subject who can say what is (take up the impossible position of the phallus, the primordial, master signifier). If we accept the earlier argument that sexual difference can be understood to be constituted structurally precisely through a relation to this signifier, the stakes for the masculine and the feminine in securing boundaries against the threat of negativity are constructed and played out differently. As Reineke notes, "the female body is a favored site to which persons have turned throughout history to reproduce their origins."[33] The bodies of women manifest the materiality used to mark and re-mark the boundaries of negativity. Departing from Reineke's more general claim that women are therefore more likely to be the victims of sacrifice, I interpret this to mean that when a thetic crisis erupts that specifically and more directly puts at stake the subject's relationship to the mother–body, women are more likely to be victims whose sacrifice enables a return of calm and order (in the Girardian sense). As Reineke indeed notes, the bodies of women become the privileged site when a threat incurs a need to go back, return, and reinscribe the very processes of negativity (*jouissance* and rejection in death-work) that secured them (those threatened by boundary failure) in the world in the first place.

It is the significance of the emergence of subjectivity as an embodied process that is so acute in Reineke's rendition of Kristeva's work. The emphasis on the creation of borders through ambivalent processes of mimesis (including the mother as model), of incorporation and ejection, fusing and re-fusing, signifies Kristeva's departure from Lacan and also from Girard, whom Reineke claims also does not attend sufficiently to the significance of soma in mimetic desire. According to Reineke's reading of Kristeva, boundary-securing processes in the face of a thetic crisis will necessarily involve the reenactment of those bodily processes that were productive of those very boundaries. The subject as social and as an apparent (imaginary) agent within the symbolic was created through moving in and out of, across and between soma; that origin, evoked through the abject marks of the maternal body, will be sought to re-mark those boundaries, to re-place soma under the control of the sign. "And only Kristeva, in focusing on death-work and its material markers, follows violence into the body and out of it again."[34]

The notion of the calm that follows the sacrificial crisis finds parallels in psychoanalysis with the concept of catharsis. Lacan notes how the original meaning of the word in ancient Greek means purification; the Cathars were the pure. Through a medical route in classical antiquity it came to take on a meaning of purging, in addition to ritual purification.[35] Purification and purgation both evoke the sense of getting rid of that which is contaminating, or evil, to retain and even protect that which is uncontaminated and therefore pristine in its association with good. Lacan cites Aristotle to emphasize the role of a certain kind of music in provoking a kind of energetic crisis within a group, which is followed by a calm:

> Well now, says Aristotle, once they have experienced the state of exaltation, the Dionysian frenzy stimulated by such music, they become calm. That's what catharsis means as it is evoked in Book VIII of the *Politics*.[36]

This dynamic of an escalation of emotion into a frenzied, trancelike state amongst a group is known to be contagious and plays a role in the abrupt shift from all-against-all to all-against-one sacrificial victim in the Girardian sense. Lacan goes on to suggest how it is not everyone who enters easily into such states of hyperexcitement, even if we are all "at least slightly susceptible." In Reineke's terms, this would mean there are differences among people in the way death-work is engaged and accomplished. Such a pattern of collective passion of affect followed by an equally collective calming is evocative of reports of the rise in domestic violence against women in New Zealand that follows a loss of a world cup rugby match; the hype and hysteria of masculine identification with the national team's success, frustrated in its climax, is cathected onto the bodies of women (even though they may well share elements of the frustration).

Sacrifice, understood as an exercise in representation, specifically places death-work under the sign in order to secure human experience against threat. In other words, the securing will be accomplished through forcing signification; sacrifice "describes a defining aspect of acts that turn bodies into signs: sacrifice kills soma in order to create symbols" through placing a boundary around, or barrier to, the threat that negativity poses.[37] "Killing substance to make it signify"[38] is cathartic when death-work is sacrificial. The mastery of the sign reinstates the (illusory) borders of the subject threatened by negativity.

Kristeva's insistence on the centrality of sexual difference to sacrificial processes is thus clearly highlighted by Reineke. In addition to the abject marks of the maternal body (literal or ritualized) being important to the mechanism of surrogate victimage, women and men are, according to Kristeva, positioned differently in relation to death-work: the "sacrificial gesture" is "deployed along sexually differential lines."[39] Mimetic violence that 'explodes' in sacrificial focus on a victim (men, women, animals) tends to align with the masculine (Reineke claims it is literally more common among men), whereas for the feminine, an implosive sacrificial process is more characteristic and means women's violence tends to turn inward (women are more likely to withdraw into melancholia and even suicide). It is important to situate this observation within the Western context. Reineke relates this sexually differentiated sacrificial logic to the positioning of the masculine and the feminine in relation to the symbolic order, in relation to the phallus. The threatened masculine subject who is shaken in his belief that the symbolic order can fully secure his subjectivity against the threat of negativity, resorts to an explosive act of sacrificial violence that acts to reinforce his power. The threatened feminine subject who *refuses* the necessity of the symbolic work involved in negativity, refuses that which is necessary for the social order (gives up on castration), may have recourse to an implosive act of sacrificial violence. It is important to acknowledge that these sacrificial processes take on their own dynamics at the social, collective level and yet are not separate or independent from their enactment at the individual level.

As Reineke interprets Kristeva, although it is inescapable for human subjects to not "live at a loss" (unless they take the route of the psychotic whose suffering in exile is far greater), not all death-work is sacrificial. A reorientation to the work of negativity within language can open subjectivity to its own ambivalence, its own internal structure of alterity, instead of projecting fears of negativity onto (the bodies of) others. I will conclude by returning to this point, but first I (tentatively) explore what is at stake when sacrificial, gendered violence is specifically *sexual* violence.

DESIRE, FANTASY, JOUISSANCE AND THE NON-SEXUAL-RELATION

> . . . the primordial matrices of fundamental fantasies organize the body imaginarily around objects that cause desire.[40]

Reineke's "theory of sacrifice" provides a Kristevan psychoanalytic account of a gendered violence that is at heart sacrificial, specifically of the feminine. In a sacrificial economy, death-work is structured in such a way that the threat posed by negativity provokes a sacrificial imperative for an imperilled subject: something must be given up, annihilated to preserve (imaginary) boundedness intact. Sexual difference is understood to be integral to this structuring of subjectivity in its relation to the symbolic order in a sacrificial economy. In such an economy where gendered subjectivity is gained at the cost of abjection, the irruption of violence *into* the bodies of women (marking the feminine in its evocation of the abject) is the corollary; the abject is ever-present with its threat of engulfment, and must be kept at bay. The abject is bodily, and to precisely keep it at bay, to fend off its power to dissipate and subsume the bounded subject, it must be symbolized: "sacrifice kills soma in order to create symbols." But what of sexual violence? Is sexual violence, understood within a psychoanalytic frame, a specific form of gendered violence that requires additional critical theorization? If a Kristevan analysis provides some insight into why it is that women's bodies might be a "favored site" of surrogate victimage, what of the specific desire that compels violence that is sexual in nature? What sort of question is the question of sexual violence?

In the psychoanalytic clinic, sexual violence cannot be a singular phenomenon. Its considerable variation (within the general categorization of the 'perversions'),[41] must be accounted for and engaged, whether violence occurs in intimate relations, incest, whether stranger violation, forms of pedophilia, exhibitionism, or the mis-en-scène of sadism and masochism. For all that psychoanalysis is first and foremost a practice, the question I pose here is a more broadly theoretical question of what might be understood about the nature of desire and the *sexual* relation with the Other, that specifically contributes to making sexual violence of any kind possible, or indeed, for some, apparently imperative. The 'whys' of any individual case will of course be unique and infinitely contingent. Although a violent fantasy of sexual desire may involve no aggression whatsoever in relation to a sexual partner, it must also be conceded that the act of sexual aggression may (will?) involve an eroticism that is both fantasized *and realized* in violent aggression towards another. It is important to understand this specifically sexual desire that is animated in violating another.[42] To approach the heart of the 'sexual' in gendered violence, I will discuss the concept of desire, Lacan's engagement with the notion of *jouissance* and the role of fantasy, the possible meaning and relevance of Lacan's "there is no sexual relation," finally suggesting some indicative pointers towards the possible stakes in acts of sexual violence, in alignment with Kristeva's sacrificial theorization.

Reineke outlines the use Kristeva makes of Freudian drive theory to make a case for the significance of the bodily phenomena of orality and anality in the infant as these are played out in the mimetic relation to the maternal body. Patterns of presence and absence, incorporation and rejection or expulsion are played out within a mimetic relation infused with anxieties of conflict as much as with pleasures of incipient agency. Through Kristeva's argument regarding the specifically bodily constitution of the subject in language through the discussion of drive theory, we learn how the drives are fully cultural and constitute the embodied being in relation to the Other. As such, the drives traverse the body, activate it, and delineate its contours. It is helpful to turn to Lacan's engagement with desire and *jouissance* to focus on the specifically sexual. Where Reineke's Kristevan rendition of *jouissance* tends to gloss its meaning as the subject's pleasure (in its inassimilable alterity),[43] we need a more nuanced engagement with this term. Firstly I turn to the question of desire.

Earlier reference was made to Girard's thesis that desire is imitative, that desire has no object; indeed the notion of mimetic desire is central to his theory of violence and the sacred, and the role of sacrifice in the founding and sustaining of culture through the very containment of violence. Lacan shares the view that desire is precisely not a matter of the object, but this is where the similarities cease. Lacanian analyst and researcher Bruce Fink writing on *The Lacanian Subject* insists: "*Desire, strictly speaking, has no object*," but he goes on to state that "desire is in constant search for something else, and there is no specifiable object that is capable of satisfying it."[44] Most of all it seeks its own continuation: to be a subject is to be a desiring subject. The parallels with Girard's concept of desire as mimetic are as striking as the departures: in a Lacanian frame, indeed, the Other's desire is what elicits desire, but it is not a *mimesis* of desire in the Girardian sense (with the object as somehow secondary, creating the conditions for the model and rival). It is rather the pure desiring-ness in itself that *elicits* desire. The desire is 'for' that which is always already beyond, "it is not so much the object looked at as the looking itself, the desire manifested in the very act of looking" that is arousing of desire, in the child.[45] Girard's rendition of mimetic desire in a sense still leaves the question of where does desire come from; it is a secondary construct. Lacanian desire is primary, with its impetus in the experience of lack; lack as primary and social.

As discussed earlier, the split subject is alienated in language. This occurs as the child confronts the Other as language. In addition to the process of alienation, Fink discusses that of 'separation,' involving the alienated subject's confrontation with the Other, this time as desire. In Lacanian analysis, desire is coextensive with lack. Without lack, without negativity or absence in Kristevan terms, there can be no desire (and no subject). The infant's wish or fantasy is to be all for the mother, to be all that she desires. As the infant becomes aware that the mother's attention is focused at least partly elsewhere (her partner, work, interests) the infant becomes aware of the lack in the Other. The Other's desire, the lack in the Other, becomes the cause of the subject's desire, furthermore, as such it becomes the cause of his or her being.[46] This needs to be explained. As Fink describes it, where *alienation* creates a kind of "forced choice" (as an either/or) whereby the only choice is to take up the position of subject within the symbolic order and thereby embrace the possibility of 'existence'[47] but to give up 'being' (the full plenitude of being), *separation* forces the alienated subject to grapple with the desire of the Other. Unlike the either/or of alienation, separation is structured as a neither/nor. The elusiveness of being comes from neither the subject nor the Other; rather the child tries to make the two lacks (that of the subject and the Other) coincide, or overlap so the one might fulfil the Other. It is the intervention of the third term (the paternal metaphor in the form of the master signifier) that enables language to effectively ensure that the mother–child dyad does not close over itself. This occurs through the substitution of a name for the mother's desire; in other words a signifier, firstly as the name-of-the-father (signifying that which she desires), which then in turn creates the conditions for the mother's desire to be symbolized, to circulate in the field of signification. Fink points out that this allows for the child to mediate the desire of the Other by symbolising 'it,' signifying in the place of its absence, and the result, he argues, is the "advent of a desiring subject."[48] The signifier of the Other's desire in Western culture is the phallus (according to Fink, this is by no means a necessary designation, and it could be otherwise and probably is in some other cultures, but the fact that it is the case in the West is, he claims, attested repeatedly in clinical psychoanalytic practice).[49] The phallus, as signifier of desire, is nothing more than a signifier; it is the signifier of lack.

There is an additional point that needs to be grasped before we can address the question of how *jouissance*, fantasy and the relation with the real might be implicated in the very act of sexual violation. This is the notion of *objet a*, the contribution to psychoanalysis that Lacan considered his most significant. As we have seen, Lacan argues that the cause of desire lies in the desiring-ness of the Other, and this also originates in some aspect or directedness of the Other's desire that seems to have nothing at all to do with the child, which in fact takes the attention of the Other away and beyond. *Objet a* is this cause of desire—in the sense of that which seems to escape the child, and creates a rupture in the (illusionary) mother–child unity. This rupture, or rift occurs because of desire, and leads to the advent of *objet a*. As Fink writes, "Object *a* can be understood here as the *remainder* produced when that hypothetical unity breaks down, as a last trace of that unity, a last *reminder* thereof."[50] It is through a "cleaving" to that rem(a)inder, to *objet a* as cause of desire, that the split subject can "sustain the illusion of wholeness," and "ignore his or her division." The important point here is that Fink underlines how "[t]hat is precisely what Lacan means by fantasy."[51] In its complex and multifaceted relation to *objet a* the subject achieves the fulfilling fantasmatic sense of wholeness and well-being:

> Fantasy [. . .] takes the subject beyond his or her nothingness, his or her mere existence as a marker at the level of alienation, and supplies a sense of being. It is thus only through fantasy, made possible by separation, that the subject can procure him or herself some modicum of what Lacan calls 'being.' While existence is granted only through the symbolic order (the alienated subject being assigned a place therein), being is supplied only by cleaving to the real.[52]

Fantasy is thus integral to the subject's achievement of a sense of being. Fantasy engages the subject's desire, manifest as it is in the relation to the desire of the Other, the Other's lack, to *objet a*. In this way, *objet a* (unspeakable, unrepresentable, unable to be signified) enters into fantasy as that which can be manipulated and played with in the way that is most pleasing to the subject, that incites the most enjoyment and excitement. The mise-en-scène of the fantasy scenario can be set to derive as much excitement and sensual pleasure as possible for the subject.[53] This is at the heart of Lacan's multifaceted use of the term *jouissance:* the exquisite sensual experience of excitement resulting from the fantasy in which the subject literally casts (in the theatrical sense) the Other's desire in whatever way that is most pleasing, or more specifically, most exciting to him or her. This excitement, this pleasure can be one that is experienced by the conscious subject as a scene of pleasure or pain; it may be a scene of horror or disgust; it may be a scene of innocent sensuality or torment and violence. Whatever it is, it is the fantasmatic formulation of the Other's desire, of *objet a* that is most exciting to the subject. *Jouissance* thus comes to substitute for the lost unity of the maternal matrix in Kristevan terms, and thus is related to deathwork.[54] As Fink notes, in accord with Lacan who stated simply that there is no whole—that nothing is whole—this 'unity' was never 'united,' as "it was a unity owing only to the child's sacrifice or foregoing of subjectivity."[55]

How does *jouissance* differ for the masculine and the feminine? In Lacanian terms, the sexual difference of masculine and feminine is nothing other than a differential structural relation to the symbolic order, as discussed earlier; in other words, different ways of being split as subjects; different positions in relation to existence as a practice of absence, in Kristevan terms. As such it has nothing to do with biological males and females. It is not about bits of bodies and how they differ. It is not about 'sexual identity,' which is rather the result of identifications constituted within the ego and thus of the order of the imaginary. Sexual identity can itself be highly self-contradictory, and is not necessarily in harmony with the masculine or feminine structure, which is of the order of sexed subjectivity.

Masculine and feminine structures, typically men and women but not necessarily, take up a different relation to *jouissance*. Lacan's concept of castration, more generally characterising a structure or logic of lack or loss, focuses most specifically on that part of *jouissance* that must be given up, sacrificed, renounced by the subject in the processes of alienation and separation; this sacrificed 'part' of *jouissance* being the greater 'part' in that what is left is described by Lacan as a "mere pittance." This is particularly the case for the masculine: the feminine position requires less renunciation of *jouissance* than is required by the masculine position—a conclusion Lacan tracks back to Freud.

In Lacan's analysis, masculine and feminine are structures positioned or defined differently in relation to loss or lack; the alienating function of language splits, and constitutes, masculine and feminine subjects differently. The masculine and the feminine take on their difference, not from one another, but from their differential relation to a third term: that of the symbolic order. This appears to be the key point with respect to Lacan's claim that "there is no such thing as a sexual relationship." With reference to Fink's analysis, men (and he is careful to be clear that this categorization is referring not to men in biological terms, but to masculine subjects in psychoanalytic terms, which includes many 'women') as masculine subjects are determined fully by the phallic function; in other words they are "wholly alienated within language."[56] They are, in their subjectivity, completely and altogether subject to the symbolic order. This Lacanian masculine structure might be analyzed in relation to Reineke's rendition of Kristevan 'death-work' discussed previously whereby she argues that sacrifice places death-work under the sign in order to secure subjectivity against threat. In Fink's rendition of Lacanian sexual difference, it is not a matter of the sacrificial, but is rather a structural imperative imposed by the nature of language. As I will discuss below, this distinction leads them to different psychoanalytic 'paths' for an ethic of being as sexed subjects that is not dependent on the violent exclusion or expulsion of the Other, paths that do appear to converge.

This masculine structuring of subjectivity has implications for men's pleasures. According to Lacan, these are limited to a phallic *jouissance* that is circumscribed, allowed by, or determined by the play of the signifier itself: the phallic signifier. The master or phallic signifier (the phallus as prohibition against incest as the Father's 'No') acts as a limit in absolute terms. As Fink writes: "Insofar as it is related to the body, phallic or symbolic *jouissance* involves only the organ designated by the signifier, which thus serves as a mere extension or instrument of the signifier."[57] At the level of the all-important fantasy, men's fantasies are confined to, or as Fink writes, "tied to" that "aspect of the real that underwrites the symbolic order,"[58] which is *objet a*. This is precisely the point that leads to the conclusion that men do not have a sexual 'relation' with women per se, but with fantasy, with *objet a* (even though the ideal of noncastration, of no boundaries and limits might, as Fink suggests, live on in each man).

Women, or the feminine structure of subjectivity, however, takes its definitional characteristic precisely through *not* being defined wholly by the phallic function, whose alienation within language is therefore not total or complete. By virtue of her different relation to the master signifier, the phallic signifier, she is not limited by it in the same way. "With respect to the symbolic order, a woman is not whole, bound, or limited."[59] As Elliot analyzes with a slightly different emphasis:

> Man can only imagine himself as a self-determining, independent subject insofar as he projects his own lack elsewhere. At the same time, woman, in assuming her status as other, as object, as cause of man's desire, repudiates her own desire and reinforces man's position as the 'one supposed to know.'[60]

This different relation means that women's *jouissance* is not limited to the solely phallic *jouissance*, but that she can access (at least in terms of structural potential) an Other *jouissance*. The "mere pittance of pleasure" left to the masculine who cannot step beyond the limits and boundaries set by language, does not comprise the same constraint for the feminine who can go beyond these limits and boundaries.[61] To return to the discussion of Kristeva, does this also mean that the feminine subject has more latitude to engage threat creatively? Is it possible that she can finesse boundaries in a seductive play? And yet given the constraints governing the masculine subject's boundaries, given his more narrowly constrained reactive boundary defences, does this mean that he will experience the feminine seductive play as precisely threatening his defences in a way that infuriates?

In psychoanalytic terms, tuned acutely and necessarily to the clinical context, this Lacanian analysis suggests that specifically sexual violence might be understood to emerge out of a collapse or implosion of fantasy and 'reality' (reality in the sense of the world of others in the social, constituted as it is by language). As we have seen, the fantasy and the *jouissance* it takes as its aim, is the subject's play featuring *objet a*. As such it *may* be violent and stage a fantasmatic murder or torture causing fantasized pain degradation or humiliation (it is, after all, engaging the fantasy of the Other's desire). Where actual sexual violence ensues it is possible that the fantasy becomes inseparable from the actuality of sexual interaction with another, and the drama of 'relationship' becomes implicated in the urgency of a fantasmatic phallic *jouissance*. This analysis is suggested by Claude Balier whose psychoanalytic work with sexually violent, incarcerated criminals is well-known in France.[62] The clinical picture he describes is one in which the sexually violent subject is in full denial of reality, and as such in full denial of absence. If existence is, as Reineke's Kristevan reading proposes, a practice of absence, and if death-work is how we live and do that practice of absence as alienated subjects, to deny reality and thus to deny absence is one sacrificial act possible for a subject threatened by boundary-failure.[63]

Feminist theorizing of sexual violence will always push beyond the pathological, which is not to deny the significance of understanding such processes but is rather to seek out questions that point towards the conditions of possibility for those pathologies and openings for sociocultural transformation. Although beyond the scope of this chapter, it is noteworthy that the observations made by Balier mentioned earlier, synchronize with current theorizations by Lacan on psychosis and modernity, by Kristeva on 'new maladies of the soul,' and Baudrillard on the state of the subject in our contemporary age of the virtual, all suggesting that the implosion or blurring of fantasy and reality might be something of a signature of a postmodern subjectivity.

I will conclude with some thoughts on what the psychoanalytic ideas presented in this chapter imply for theorizing sexual violence, focusing on the ethical and political transformations they suggest.

VIOLENCE OF BEING BETWEEN LANGUAGE AND JOUISSANCE—FRAMING QUESTIONS

> The analytic approach I am advocating posits women and men as subjects of possibility, neither masters of ourselves nor victims of some predetermined social or biological necessity.[64]

Through Reineke's analysis and critical engagement with the works of Kristeva for her own project of understanding of the gendered nature of sacrificial violence, she highlights one aspect of Kristeva's work where she departs from that of Lacan. Like Lacan, Kristeva emphasizes the significance of the bodily drives to the entire psychoanalytic project, but beyond this she insists on the ongoing influence of the negativity associated with the semiotic in its abjected maternal materiality. Such an emphasis suggests that women's bodies are either more likely to be scapegoated and sacrificed in the Girardian sense, or they at least represent a site where a particular dynamic of gender is at work in the violence of this process. This employment of the Girardian analysis of sacrifice and violence opens on to the intrinsic connection between psychoanalysis and the sociocultural, political, economic domain: sacrifice is essentially about the projection of fear, or more accurately dread, onto another. This dynamic, analyzed so clearly by Girard in the domain of culture, can be seen to be reflected in the psychoanalytic domain as a dynamic bearing on the intimate structures of (sexed) subjectivity.

This violence of asserting presence to counter the threat of absence is endlessly repeated when that very countering, the death-work, is structured within a sacrificial economy, when the boundary of presence is 'rescued' or shored up through a process of making bodies signify—killing, or subduing, controlling, directing, moulding, substance to make it signify. The suggestion by Kristeva that death-work does not have to be sacrificial, and how this might become possible, is developed in her writings following *Powers of Horror* and *Tales of Love* (in *Strangers to Ourselves* and *Nations Without Nationalism*).[65] The trope of maternity is used in Kristeva's *Sabat Mater*[66] to point to a way for the reconfiguration of difference as that which is outside, separate, other and strange, to that of difference within: "an imprint of the other within the same."[67] Kristeva presents an ethic of subjectivity that, instead of finding the 'cause' of suffering, or the origin of threat, in (any) other(s), in she or he who is foreign, different, strange, the incitement is to recognize the otherness within: "I must tame the demons within myself."[68]

The psychoanalytic path to 'realize' the 'Truth'[69] of being a sexed human subject in the work of Lacan evokes what is possibly, and not surprisingly, a similar ethic to that of Kristeva. The task is articulated differently, and importantly involves different paths for the masculine and feminine structures, according to Fink. For the masculine, the cause of desire is to be made one's own, becoming one's own cause. In Freud's words: "Wo Es war, soll Ich werden" which Fink translates as "where the Other pulls the strings (acting as my cause), I must come into being as my own cause."[70] The ethical component for Lacan here is simply "one is always responsible for one's position as subject."[71] This process is one Fink refers to as "subjectifying" one's own cause; making otherness one's own; to create a new relation to the object. This has some similarity to Kristeva's stranger within. The feminine is also invoked to make one's own of otherness, but requiring a somewhat different subjectification. The ethical task for the feminine is to subjectify the previously unspoken, unwritten real that manifests in the Other *jouissance*, in the Other 'sex'—to symbolize, represent the real of their experience, through a path of sublimation; to create a new relation to the signifier.

In each case, both that suggested by the work of Kristeva and of Lacan discussed here, the subject confronts the possibility of relinquishing the sense of itself as a breach against otherness, in the masculine as that which must be defended, secured and sutured, and in the feminine as that which is subjected.

A central debate within psychoanalytic feminism since the 1980s is the question of phallocentrism: the inevitability or otherwise of the privileged status of the phallus as master signifier within the symbolic order. Is it the case that gendered subjectivity must be structured in relation to the phallus?[72] As a contributor to this debate, Jacqueline Rose, writing in 1982, expressed the conclusion that "if the status of the phallus is to be challenged" it must be "by means of a different symbolic term (in which case the relation to the body is immediately thrown into crisis)" or else "by an entirely different logic altogether (in which case one is no longer in the order of symbolisation at all)."[73] Such a view is consistent with Lacanian psychoanalytic thought, and it is also the case that Kristeva did not propose that gender in some way can be understood to be prior to language, prior to the symbolic, constituted as it is by/within language. Possibly the central question for psychoanalytic feminism, in consideration of sexual violence, that is suggested by this discussion is not the question of phallocentrism and how to challenge the inevitability of the privileged status of the phallus. Rather the question of importance might be *how* to confront the inevitability of negativity, of 'living at a loss,' through a paradoxical ethic that refuses a detour from the death-drive, that traverses the fantasy and that fully enables a subjectivity that is split by language and divided by desire. To engage the challenge such an ethic presents would lead away from the possibility of blaming the other as the cause of suffering, so detested by Nietzsche, would obviate the possibility of being a victim of another's anger or hatred and violence, and would thus reverse the possibility of a politics of *ressentiment*. The pain and suffering would be experienced, the act of violence responded to, reversed through being challenged to death possibly, all the while knowing that there cannot be a 'knowing' of its 'cause.'

NOTES

1. Friedrich Nietzsche, *On the Genealogy of Morals*, trans. Walter Kaufman and R.J. Hollingdale (New York: Vintage Books, 1967 [German original 1889]).
2. Ibid., 118.
3. Martha Reineke, *Sacrificed Lives, Kristeva on Women and Violence* (Bloomington, IN: Indiana University Press, 1997).
4. Patricia Elliot, *From Mastery to Analysis: Theories of Gender in Psychoanalytic Feminism* (Ithaca, NY: Cornell University Press, 1991).
5. Jouissance is italicised because it is a French word, considered to be untranslatable in a single word in English. It will be discussed further in this chapter.
6. René Girard, *Violence and the Sacred*, trans. Patrick Gregory (Baltimore, MD: The Johns Hopkins University Press, 1977 [French original 1972]), 151.
7. Chambers *Dictionary of Etymology* (Edinburgh, UK: Chambers Harrap Publishers, 1988).
8. See Jean-Jacques Walter, *Psychanalyse des Rites, La Face Cachée de l'Histoire des Hommes* (Psychoanalysis of Rituals, The Hidden Face of the History of Humankind; Paris: Denoël/Gonthier, 1977).
9. Girard 1977 (French original 1972), op. cit., 81.
10. René Girard, *Things Hidden Since the Foundation of the World*, trans. Stephen Bann and Michael Metteer (Stanford, CA: Stanford University Press, 1987 [French original 1978]). See chapter two of Book III.
11. Ibid., 299.
12. Ibid., 307.
13. Ibid., 307.
14. Julia Kristeva, *Nations Without Nationalism*, trans. Leon S. Roudiez (New York: Columbia University Press, 1993). I note that this quote prefaces Martha Reineke's book on Kristeva, women, and violence.

15. Elliot, op. cit.
16. Cleo Kearns, "Kristeva and Feminist Theology," in *Transfigurations: Theology and the French Feminists*, eds. C.W. Maggie Kim, Susan M. St Ville, and Susan M. Simonaitis, (Minneapolis, MN: Fortress Press, 1993), 49–83.
17. Kelly Oliver, *Reading Kristeva: Unravelling the Double Bind* (Bloomington, IN: Indiana University Press, 1993).
18. Reineke, op. cit., 6.
19. Ibid., 19.
20. See Bruce Fink, *The Lacanian Subject, Between Language and Jouissance* (Princeton, NJ: Princeton University Press, 1995).
21. Ibid., 41.
22. This view originated with Freud, who was clear that the unconscious, which contains repressed wishes or drives, does not contain thoughts or affects as such but rather "representatives of the (re)presentation or idea"; Lacan understands these representatives of the drives as signifiers, words that stand in for the drives (see Fink, op. cit., 73). In Ellie Ragland's reading of Lacan, that which is repressed is precisely unsymbolized meanings; "meanings that have not yet been translated into language" (98–99). See Ellie Ragland, *Essays on the Pleasures of Death, Freud and Lacan* (New York: Routledge, 1995).
23. Ibid., 46.
24. Reineke, op. cit., 19.
25. Against the notion of the semiotic as the reading of signs as in medicine or linguistics, Kristeva employs the term to refer to the irrepressible eruption of the nonrepresentable being-in-the-real.
26. Ibid., 22.
27. Elliot, op. cit., 53.
28. Reineke, op. cit., 55.
29. Elliot, op. cit., 191.
30. Reineke, op. cit., 49.
31. Soma meaning of the body, bodily.
32. Ibid., 69.
33. Ibid., 68.
34. Ibid., 85; also see Jean-Thierry Maertens for an in-depth elaboration of these processes in numerous cultural contexts (Jean-Thierry Maertens, *Ritologiques* [*Ritologics*; Paris: Aubier, 1978]).
35. See Jacques Lacan, "The splendor of Antigone," in Book VII *The Ethics of Psychoanalysis*, 1959–1960, trans. Dennis Porter (New York: Norton, 1992 [French original 1986]).
36. Ibid., 245.
37. Reineke, op. cit., 70.
38. Ibid., citing Kristeva.
39. Ibid., 91.
40. Ragland, op. cit., 93.
41. See James Penney, *The World of Perversion: Psychoanalysis and the Impossible Absolute of Desire* (New York: State University of New York Press, 2006), for an in-depth analysis of, and argument for, the value of the psychoanalytic notion of the perversions, against Foucault, and for the political strategies of queer theory.
42. For a psychoanalytic discussion of the connections between anger and libido, see the work of Lacanian analyst Gerard Pommier, *Erotic Anger*, trans. Catherine Liu (Minneapolis: University of Minnesota Press, 2001).
43. See all references to jouissance indexed by Reineke, op. cit.; for example, pp. 24, 52 (index to 'defined' on p. 19 appears to be erroneous).

44. Fink, op. cit., 90, I have chosen to base this discussion on Fink's analysis of the Lacanian subject, because his work is, in my view, one of the most pertinent accounts focussing on the specific aspects of Lacan's work of importance for this project.

45. Ibid., 91.

46. Paul Verhaeghe, among others, comments on Lacan's notion of 'cause,' consistent with Lacan's relentless deflection of any pretence to a master discourse, 'cause' in the Lacanian lexicon is more accurately rendered by a nondeterminism; to seek a cause is to seek that which is undetermined. The Lacanian cause is exactly not that cause conceptualised as a determination apparent in sets of relations observable in 'reality.' When fissures and gaps appear in this appearance, where nondetermined elements arise, this is what Lacan invokes by the concept of cause. See Paul Verhaeghe, *Beyond Gender, From Subject to Drive* (New York: Other Press, 2001), 127–128.

47. Existence in the etymological meaning: outside of a state of being, ex (outside of), stence (state), the deity does not exist.

48. Fink, op. cit., 58.

49. Ibid., 102.

50. Ibid., 59.

51. Ibid.

52. Ibid., 60.

53. This discussion relies on Fink's interpretation, see p. 60.

54. Ragland, op. cit. 99, reiterates this point in the following way: "Jouissance effects bespeak a knowledge of loss so fundamental in the grounding of one's illusion of being a being, that people never quit trying to recapture or maintain a sense of Oneness in all things."

55. Ibid.

56. Ibid., 106.

57. Ibid., 106–107.

58. Ibid., 107.

59. Ibid.

60. Elliot, op. cit., 84.

61. Verhaeghe (op. cit., 104) notes that in his view a "post-Lacanian hype" surrounding 'feminine jouissance' can only be understood as an "hysterical attempt to recuperate something that, due to its very nature, cannot be recuperated." This reflection signals the importance of precisely not treading a non-Lacanian path with Lacanian concepts.

62. Claude Balier, *Psychanalyse des Comportment Sexuels Violents: une Pathologie de l'Inachèvement* (Psychoanalysis of Violent Sexual Behavior: A Pathology of Non-achievement), 3rd edition (Paris: Presses Universitaires France, 1999 [French original 1996]).

63. Balier, ibid., argues for a new categorization for those prone to sexual violence, suggesting it represents a highly specific pattern of pathology that is close to the psychotic but not to be confused with it, and is to be distinguished from the 'sexual perversions,' including fetishism, and from the 'moral perversions.'

64. Elliot, op. cit., 240.

65. See Julia Kristeva, *Strangers to Ourselves*, trans. Leon, S. Roudiez (New York: Columbia University Press, 1991); also *Nations Without Nationalism*, trans. Leon S. Roudiez (New York: Columbia University Press, 1993).

66. Julia Kristeva, "Sabat Mater," in *The Kristeva Reader*, ed. Toril Moi (New York: Columbia University Press, 1986), 160–186,.

67. Cited in Reineke, op. cit., 174ff.

68. Ibid., 177.

69. Truth in Lacanian discourse is solely about truth related to desire. It is not a universal truth; it does not precede its discovery somehow preformed; it is rather produced in the dialectics of the psychoanalytic encounter. In this sense it is an individual truth, as Dylan Evans writes, "unique to each subject" (215). To confront the truth is to come to know the truth of one's desire. See Dylan Evans, *An Introductory Dictionary of Lacanian Psychoanalysis* (London: Routledge, 1996).
70. Fink, op. cit., xiii.
71. Cited in ibid., 47.
72. See Elliot ibid. for a discussion of this debate in 1991, especially Chapter Two.
73. Jacqueline Rose, "Introduction II," in *Jacques Lacan & the Ecole Freudienne, Feminine Sexuality*, eds Juliet Mitchell and Jacqueline Rose (London: Macmillan Press, 1982), 56.

3 'Reality Check'
Rethinking the Ethics of Vulnerability

Ann V. Murphy

Contemporary feminist theory is replete with references to the vulnerable body, and many writing within the tradition of feminist philosophy are presently preoccupied with this motif. Several feminist theorists are thinking through what it means to claim that vulnerability is constitutive of subjectivity, and the ethical consequences of this claim. A number of feminists, including Debra Bergoffen, Judith Butler, Rosalyn Diprose, and Kelly Oliver have recently published material that critiques the individualism and autonomy of the late modern subject through an appeal to figures such as vulnerability, generosity, witnessing, and dispossession. Bergoffen has argued for a new conception of politics that favors vulnerability over autonomy as the basis for personhood.[1] Rosalyn Diprose has considered the various ways in which political liberalism, and other contractarian political models, conceal a primordial corporeal generosity that is constitutive of human subjectivity.[2] Butler has asked, "What politics might be implied by staying with the thought of corporeal vulnerability itself?"[3] And most recently, in *Women as Weapons of War*, Kelly Oliver has similarly argued for a reconception of ethics based on the fundamental interdependence and mutual vulnerability that all human beings evince.[4] What follows is a critical diagnosis of the ethical consequences of the 'return' to vulnerability in contemporary feminist theory, particularly when thought in light of the political realities of sexual violence.

Vulnerability is not a novel theme in philosophy, nor is there anything particularly surprising in feminists choosing to engage this theme. Feminist philosophy has its own specific interest in discourses on care and dependency, and has had for some time.[5] Nonetheless, there is something novel in the way in which feminists are presently approaching this motif. In the past, vulnerability has been figured as something that plagues women disproportionately. Women's embodied vulnerability to various types of sexual violence and oppression has been figured as a liability in need of redress. In the last decade, however, a different feminist position on vulnerability has emerged, one that looks to the experience of vulnerability for what it may provide in terms of ethical and political provocation. Feminists suggest that the motif of vulnerability may be productively mined by those interested in exploring the possibility of an ethics of nonviolence. The claim would be that there is something in the experience of one's own vulnerability that allows for an appreciation of the vulnerability of others. Hence the challenge implicit in the recent feminist 'return to vulnerability' is to delineate a movement from the experience of vulnerability to an ethical comportment that respects and does not abuse the vulnerability of others. Withal, the contemporary return to vulnerability in feminist theory is both redemptive and aspirational. As such, it echoes a long-standing concern in feminist ethics, namely the idea that culturally feminine—and hence undervalued—traits such as interdependence, community mindedness and vulnerability should be given their due, and that traditionally masculine traits such as independence and autonomy have been overvalued in the domain of ethics. While the return to vulnerability is consistent with this long-standing feminist agenda, and provocative in many respects, it can also be problematized in the domain of ethics.

This chapter argues that from the perspective of ethics, the recent 'return to vulnerability' is complicated and ultimately ambiguous. This argument proceeds in three stages. Firstly, experiential narratives lay bare the fact that there is frequently an impulse towards retributive violence that follows close on the heels of many instances in which one is forced to contend with one's own vulnerable body. There is absolutely no guarantee that the realization of one's own vulnerability will motivate an attempt to respect the vulnerability of others. Indeed, there is ample evidence to the contrary. A sense of one's own dispossession, availability to others, and vulnerability may incite violence just as readily as it does empathy, care, or tolerance. A second and related claim follows: from the perspective of ethics, there is no normative or prescriptive force to be mined from these experiences. To argue that one is inherently vulnerable and dispossessed is not to say anything about the ethics or politics that follow upon such a claim. Finally, from an ethical standpoint, assuming the profile of the vulnerable body without appreciating the different ways in which different bodies are vulnerable risks generalizing the motif of vulnerability to the point of abstraction and inefficacy. Feminist theorists must be particularly vigilant in this regard as they work with a category—'woman'—that is radically animated along other critical axes. To blithely speak of "violence against women," for instance, runs the risk of effacing racial or class differences.

Much of this argument proceeds in a domain where ethics and politics overlap, and this is entirely consistent with the long-standing insistence on the part of feminist ethicists that ethics must "come down to earth" and speak to the particular configurations of power and political circumstance in which ethical aims are articulated. Feminists have long insisted that ethics, as that domain of thought that attends to questions of right and wrong, and of what it means to live a good life, is entangled with politics. The notion that the domains of ethics and politics could ever be discrete has justifiably been eyed with suspicion. Traditionally, moral philosophers have tended to favor universal, generalized descriptions of the ethical subject. The attempt to formulate a moral code that would be universally binding has necessarily tended to import an abstract and universal conception of ethical subjectivity. Since feminist theory is preoccupied with the dynamics of power at play in the articulation of sexually specific bodies and the various kinds of violence that these bodies both suffer and enact, a different conception of ethics follows, one that resists the pretense of abstraction and that aims to more meaningfully address considerations of power and politics.

The theorization of sexual violence in particular demands that one attempt to speak to the myriad ways in which ethics become altered as they are actualized in the political domain. The argument here is that while the renaissance of interest in vulnerability is in many ways promising, when the ethics of vulnerability are thought in the domain of politics, or in light of the reality of sexual violence, their promise appears to be ambiguous. Indeed, there is an irreducible singularity in the experience of vulnerability, one that belies any categorical account of how it is that vulnerability and dispossession are lived. This chapter argues that the return to vulnerability must constantly be subjected to a 'reality check' in order that it resist its own universalizing tendencies. Simply stated, it is ethically unclear what an affirmation of universal exposure suggests. When questions of right and wrong are thought in light of concrete circumstance, an appeal to vulnerability becomes complicated in terms of the diversity of experience it conjures, the ethical impulses that result, and the profile of the vulnerable body that is assumed in such appeals. The three sections of this chapter respectively address these three ambiguities. The title of this chapter suggests that an ethical appeal to the reality of vulnerability is an appeal to a 'reality' that is always already circumscribed by the interests of some but not all. For this reason, 'reality' should never be conceived as a neutral ground from which to commence the articulation of a feminist ethics.

FEMINIST ETHICS AND THE RETURN TO VULNERABILITY

Thinking surrounding embodiment could surely be credited with governing the evolution of feminist theory in some sense. For much of the 1980s and 1990s the debate over social constructionism was at the fore of feminist theory, and a critique of the nature/culture binary was dominant in thinking about the body. [6] The central concern in feminist philosophy at that time was the worry about what different discourses—from phenomenology to poststructuralism to psychoanalysis—had to say about the various ways in which gendered bodies were sculpted through sometimes violent means by various discursive and social institutions. If critical engagement with the nature/culture binary governed discourse on the social construction of the body for much of the nineties, the body is now also being figured in light of another binary, that of vulnerability and aggression. Hence although the focus on the body in feminist theory has not diminished, the 'body' under investigation has changed. It is not enough, however, to simply suggest that a new binary has ascended to predominance; such a claim would elide not only the forceful criticism of binary thinking with which feminists have been preoccupied for decades, but also the relation between the debates on social construction of the 1990s with current feminist thinking on violence. Of course bodies do not emerge ex nihilo as differentially violable or violent; they are socially constructed as such. The debates surrounding social construction continue to play out on theoretical terrain marked by an interest in violence and vulnerability.

Recently, feminist philosophers have become interested in how experiences of dispossession, vulnerability and exposure can motivate retributive acts of aggression and violence. One critical impulse has been to critique these instances of violence via recourse to the opposite that is via an appeal to the realities of vulnerability and passivity that a patriarchal culture of violence and domination tends to denigrate. To be sure, even though there must be an enduring effort to advance claims to bodily integrity and self-determination on the part of women (and while these claims undoubtedly inform much of feminist politics), there is a sense in which the body we defend as our own can never be only that. As embodied, we are necessarily exposed to others; we struggle for recognition, and suffer for the lack thereof. Hence while feminist theorists acknowledge the importance of claims to bodily integrity, they also suggest that there must be another normative aspiration that rests alongside these claims to autonomy and self-determination. Claims to autonomy and integrity must be coincident with the acknowledgement we are radically dependent on others for the formation and persistence of our social selves.

In this sense, the resurrection of the theme of vulnerability in recent feminist theory marks a departure from the manner in which that motif has been deployed in the past, where women's exaggerated vulnerability to sexual violence served as the principal locus of redress. Indeed, the "feminist contentions" of the 1990s were grounded in debates concerning which type of theory would best address the vulnerability of women, both as subjects positioned in language, and as a victims of physical abuse or neglect.[7] Hence this return to vulnerability is remarkable in many respects, not least because it emerges in a tradition of feminist thinking that has taken the ideal of bodily integrity to be an almost unquestioned good, a right that women should demand, and moreover one that is constantly under assault. Hence while some may laud the virtues of vulnerability, there are others for whom vulnerability remains a more precarious and threatening reality. As noted previously, feminists have long taken as one of their guiding aims the address and amelioration of women's embodied vulnerability to various types of violence. This concern is evident in the rhetoric of 'wholeness' and integrity that informs feminist discourses on recovery from rape and sexual assault.[8] It is for this reason that the recent revaluation of the motifs of dispossession and vulnerability is particularly provocative in the context of contemporary feminist thought. Especially in regard to the issue of sexual violence, this return to vulnerability appears precarious; it is a return to a theme that is deeply vexed in the history of feminist theory.

The inherently ambiguous nature of embodied vulnerability is particularly obvious when it is viewed through the lens of phenomenology, a branch of philosophy that champions experience as the privileged locus of theoretical investigation. Here one might consider any one of several accounts of oppression and vulnerability that emerge from the tradition of existential phenomenology, including Simone de Beauvoir's investigation of sexed embodiment, as well as Frantz Fanon's descriptions of black embodiment under colonialism.[9] For Fanon, the experience of dispossession was one of horror and despair. Describing the experience of racialized objectification in the eyes of the colonizer, he writes that his body is given back to him "sprawled out, distorted, recoloured, clad in mourning."[10] Fanon's descriptions of embodiment are rife with images of amputation, excision, and dislocation. In short, they are metaphors of dispossession that bring home its most violent dimension. Similarly, Beauvoir's discussion of the body in *The Second Sex* is rife with accounts of the dispossession and alienation that women may feel as they confront a masculine gaze that robs them of their authority and agency.[11] These experiences of dispossession challenge the virtues of a return to vulnerability, as would the narratives of women whose reproductive rights are under assault, or the testimony of refugees or the homeless, for whom dispossession is an all too real experience of dislocation and despair. This much is clear given the significance of a language of possession and ownership being used in current discourse on the body by those experiencing such dispossession. One can hardly speak coherently of dispossession without acknowledging that there is something sacrosanct in possession itself, particularly when it comes to one's own rights over one's body.[12] This is one sense in which an appeal to vulnerability is experientially complicated; for some, a sense of dispossession may be accompanied by a sense of communion with others, or by empathy for others' suffering; for others it may be experienced solely as violation and terror. It consequently remains unclear what type of politics the realities of dispossession and exposure gesture towards.

What, then, does the ambiguity at play in embodied vulnerability mean for ethics? What warrants the return to this motif in theory? Moreover, what does it mean to conceive vulnerability as a basis for community? Judith Butler's thinking on vulnerability in her recent texts *Undoing Gender* and *Precarious Life* is informed by a concern to critique the kinds of violence that are motivated by various attempts to foreclose, shore up, or conceal one's own vulnerability. In other words, she suggests that there is some ethical merit in "tarrying with," "attending to," or "remaining exposed" to the reality of one's own vulnerability. Instead of the primacy that autonomy and independence have been afforded in traditional elaborations of ethics, Butler argues that it is an inevitable interdependency, a primary vulnerability, which might instead be acknowledged as the basis for global political community.[13] While she confesses to not knowing precisely how to theorize this interdependency, she is convinced of the necessity of imagining the possibility of community on the basis of vulnerability and loss.[14] This condition of vulnerability and mutual interdependence is not one with which we can argue. Indeed, Butler claims that the ubiquitous attempts to nullify or diminish this interdependence are not only counterproductive but also ethically bankrupt.

Undoing Gender is concerned with various modes of *dispossession* that are actualized in the modern subject. Gender and sexuality qualify as modes of dispossession, or ways of being disposed towards others. This sense of dispossession is inherently corporeal, as it is "through the body that gender and sexuality become exposed to others, implicated in social processes, inscribed by cultural norms, and apprehended in their social meanings."[15] Of course it is equally through the social that embodied gender and sexuality become constituted via interactions with others. Hence important political struggles in the name of bodily integrity must contend with the fact that as embodied, we are necessarily dispossessed and available to others:

> The body implies mortality, vulnerability, agency: the skin and the flesh expose us to the gaze of others but also to touch and to violence. The body can be the agency and instrument of all of these as well, or the site where 'doing' and 'being done to' become equivocal. Although we struggle for rights over our own bodies, the very bodies for which we struggle are not ever quite our own.[16]

If dispossession is a requisite dimension of embodied life, Butler is cognizant of the fact that experientially this sense of dispossession has the potential to be both jubilant and terrifying. Vulnerability and aggression often emerge in precarious tandem, or as Elaine Miller suggests "this is to say that as the other of violence, vulnerability may itself constitute or be constituted by violence in a way that puts its appeal into question."[17] This experiential reality leads to a further complication when thinking through how it is that vulnerability might be said to ground an ethics of nonviolence, namely the fact that there is nothing normative or ethically prescriptive in pointing to vulnerability as an intrinsic dimension of human existence.

THE ETHICAL AMBIGUITY OF VULNERABILITY

Butler's recent work provokes serious reckoning with the fact that there is not any *specific* ethics or politics that are implied by "staying with the thought of corporeal vulnerability." While it is tempting to argue that there is some definitive sense of responsibility that should follow from the recognition of one's own vulnerability, and the similar vulnerability of others, there is in fact no particular ethics that is suggested by an ontology of vulnerability. One is thus in bad faith to claim that the recognition of one's own vulnerability provides a sense of responsibility for the similarly vulnerable other. Butler would herself claim that this leap is in bad faith; there is too much evidence in front of us to the contrary. To simply nod in the direction of dispossession or vulnerability is not good enough.

Butler frequently notes that a heightened sense of vulnerability is one that is often coincident with a similarly heightened sense of aggression, which is evidence of the fact that there is nothing in the acknowledgement of one's own embodied vulnerability that necessarily inspires generosity, empathy, or tolerance. Nonetheless, she suggests that "the fact that our lives are dependent on others can become the basis for non-militaristic political solutions, one which we cannot will away, one which we must attend to, even abide by, as we begin to think about what politics might be implied by staying with the thought of corporeal vulnerability itself."[18] This is not to herald or elevate passivity, nor is it to suggest that one must resign oneself to it; it is rather to suggest that the paradox that passivity presents, or the experience of passivity, is ethically provocative.

Butler's investment in vulnerability stems from a correlative interest in the roles that grief, loss, and mourning play in politics, even as these roles are frequently obscured. The instances of grief that follow upon the realization of vulnerability often motivate retaliation, but Butler remains convinced that other avenues are opened by grief as well:

> To grieve, and to make grief into a resource for politics, is not be resigned to a simple passivity or powerlessness. It is, rather, to allow oneself to extrapolate from this experience of vulnerability to the vulnerability that others suffer through military incursions, occupations, suddenly declared wars, and police brutality. That our very survival can be determined by those we do not know and over whom there is no final control means that life is precarious, and that politics must consider what forms of social and political organization seek to best sustain precarious lives across the globe.[19]

Butler frequently hones psychoanalytic resources to demonstrate the depth of our attachment to what we disavow, as well as the violence that can be spawned when the possibility of grieving lost attachments is thwarted or foreclosed. If the foreclosure of grief can motivate violence, Butler's claim is that staying with the thought of grief, and settling into the realities of vulnerability, may illumine a sense of responsibility for the similarly vulnerable other. The suggestion is that there is some moral virtue in learning to tolerate or "stay with" vulnerability as opposed to lashing out in an attempt at retribution.

The sense of dislocation or dispossession that comes with grief is one wherein one is forced beyond oneself, undone. Importantly, Butler claims that one might "allow oneself to extrapolate from this experience" to the vulnerability of others, and that there is something in this extrapolation that is ethically and politically promising. But to argue thus is to pre-suppose that there are some orders of political life that best take up the realities of human vulnerability, and it is less than obvious what these would be. Hence if the need for such an "extrapolation" is clear enough, its means are not.

In the absence of normative claims there is no clear extrapolation from the reality of embodied vulnerability to a just politics. This is because there is nothing prescriptive—or at all normative—in the acknowledgement that we are dispossessed and vulnerable before others. If dispossession enables care, love, and generosity it equally enables abuse, intimidation, and vio-lence. So while it is doubtless the case that many could stand to be reminded of the ties that bind one to another, and while this recollection appears to be a requisite ethical consideration, this appeal to vulnerability cannot in and of itself proffer an ethics:

> Mindfulness of this vulnerability can become the basis of claims for non-militaristic political solutions, just as denial of this vulnerability through a fantasy of mastery . . . can fuel instruments of war. We can-not, however, will away this vulnerability. We must attend to it, even abide by it, as we begin to think about what politics might be implied by staying with the thought of corporeal vulnerability itself.[20]

Butler claims that the fact of embodied vulnerability can become the basis for non-militaristic political solutions, and indeed may even serve as the provocation for a politics of nonviolence. But consider that attending to one's vulnerability can also promote all manner of violence, a point that Butler likewise acknowledges. What is left unsaid is how, exactly, mindful-ness of vulnerability can become the basis for any politics. If "staying with the thought of corporeal vulnerability" is meant to return us to a sense of collective responsibility for the physical lives of others—a possibility that Butler clearly gestures towards—it cannot do so in the absence of norms that would delineate how the realities of vulnerability are to be taken up politically, and these norms would themselves be injurious, as Butler herself has argued elsewhere.[21]

In *Undoing Gender*, Butler stresses the bivalent nature of norms: if there is one sense in which norms are aspirational, there is another in which they necessarily inflict a type of constitutive violence. They may indeed guide our actions and deliberations, but they also legislate what appears as normal, or even intelligible, and this legislation can be cruel. How is one to dissociate the norms that "permit people to breathe, desire, love and live" from those which restrict these possibilities, when norms of necessity do both, and the same norms can do both at once? Vulnerability and violence are intrinsically coupled, and there is no clear solution to the paradox of dispossession. The ethical subject should not be motivated by an attempt to foreclose vulnerability; conversely, ethics cannot consist in a naïve appeal to this motif; hence it remains unclear what norms would be at play in an attempt to derive a substantive ethics (or politics) from a constitutive and primordial exposure to others.

One might claim that a recognition of my own vulnerability commands my recognition of the same in others, and that I am compelled by this realization to have some trust in them as they are entitled to have of me. In such an instance, the politics of dispossession becomes an issue of trust, trust that one's own vulnerability will be respected and not subject to abuse. But this trust and this faith are less real for a subject whose own experiences of dispossession and vulnerability have been injuriously actualized as suffering at the hands of others, particularly in the case of sexual violence. Hence there is an important respect in which the possibility for trust, for the experience of trusting others, and of keeping the faith is anchored in a phenomenological history of care and hospitality. Concretely, there are simply too many for whom such a leap of faith is unimaginable, and too much evidence in front of us now that testifies to the tragic undoing of faith and trust through violence. We are in bad faith to assume safe passage from the primordial vulnerability and exposure that constitutes the embodied subject to a model of justice wherein this ethical corporeity is universally respected. To force some remembrance of our primordial ties to one another is one thing, but in and of itself, this retreat to vulnerability and exposure does not readily conjure any particular ethical sensibility. If the vulnerable body must be ethically accommodated, and perhaps even can be seen as the provocation for a theory of justice, it does not in and of itself prescribe the contours of ethical or political life.

VISIBLE VULNERABILITIES

It has been argued thus far that the return to vulnerability in contemporary theory is ambiguous not only in its experiential aspect—as dispossession can be lived in both jubilant and horrifying ways—but also insofar as a critical ontology of vulnerability does not imply any specific ethics. The return to vulnerability is further complicated when one considers the difficulties that arise through endeavors to make sexual violence, and its abuse of particular sites of violability, visible as such. To theorize sexual violence is no straightforward enterprise; indeed, the title of this volume brings together terms that many conceive as antithetical. Many feminists have voiced a suspicion of what it is that theory could bring to a problem as concrete as sexual violence. The suspicion is commonplace, manifest in the accusation that theory has become detached from the experience of 'real' women and the violence of the 'real' world, an accusation implying that theory operates at a remove from concrete political concerns such that its efficacy is suspect. This accusation is obviously not innocent; its very terms obscure the fact that it is precisely the idea of a 'real woman' that feminist theory subjects to scrutiny. To theorize sexual violence is thus to theorize the vacillating boundaries of legitimacy that enable the visibility of certain vulnerabilities and the invisibility of others. Bringing theory to bear on the problem of sexual violence brings certain dimensions of this problem into relief that may otherwise remain veiled, among them, who counts as a victim of sexual violence, and which women are 'real' enough within the purview of our cultural imaginary to warrant attention. This is crucial, given that it may be the case that the degradation of women is so much a part of the social realm that violence against them is not even recognized as such.

There are images of rape, abuse, and torture that demand our attention and that cry for an ethical response to sexual violence. And there is a different violence—no less cruel and no less sexed—involved in rendering certain individuals invisible such that their availability to violence does not even register in the cultural imaginary. These images of suffering do not appear in the media, they are not privileged objects of analysis by academics, and they do not solicit cries of outrage. They are invisible. To theorize sexual violence is to seek redress and recognition for the heightened vulnerability to sexual violence evinced by certain groups. It is also to remain vigilant to the ways in which a logic of exclusion can still operate in those discourses whose purpose is this very recognition and redress. From the perspective of ethics, this differential economy of recognition and its attendant concern with visibility demand that one acknowledge that one cannot advocate an investigation of the ethical promise of vulnerability without attending to the different ways in which different bodies are represented as vulnerable.

Feminist theorists must continue to demand recognition and redress for the problem of women's disproportionate availability to various types of violence. But we must do so in a context that acknowledges the increasing awareness of women as agents of violence. One can think here of a smiling Private Lynndie England jeering at the humiliation of Arab prisoners in Abu Ghraib. Conversely, one can think of the increasing frequency with which women are the perpetrators of suicide bombings. The presence of women at every level of the Abu Ghraib prison scandal, as well as the increasing frequency of female suicide bombers in the Middle East, attest to the insufficiency of paradigms wherein women are categorically understood as figures of vulnerability and violability. The figuring of female suicide bombers in the media is particularly provocative in this regard. Media responses to women who perpetrate violence are contradictory. The women are presented either as figures of monstrosity and unbearable transgression ("they are like stealth bombers" says one source), or as women whose actions are overtly framed by considerations of their beauty and suffering, with one reporter from *The Guardian* going so far as to comment on the "the delicate Audrey Hepburn face" of suicide bomber Leila Khaled. These responses betray the unease that many feel with the idea that women's bodies are increasingly made public as sites of aggression. What must be theorized is the ubiquity of these images—images that present women as aggressors—alongside an increasingly noticeable call to take embodied vulnerability as a site of ethical promise, or a locus from which we may commence a rearticulation of feminist goals. The previous examples obviate the need to note that the profile of the vulnerable body is a far cry from general; gender, race, and nation, along with myriad other dimensions of identity, constitute the vulnerability to which ethics appeals. It is precisely the singular nature of embodied vulnerability that complicates the ease with which this figure can be invoked in the service of ethics. These specificities and differences inform the representation of vulnerability as much as they do one's experience of one's own vulnerable body.

For feminists such as Butler and Catharine MacKinnon, there is a kind of violence at play in the very representation of women. Where these feminists would differ, however, is in thinking through how problems of representation, recognition, and misrecognition should be remedied. For all the contention that may occasionally mark the difference between these various feminist approaches to violence, all claim an investment in thinking through the ways in which 'woman'—as a category of feminist analysis—is circumscribed. If women can be said to be united in their vulnerability to various forms of sexual violence, it is also the case that this mutual availability is differentially allocated along axes other than sex and gender in ways that complicate the ease with which one can advocate a general return to vulnerability as the basis for an ethics. To think through the realities of vulnerability, to represent sexed vulnerability, or put it forward as an object of analysis, is to acknowledge that some sexual vulnerabilities are more visible than others. Hence the challenge is to identify the kind of vulnerability to which we are being asked to return. When thought in a universal sense, vulnerability itself becomes dangerously abstract.

This concern with the emergence of vulnerability, its representation and recognition, marks an affinity between the aims of many feminist thinkers whose projects may otherwise collide significantly. Feminist theorists have long negotiated a perceived rift between materialist politics and an allegedly more symbolic politics, but the implied breach here is potentially dangerous. It runs the risk of playing the violence of rape or abuse against the violence of misrecognition or cultural abjection. Moreover, as divisive an issue as violence might be, it is surely also an issue in which feminists may find a source of solidarity, however complicated. Despite the divergent approaches to this issue, violence and vulnerability are essential themes around which feminism may begin to take up the demand for the rearticulation of its goals in light of accusations of exclusion that have consistently plagued feminist theory historically.

While some feminists prefer to work for legal reform and more sweeping social agendas, others are intent to focus on the very contingent and particular arrangements of power that govern certain cultural discourses on representation and recognition. To be sure, there are times when these two approaches very happily coincide, and there are surely others when a tension persists between the two. By placing Catharine MacKinnon and Judith Butler in dialogue on the issue of sexual violence, it becomes obvious that vulnerability itself is a complex figure, manifest in myriad ways. The current charge to feminists is to remain vigilant to the various ways in which vulnerability is articulated, and to reject an approach to the issue that is myopic, narrow, and exclusionary. This is easier said than done, but such an attempt is requisite in any ethical response to the issue of sexual violence. Still and always, feminist theorists will favor certain figures of vulnerability in their analyses, but an attentiveness to the interconnectedness of these figures is necessary if one is truly to redress issues of sexual violence. For instance, even if MacKinnon's aspiration is to allow for legal action on the part of women who have suffered sexual violence as a consequence of the distribution of pornography, her arguments to this effect cannot help but begin in an examination of how it is that pornography advances and normalizes images of women that motivate sexual violence against them. In this sense, discursive violence and material violence intersect radically. One cannot be thought without the other.

MacKinnon situates the vulnerability of women in part in their subordinate status before the law, and so there is a straightforwardly legalistic bent to her agenda. But this fact does not justify the claim that MacKinnon is more concerned with the violence confronted by 'real' women, or the violence of the 'real' world. This is because it is precisely MacKinnon's own vigilance surrounding the power-laden artifice that is the 'reality' of sex that motivates much of her work. Indeed, her renowned arguments against pornography are grounded in the belief that "power constructs the appearance of reality by silencing the voices of the powerless."[22] MacKinnon's point is precisely that the subordination enacted as gender inequality is rendered invisible, and "dissent becomes inaudible and rare."[23] In this sense, MacKinnon worries that the subjugation and social inferiority of women simply appears as a benign difference between the sexes. With her particularly provocative claim that rape, battery, and sexual assault are simply understood as 'sex' within the confines of a misogynist cultural order, MacKinnon illumines the gross inequity and violence that pervades what many conceive as innocuous images of sex. The point, then, is that 'reality' is not neutral, benign, and simply given; rather it is shaped in the service of certain cultural institutions whose own investments in this particular representation of things is obscured. MacKinnon famously argues that this dynamic is particularly obvious in the case of pornography:

> In pornography, there it is, in one place, all of the abuses that women had to struggle so long to begin to articulate, all the unspeakable

abuse: the rape, the battery, the sexual harassment, the prostitution, and the sexual abuse of children. Only in the pornography it is called something else: sex, sex, sex, sex, sex, and sex respectively. Pornography sexualises rape, battery, and sexual harassment . . . it thereby celebrates, promotes, authorizes, and legitimates them. More generally, it eroticises the dominance and submission that is the dynamic common to them all. It makes hierarchy sexy and calls that 'the truth about sex' or just a mirror of reality. Through this process pornography constructs what a woman is and what men want from sex. This is what pornography means.[24]

She further claims that "pornography is not imagery in some relation to a reality elsewhere constructed. It is not a distortion, reflection, projection, expression, fantasy, representation, or symbol either. It is a sexual reality."[25]

Of interest here is less the validity or efficacy of MacKinnon's case against pornography, and the specificities of her argument to make it legally actionable, than the conception of sexed vulnerability that motivates such claims. 'Reality' is not an ethically neutral entity, and a blind appeal to it does not suffice for one invested in the creation of more ethically and politically just modes of life. Indeed, agree or disagree, MacKinnon's work stands as one of the most powerful reminders of the violence at play in certain representations of 'real' women, as the very appearance of reality, for her, invokes a representational exclusion and a concomitant silencing of the victims. Requisite for a politics that would redress this silencing is the radical critique of what passes for reality, an interrogation of the violence that is manifest in the crafting of reality in accord with certain interests that obscure their own violence. At one level, there is a striking symmetry here between Butler and MacKinnon when it comes to their vigilance surrounding naïve appeals to reality. Butler claims:

> The construction of gender operates through exclusionary means, such that the human is not only produced over and against the inhuman, but through a set of foreclosures, radical erasures, that are strictly speaking, refused the possibility of cultural articulation. Hence, it is not enough to claim that human subjects are constructed, for the construction of the human is a differential operation that produces the more and less 'human,' the inhuman, the humanly unthinkable. These excluded sites come to bound the human as its constitutive outside, and to haunt those boundaries as the persistent possibility of their disruption and rearticulation.[26]

It is not simply that bodies themselves emerge through a violent foreclosure of unthinkable identities, but that these foreclosures enact and inspire further violence, manifest either in the case of physical violence against groups deemed abject or as a phenomenological suffering of the unlivability of one's gender:

On the level of discourse, certain lives are not considered lives at all, they cannot be dehumanised; they fit no dominant frame for the human, and their dehumanisation occurs first, at this level. This level then gives rise to a physical violence that in some sense delivers the message of dehumanisation which is already at work in the culture.[27]

As embodied, we are always beyond ourselves to some extent, open to others, and vulnerable before them, in ways we cannot control. As Butler put it most recently in *Undoing Gender,* "to be oppressed means that you already exist as a subject of some kind, you are there as a visible and oppressed other for the master subject, as a possible or potential subject, but to be unreal is something else again."[28] The paradigm of recognition calls to mind a violence at the level of one's very emergence as an intelligible social subject. It is for this reason that Butler becomes concerned with the violence of the exclusionary logic that comes to circumscribe the domain of the human.[29] Indeed, she understands the main task of feminist theory to be its opposition to the unwanted and exclusionary legislation of identity. From her early criticisms of the notion of a "natural woman" in *Gender Trouble* to her more recent considerations of the theme of vulnerability, Butler has aimed to promote the reality and integrity of certain relations. Her concern is to critique those norms that are used to restrict and eviscerate the conditions of social intelligibility. This requires attending to the vulnerability that women evidence to forms of violence that might not qualify as instances of physical or material abuse or neglect, but which rob them of their freedom and integrity in equal measure. Hence both Butler and MacKinnon would insist that feminists who advocate a return to reality— a 'reality check'—must also note that an appeal to reality is an appeal to a world that has been constructed through the violent prohibition of some bodies and some lives that for whatever reason do not count as full persons, whose voices are silenced, and who are dehumanized.

This affinity is undercut by a serious difference between Butler and MacKinnon when it comes to the respective ways in which they understand the redress of certain kinds of violence. Insofar as both Butler and MacKinnon are concerned with the exclusionary mechanism of gender norms, and the perpetuation of these norms at the level of cultural representation, the difference lies in what each conceives as the possibility for altering these norms. Butler's criticism of MacKinnon in *Excitable Speech* concerns the claim that MacKinnon does not allow for the resignification of norms, or for their altering in different contexts, their emergence in accord with different aims.[30] Butler's understanding of the iterability of gender norms informs her claim that the force of sexual norms is in itself vulnerable to distortion and unfaithful repetition. In this sense, the way in which pornographic images 'act' is never monolithic. This worry is what motivates Butler's critique of MacKinnon. There is no contestation of the claim that images do act; Butler is simply interested in the fact that images can do different things at different times and places. The force that certain images of sex can exercise is thus inseparable from their context, and this highlights quite different conceptions of the performative in Butler and MacKinnon. Butler is suspicious of any account that attributes a homogenous or unilateral kind of violence to the production and repetition of certain images. MacKinnon, on the other hand, seems to grant some sovereignty to the power of pornography. Butler claims that "MacKinnon's use of the performative engages a figure of the performative, a figure of sovereign power that governs how a speech act is said to act—as efficacious, unilateral, transitive, generative."[31] On her account, what violence, if any, is exercised by these images is in many ways contingent, not necessary. There can be no unilateral or categorical argument made for the way in which images of sex exacerbate the vulnerability of certain groups to various types of violence. Indeed the images themselves are not the issue; rather, it is a question of contingency when it comes to how the images are interpreted in the context in which they appear, considerations that render the norms themselves vulnerable to change. However, given Butler's own criticism of MacKinnon—namely the accusation that MacKinnon does not grant sufficient attention to the ways in which images are altered depending on contingency and circumstance— it is interesting to note that Butler's recent engagement with the motif of vulnerability refrains from engaging this theme in particular contexts. Just as Butler claims that MacKinnon's argument suffers from generalizations about harm and violence that seem ignorant to circumstance, the return to vulnerability is arguably guilty of this same kind of abstraction. Arguably, attention to the differences that mark vulnerable bodies is requisite if one is interested in mining this motif in the service of ethics. A more general appeal cannot suffice, for reasons that Butler's own engagements with MacKinnon make clear.

Moreover, if there is a sense in which these various elaborations of the performative and injurious dimension of sexual norms seem inimical, it is important to bear in mind that an affinity does persist between them, an affinity that is most notable when thought in light of the recent return to vulnerability in feminist theory. Any attempt to ascertain the vulnerability of different groups in relation to sexual violence must contend with the fact that there are certain norms that render particular identities disproportionately violable. Butler and MacKinnon would agree that there is an intrinsic violence at play in the appearance of 'reality,' an insidious violence that conceals its operation as such. For this reason, though the difference between them is quite substantive, they both insist on the multiple vulnerabilities at play in the emergence of sex and gendered norms. For this reason, a 'reality check' will always be useful feminist methodology.

It is precisely with the problem of 'real' women that recent feminist theory has been preoccupied, as feminism is dedicated to the interrogation of the vacillating boundaries of legitimacy that circumscribe the domain of the subject in ways that dehumanize and exclude some from the realm of personhood altogether. What must be resisted is the claim that 'real women' and 'real violence' are the only viable categories in the theorization of sexual violence, as if these notions designate static identities. Such an approach makes the dangerous mistake of playing the violence women confront at the level of cultural representation against the erasure and physical assault of individuals who may not be intelligibly gendered at all. This should be intolerable to feminists. We cannot risk idealizing certain gendered expressions that in their own turn become instruments of violence and exclusion. For this reason, the renaissance of interest in vulnerability must be viewed critically, for vulnerability is manifest along many axes, some of which render others invisible. This much must be taken into account as we seek to redress the many instantiations of sexual violence.

One of the more abiding merits of feminist ethics is the insistence that ethics cannot be thought apart from political reality and thus cannot be theorized in a way that ignores the ways in which power plays out in different concrete circumstances. It is in the service of this agenda that contemporary feminist theory has returned to the motif of vulnerability with some hope, in an attempt to begin to outline what ethics emerge when vulnerability and interdependence are given priority. Importantly, however, a critical analysis of this return to vulnerability also obviates the need to recognize the vastly different configurations of power and politics within which vulnerability is animated and recognized. This chapter has argued that these political complexities render the ethics of vulnerability ambiguous. Apart from the deep experiential ambiguity of vulnerability—that is its tendency to be announced in ways both promising and perilous—there is the further fact that there is nothing necessarily normative in asking individuals to remember or "tarry with" their own vulnerabilities. The attempt to elaborate an ethics grounded in the experiences of the vulnerable body is also deeply problematized by the fact that vulnerability is inscribed on different bodies in radically different ways, a fact that belies the notion that there may be a general or universal virtue at stake in vulnerability's recognition. There is no question that the feminist thinkers engaged here recognized this, but it is also the case that the return to vulnerability that is currently being advocated might be, and must be, subjected to a reality check of its own as it continues its efforts to situate the ethical on the terrain of power and politics.

NOTES

1. Debra Bergoffen, "The Politics of the Vulnerable Body," *Hypatia* 18, 1 (2001): 116–134.
2. Rosalyn Diprose, *Corporeal Generosity* (Albany: State University of New York Press. 2002).
3. Judith Butler, *Undoing Gender* (New York: Routledge, 2004), 29.
4. Kelly Oliver. *Women as Weapons of War* (New York: Columbia University Press, 2008).

5. See Eva Feder Kittay, *Love's Labor: Essays on Women, Equality and Dependency* (New York: Routledge, 1999).
6. See Judith Butler, *Gender Trouble* (New York: Routledge, 1999); Judith Butler, *Bodies That Matter* (New York: Routledge, 1993); Rosalyn Diprose, *The Bodies of Women* (New York: Routledge, 1994); Moira Gatens, *Imaginary Bodies* (New York: Routledge, 1996); Elizabeth Grosz, *Volatile Bodies* (New York: Routledge, 1993).
7. See Seyla Benhabib et al., *Feminist Contentions* (New York: Routledge, 1995).
8. Ann Cahill, *Rethinking Rape* (Ithaca: Cornell University Press, 2001).
9. Frantz Fanon, *Black Skin White Masks*, trans. Charles Lam Markmann (New York: Grove Press, 1967).
10. Ibid., 113.
11. Simone de Beauvoir, *The Second Sex*, trans. H.M. Parshley (New York: Random House, 1989).
12. Though the language of 'possession' entails some acknowledgement that one is still working within the liberal paradigm, however critically.
13. Judith Butler, *Precarious Life* (London: Verso, 2004), xiii.
14. Butler, *Undoing Gender*, 20.
15. Ibid., 21.
16. Ibid.
17. Elaine Miller, "Bodies and the Power of Vulnerability: Thinking Democracy and Subjectivity Outside the Logic of Confrontation," *Philosophy Today* 46, 5 (2002): 102–112, 102.
18. Butler, *Undoing Gender*, 23.
19. Ibid.
20. Ibid., 29.
21. See Catherine Mills, "Normative Violence, Vulnerability, and Responsibility" *differences* 18, 2 (2007): 133–155.
22. Catherine MacKinnon, *Feminism Unmodified* (Cambridge MA: Harvard University Press, 1987), 164.
23. Ibid., 166.
24. Ibid., 171.
25. Ibid., 173.
26. Butler, 1993, 8.
27. Butler, *Undoing Gender*, 25.
28. Ibid., 30.
29. While concerned with the designation of the human, she explicitly notes that "the rethinking of the human . . . does not entail a return to humanism" (*Undoing Gender*, 13).
30. Judith Butler, *Excitable Speech* (New York: Routledge, 1997).
31. Ibid., 74.

4 Of Shards, Subjectivities, and the Refusal to 'Heal'

Refiguring the Damage of Incest

Melanie Boyd

> In our journey from victim to survivor, we have often had to take that which once enabled us to live and reconceptualize it as something to be broken through, a crutch from which we must liberate ourselves in order to take back our creative power.
>
> Margaret Randall[1]

> maybe my broken parts teach me things invisible to you who are whole healthy happy and maybe my speaking is something you do not wish to hear precisely because my speaking is true and maybe i am both paranoid and prophetic
>
> Darlene Dralus and Jen Shelton[2]

Feminist narratives of father–daughter incest have conventionally anchored their politics in three tropes: *helplessness*, which attests to the child's innocence; *damage*, which identifies incest's wrong; and *recovery*, which redresses personal victimhood while offering a parable for cultural transformation. These texts are, moreover, testimonial: both plot and politics cohere out of the ethical imperatives of bearing witness. Reflecting the premise of the speak outs from which they evolved, the incest memoirs of second-wave feminism address themselves to a supportive audience, interpellating a readership who will respond to the victim's wavering narrative of suffering with empathy, encouragement, and action. The conventional address insists that readers recognize the victim's innocence despite her self-doubt, grieve her wounds when she denies them, be sure of her final transcendent recovery even as she succumbs to despair. And indeed, by following the models laid down by the friends, therapists, and support group members who populate these accounts—and by taking note of the subtitles, jacket copy, and the material reality of a published "recovery story"—readers can be steadfast where the damaged narrator cannot. The textual assertion of helplessness solicits agency: it is the sentimental mechanism by which these memoirs construct the very audience they address. Submitting themselves (ourselves) to the demands of this intimate address, taking on the assigned tasks, readers become a responsive feminist public, poised to listen, respond, and act.

I offer this compressed background in order to begin with the following question: what happens to feminist testimonial politics when victim–narrators divest themselves of the conventional tropes of helplessness, damage, and recovery? For divest themselves they have: not all, of course, but many feminist incest writers have, of late, jettisoned the familiar rhetoric of innocent victimhood; prominent examples include Sapphire's *Push*, Kathryn Harrison's *The Kiss*, Dorothy Allison's *Bastard Out of Carolina*, and Carolivia Herron's *Thereafter Johnny*.[3] Rejecting the quest for recovery and thus suspending the conventional appeal for readerly support, such accounts seek to exploit, rather than transcend, the damage of abuse. In so doing, they propose that agency and victimization can coexist. This new paradigm is rhetorically startling and theoretically urgent—it is, in this chapter, my primary object of analysis. And yet I would like my analysis of the victim–narrator's agency to be haunted by this initial concern with testimonial address and politicized readership. Postconventional incest accounts are powerful but also powerfully unsettling. Even readers relieved to set aside the sentimental dynamics of conventional feminist incest accounts— relieved, that is, to escape an address in which the reader's agency is constructed out of the victim's powerlessness—even those readers might well be disconcerted. In the absence of that urgent address, what becomes of our response, of our politics?

With the question of testimonial politics suspended at the edge of our concerns, we can move into less rushed analysis of agency—both represented and enacted—within feminist incest narratives. In the sections that follow, I begin with an overview of conventional rhetorics of helplessness, damage, and recovery in a variety of texts. I go on, in greater detail, to explore the postconventional turn as exemplified in Sapphire's *Push* and Kathryn Harrison's *The Kiss*. In closing, I offer a pair of conclusions that reconsider agency and address in light of the postconventional reformulations. Throughout, I theorize the trio of victimization tropes—helplessness, damage, and recovery—as political and aesthetic practices rather than ontological or psychological truths. My reframing of damage and recovery, terms we generally use to register sensitivity to the victim's trauma, may seem callous; my desire to set aside helpless innocence may seem ill considered, particularly from a juridical standpoint. Certainly, I do not mean to disregard the suffering and resilience represented in these texts, nor do I wish to dismiss the gains secured by victims' ability to appear innocent in a wide range of settings. Nonetheless, I propose that we can most usefully understand those critically important experiences and responses by refusing to imagine any of these terms as fixed psychological, juridical, or even neurological effects; indeed, I would suggest that the conventional strategy of 'fixing' innocence has excessively restricted our understanding of victimhood, especially in relation to agency. In attempting to denaturalize painful damage, transcendent recovery, and helpless innocence, I follow theorists such as Sharon Marcus and Renee Heberle, who insist we must deconstruct our cultural stories—even feminist stories—of sexual violence in order to insist upon their mutability.[4] To create the possibility of change, Marcus insists, we must "ask how the violence of rape is enabled by narratives, complexes, and institutions which derive their strength not from outright, unbeatable, immutable force but rather from their power to structure our lives as imposing cultural scripts."[5] Extending her intervention from the domain of violence to that of victimhood, I attempt to set aside psychological paradigms of trauma and juridical binaries of culpability and innocence, while nonetheless retaining the political framework of testimony. In what ways are experiences of victimhood structured and deployed, I ask, and to what effect?

"LIKE PHOENIXES RISING FROM THE ASHES"[6]: CONVENTIONS OF DAMAGE AND RECOVERY

Unimaginable as it may seem from this vantage point, feminist antiviolence activists of the 1970s had to combat a popular view (often originating in 'expert' analysis) that father–daughter incest is rare, even exotic, and really not so bad: girls usually aren't hurt, or so runs this logic, except possibly by prudish responses; indeed, they might even benefit from the extra paternal attention.[7] In response, both theorists and memoirists emphasized the profoundly damaging impact of incest upon women and girls, thus insisting that incest mattered.[8] Feminist accounts of incest's damage combined with new data on incest's frequency to shape a new public perception of incest as a particularly horrific form of abuse; at the same time, father–daughter incest began to register within feminist discourse as a heuristic for the abusive nature of patriarchy itself.[9]

With damage as the emphatic measure of incest's wrong, recovery quickly became a symbol of incest's eradication—and, with healing conceptualized primarily as the process of telling one's story, became not only the symbol but also the practice of much anti-incest activism. At the heart of the feminist recovery paradigm is the entwined personal and political act of 'breaking silence,' in which healing is the byproduct of telling (and learning to believe in) the story of one's own innocence to an attentive listener.[10] Inherently relational, testimonial recovery mobilizes via the victim's need: its address levies an ethical demand that listeners hear, feel, and respond. To break silence is thus to begin a chain reaction, one triggered not just by the factual content of the testimony, but by its performative enactment of courage, suffering, and expectation: "Every woman who can share her experience with this ugly reality," as the introduction to one collection of testimonials asserts, "surely gives increased permission to others still frozen in silence."[11]

In its demand for response, the testimonial vocative of these now unfrozen speakers fuses therapeutic and political agendas by binding individual healing to cultural transformation. Writing of an early speak out, for example, activist Nikki Craft describes the impact of hearing women's stories of sexual violence:

> There were many tears that weekend and then our tears turned to rage. There would be no more years of silent anger, guilt, anguish and fear ... no more willing victims ... 'WE MUST FIGHT TOGETHER, OR BE ATTACKED ALONE' became our battle cry.[12]

As Craft makes clear, the testimonial address mobilizes not individual listeners but a feminist public constituted in the act of responding to the victim's suffering.[13] This reflexive dynamic persists strongly in written memoirs, where readerly participation emerges as a necessary textual element upon which both recovery and politics rely. Margaret Randall, who writes as both a victim and an expert, casts the shared pain of authorial telling and readerly responding as an essential part of her memoir's narrative progression. "Writing about incest is at once necessary ... and painful," she writes. "For the listener or reader it is uncomfortable, perhaps demanding ... There is a need for great literalness. Step by step. Here, I will take you by the hand."[14] To be an ethical reader of this or any other conventional text is to accompany the narrator into suffering—to be moved by the recognition of that pain to fight against the sexual abuse of women and children. As one anthologist insists, as readers "we cannot close ourselves off and hope for the best. We are in danger."[15] Stressing the agency exercised in the audience's elicited support, testimonial rhetoric wards off the threat that political change might be preempted by therapeutic palliatives: the interpellated mutuality of bearing witness becomes its own evidence of collective progress, ratifying the political potency of the testimonial endeavor even as it rests on the narrated powerlessness of victimhood.[16]

Under pressure as both the symbol and the practice of anti-incest work, recovery quickly became idealized as an individual's *complete* transcendence of her abusive past. Consider, for example, the goals of feminist psychologist Christine Courtois' 1988 *Healing the Incest Wound*, a weighty clinical guide that lays out the process by which a therapist can "move a victim from the status of victim to the status of survivor." To achieve this transformation, she writes, "the survivor must psychologically separate from the past in order to develop her unique self, separate from the abuse and its supporting family ethic." While we might read Courtois' central metaphor of "the incest wound" as a departure from her emphasis on separation—a wound is, after all, still a part of one's body—Courtois actively forecloses such a reading by casting the wound as a site of contamination. The necessary therapeutic work is thus that of "cleaning and disinfecting."[17]

Political recovery emphasizes the power of rigorous intervention: once the polluting impact of incest can be eliminated, once the damage is cleared away, the victim will heal cleanly, becoming, in the words of so many conventional narratives, "the person she was fully meant to be."[18] The narrators of conventional recovery memoirs might not actually accomplish this transcendence within the pages of their texts (indeed, they rarely do) but it is nonetheless the persistent goal.

Embedded within this transcendent telos is a firm distinction—both ontological and temporal—between the victim and her damaged state, between essential self and abusive experience. Echoing the presumptions of trauma theory, the feminist recovery paradigm presumes an idealized pre-traumatic self toward which healing can strive; even in cases where incest began in infancy or occurred within an already violent life, an unharmed self is imaginatively visualized as that to which one returns. This political therapeutic relies upon an essentialist unitary self, an innocent subjectivity against which to calibrate first the damage of patriarchal abuse and then the power of feminist recovery.

The presumption of unitary selfhood becomes explicit in the language of empowered 'wholeness' that runs through conventional recovery literature. The vision of recovered wholeness, along with the empathetic portrayal of the fractured helplessness of those-not-yet-recovered, takes especially clear shape on the pages of feminist self-help workbooks, which mirror the memoir's testimonial stance by adopting and articulating the responsiveness of an ideal feminist public. The workbook narrators speak of both sympathy and outrage, all the while exuding a steady confidence that their fragmented, self-doubting readers can be ushering along a well-marked path to the wholeness of recovery. This is the promise, for example, with which Ellen Bass and Laura Davis end their unswervingly encouraging introduction to *The Courage to Heal*:

> The other morning, when Ellen listened to the messages on her answering machine, there was one that said, "I called to let you know that I really *am* healing. And this is the sweetest feeling I have ever known—to be whole."
>
> You deserve this feeling.[19]

As performative as it is descriptive, this anecdote affirms survivors and supporters, even as it implicitly registers the agency of both against the powerless suffering of victimhood.

Bass and Davis' emphasis on collaboration is conventional: the endpoint of wholeness is reached through the ethical encounter between the urgency of the victim's need and the steady confidence of her interlocutors. Introducing another self-help text, for example, Randall describes the struggle by which "the strong, healthy, *whole*, creative being who was lost by virtue of the crime committed against her is remembered, reclaimed, found."[20]

Randall's passive construction is, as I read it, a note of reassuring support—the victim herself need not remember, reclaim, nor find, only prepare for discovery.

Notice, too, that the political work of 'wholeness' is not only procedural, but extends to the state itself. Wholeness is a vindication of innocence, the long-awaited instantiation of justice. The ontological purity of transcendent recovery stands as evidence of incest's offense by revealing the innocence that was violated, even as it redresses that damage by restoring that lost condition. "In [testimonial] telling she can reclaim her innocence," avers Louise Thornton, in another introduction. "She *is* innocent. She has always been innocent. Both the burden of the crime and the crime itself are lifted from her shoulders." On multiple levels, then, transcendent recovery thus is both an allegory of and a mechanism for cultural transformation. If a damaged victim can be healed, so too can a culture, especially one organized into an intimate collective.[21]

These political and emotional maneuvers resuscitate those used by an earlier generation of women writing for change: nineteenth century female abolitionists, whose sentimental accounts of slavery invoked the relational ideals of the domestic sphere to argue for sweeping change in the public realm. The use of suffering to bind narrator and reader, the construction of a female and feminist public from that interpellated mutuality, the conversion of affect into political outrage and action—all these are hallmarks of sentimental politics. Recognizing this political and rhetorical heritage illuminates both the potency and the limits of the conventional incest accounts. Their emotionally-laden narratives mobilize their audiences, but are all too easily caught in what Lauren Berlant identifies as the "paradoxes of liberal sentiment":

> When sentimentality meets politics, it uses personal stories to tell of structural effects, but in so doing it risks thwarting its very attempt to perform rhetorically a scene of pain that must be soothed politically. Because the ideology of true feeling cannot admit the nonuniversality of pain, its cases become all jumbled together and the ethical imperative towards social transformation is replaced by a civic-minded but passive ideal of empathy . . . Suffering, in this personal–public context, becomes answered by survival, which is then recoded as freedom.[22]

Second-wave rhetorics of sexual victimhood resist this devolution into passive empathy, it seems to me, by insisting upon the radical nature of 'survival' itself—a term cast in opposition to victimhood by the sheer force of feminist community, by the agency unleashed by empathy. Notably, the oft-invoked transformation from 'victim' to 'survivor' can designate either (a) a feminist intervention in cultural meaning, denoting a bodily state in order to emphasize the agency required 'merely' to survive violence (in this context, a woman is a survivor as soon as the violent episode ends), or (b) a communal process through which individual women struggle to transcend the trauma and helplessness of violence to take up positions as agential subjects (here, a woman only becomes a survivor later, after she leaves her damage behind).[23] The ambiguity of feminist usage is both tacit and critical: the disjointed temporality links an idealized future to a traumatic present, even as the incommensurate meanings of survival more deeply embed personal recovery within the politics of cultural intervention.[24]

And yet these careful maneuvers do not evade Berlant's paradox. Indeed, we can recognize the core nineteenth century problematic at work in both definitions of survival, each of which—like the rhetoric of shattered victims and whole survivors—constructs political agency in opposition to the damaged victimhood that prompts it. The conventional political address of incest narratives secures its agential audience by reifying victimhood into helplessness—a reification that is not incidental, but foundational, to their testimonial paradigm. In the sections that follow, I propose we read postconventional incest narratives not simply as transcending but rather as struggling with this legacy. Through a multitude of different techniques, both *Push* and *The Kiss* invoke the testimonial promise of sentimentality only to disrupt the interlocking rubrics—helplessness, damage, and recovery—through which that promise is made.

"AT LAST, BROKEN"[25]: THE POSTCONVENTIONAL EMBRACE OF DAMAGE

If the politics of feminist recovery manifest themselves in the language of wholeness, what do we make of the following imagery?

> Broken
> I think everything in me has been broken. The shiny ceramic red heart lies on the floor in shards, its light that used to flash electric now glows steady in the dark. Outside the window I watch the souls of my mother and father wrapped in black shawls ride down the river, weird water, in strange boats. They are without hearts, liver, feet—except soles, they are all souls now. I am here in my time, lit, broken, fire burning, full of holes. Vibrating, at last, light, life, mine. At last, broken.[26]

Sapphire, the author of this prose poem, is an African American poet and novelist who writes with an autobiographical inflection about incest, poverty, racism, and sexism. The combination of identity, topics, and genre (a black woman writing autobiographically about suffering) makes it almost inevitable, I would argue, that her work be viewed through a sentimental lens that emphasizes (for both speaker and addressee) the power of emotion and fortitude. We can thus understand the impulse behind the endorsement emblazoned upon the back cover of the volume in which "Broken" appears:

"At turns alarming and inspiring, the raw lyrics and piercing wisdom of *Black Wings and Blind Angels* remind us of Sapphire's place as our most fearless poet." These bifurcated descriptions—the alternation of alarm and inspiration, of raw lyrics and piercing wisdom—affirm the familiar distinction between trauma and response, between suffering and survival, between *victim* and *abuse*, upon which transcendent recovery depends.

And yet Sapphire's poems do not draw this distinction. Rather, they persistently locate alarm and inspiration in the same moment. "Broken," for example, articulates a survival that does not transcend the impact of the speaker's abuse. Unlike her parents, who are embarked on a radically transformative journey, this victim settles herself in the potent time and space of aftermath: "I am here in my time, lit, broken . . . Vibrating, at last, light, life, mine."[27] The poem's embrace of this broken subjectivity contests not only the distinction between trauma and survival, but also that between trauma and victim/survivor. There is no clean-up, no repair, only a speaker whose shards vibrate with the power of her shattered state.

The unexpectedness of Sapphire's shards is especially clear in comparison to a parallel passage from Elly Danica's 1988 *Don't: A Woman's Word*, a memoir that experiments with form but upholds the conventional teleology of recovery. *Don't* introduces the image of shards early in its fragmented narrative, initially crafting a metaphor in which the alien impact of incest lodges within the body, an intrusion upon essential wholeness:

> I find one shard implanted under my skin. I rejoice. I remove with care. I try not to leave scars . . . I try to heal the wound. Why no relief? There are two? I will remove the second then. Still no relief. There are more? Still more?

Quickly, though, the distinction between the intruded-upon self and the penetrating shard blurs. The narrator begins to fear that she simply *is* her damage:

> The woman made of potshards. Pieces. Not herself. Never herself. Who is herself? Only broken pieces . . . The wounds fester. There is no healing. The bleeding cannot be staunched . . . The pieces cannot be removed. Can't cut out your soul. What soul? . . . Only the pieces. Only the pain.[28]

This description is akin to Sapphire's image of the broken self, yet there is a crucial difference in textual effect. In *Don't*, this is a conventional encoding of despair, in which the narrator's failure to distinguish shard and self is itself a measure of damage, a dire misconception that must be corrected. The narrator's hopelessness is thus a cue for reassurance, an instance of the paradigmatic need that elicits the readerly support out of which testimonial politics cohere. Indeed, the subsequent address is direct and explicit. "If I'm gone too long, come for me," she instructs, then sets off on the path to recovery, chanting "Faith in the process. Descend. Enter. Memory."[29] Standing outside the vicissitudes, readers are asked to make sure the narrator arrives at her transcendent destiny.

Against the image of Danica's alien shards, the unconventionality of Sapphire's formulation stands out in sharp relief: the shards of "Broken" are not the contamination of her past, to be removed with care, nor even the raw material of her future, to be pierced together in recovery, but rather the animating force of her potent present. "Broken" abandons the conventional distinctions that would hold the victim apart from her abuse, portrayed as damaged but with an essential core of innocent subjectivity in protective abeyance. Instead, this poem posits damage as an indigenous element of the self—critically, it supports the speaker's identification with her own damage, refusing to undermine her narrative authority by ringing therapeutic alarms. In so doing, "Broken" reformulates trauma as constitutive rather than simply interruptive; it thus invokes a subjectivity more complex than that of innocent victimhood, one neither unified nor pure. The notion of a fragmented, nonessential self has long been the dominant model within contemporary feminist theory, and yet the affect-laden politics of recovered wholeness have protectively shielded victims from such paradigms. In dispensing with such protection, the exultant "at last, broken" reimagines not only victimhood, but also recovery, arguing that transcendence may be not only impossible but undesirable.

Representations of constitutive victimhood push us towards a newly agential understanding of the childhood experience of incest, one that consolidates the girl's responses alongside the father's actions by understanding her to be a participant within the dynamic of abuse. This is not to argue that the child consents to or is even complicit in the abuse but rather to refuse to see her only as a passive object. By uncoupling victimization from helplessness, constitutive victimhood emphasizes the operation of the girl's agency, however limited or intermittent it may be, within the context of abuse. Conventional formulations of victimhood affix agency to the transcendence of recovery, imagining that a helpless victim becomes an agential survivor precisely to the degree that she can sever the links between self and abuse; in contrast, the postconventional paradigm seeks agency in the exploration and manipulation of those links. At the simplest level, this can take the form of unexpectedly locating things of worth amid the destruction of abuse. Carol Rambo Ronai, for example, writes in her 1995 account: "if I define myself as having taken a crash course in empathy, I can reframe my experiences as having something positive about them."[30] More jarringly, though, postconventional narrators move beyond the itemization of positive or negative effects, setting aside that evaluative question to measure instead utility. Damage, they discomfitingly suggest, may itself be useful. Politically, this move is fraught. It threatens to devolve into the intolerable suggestion that incest can be a good thing. And yet it is also potent: the willingness to use the damage of incest is, in these texts, a necessary precondition for the emergence of victim agency.

To look for agency within the aftermath of abuse rather than in a departure from that damage is to move—unnervingly—beyond our familiar paradigms for agency and damage both. Writing in the broader context of theorizing "the loss of loss itself," Judith Butler frames the problem thus:

> A fractured horizon looms in which to make one's way as a spectral agency, one for whom a full 'recovery' is impossible, one for whom the irrecoverable becomes, paradoxically, the condition of a new political agency.
>
> But what precisely is irrecoverable, and what form does this new political agency take?[31]

I offer Butler's enigmatic formulation as a stepping stone into the next two sections—close readings of two incest accounts that seek to identify the actual workings of agential damage. The two texts—Sapphire's *Push* and Kathryn Harrison's *The Kiss*—are themselves ambivalent, which makes them ideal grounds for this theoretical exploration.

Despite the appeal of transcendent relief, both texts ultimately make more use of the discomfort embedded within the experience of damage; similarly, I will argue, the theoretical and political value of *Push* and *The Kiss* lies not in a utopian promise, but in their interpellation of a discomfited readership.

"TELLING YOUR STORY GIT YOU OVER THAT RIVER, PRECIOUS"[32]: TESTIMONIAL EXHORTATIONS AND REFUSALS

The exploration of damage—and of its potential utility—is the core of Sapphire's 1996 *Push*, an autobiographically-inflected novel that elaborates on the image she sketches in "Broken" by toying with narrative recovery but finally relying on damage as the framework for post-abuse existence. *Push* grapples especially closely with a key question within contemporary trauma theory: what happens if we no longer assume that traumatic events are "outside the range of human experience?"[33] As discussed earlier, transcendent recovery is predicated on this traditional understanding of trauma— here, incestuous abuse—as the exception within a life; its lessons must be unlearned for the individual to function in the nontraumatic world. Like many postconventional incest narratives, *Push* operates instead on the presumption that the world is fundamentally unsafe; innocence loses its value here, marking not purity but vulnerability.

An explicit reworking of Alice Walker's transcendent *The Color Purple*, *Push* begins by invoking the promise of narrative recovery.[34] The novel presents itself as a multilayered autobiography: an oral narrative interrupted and eventually supplanted by the laborious diary entries of the ironically-named Precious, a young illiterate African American woman whose emergence from her impoverished and abusive family parallels her entry into the world of written language. The central text of *Push* is supplemented by an appendix, a collection of "Life Stories" assembled by the literacy class that—like the conventional speak out—multiplies Precious' individual story into collective testimony about the abuses of poverty, sexism, and racism.

Push is at times a text with genuine hopes for survival, even transcendence. Despite the dismal histories and dim prospects of the literacy students, for example, these young women survive and even flourish in a series of successes that *Push* aligns with their new mastery of language—the text celebrates the power of narrative "to make sense."[35] With the training it offers in constructing both plot and scene, writing helps Precious overcome one of her biggest quotidian difficulties: despite her express desire to pick a starting place for her story and move steadily forward, her early oral narrative is constantly swept away by floods of memory that she then must interrupt. "But thas the first day I'm telling you about," she says in a characteristic attempt to get back on track. "Today is not the first day, and like I said I was on my way to maff class when . . ." (5). In the early stages of her narrative, Precious' mind wanders repeatedly to horrific memories of the past or to formulaic MTV-inspired fantasies of an unlikely future; however hard she tries, Precious cannot focus her attention on the present moment. These interruptions effectively mark Precious' devastation in two ways. First, the memories provide readers with details of the shattering abuse she has suffered. Second, the apparent inability to maintain focus—either as a narrator or as an actor within that narrative—becomes a calibration of damage itself. In *Push*'s initial interpretive framework, the impact of abuse emerges conventionally as the loss of control, not only of one's life but also of one's story; literate testimony is cast as a learned practice of both experiential and narrative control.[36] The ability to write is, conventionally enough, the ability to narrate the story, to overcome trauma by reinstating the temporality it has destroyed.

Yet even as *Push* invokes the conventions of the recovery memoir, it offers Precious herself as a resistant element: the novel supports her defiant refusal to behave as a victim in recovery should. The most immediate evidence of this is the hostile suspicion she turns on most offers of help. This wariness alone is enough to topple the narrative arc of recovery, sustained as it is by a faith in an ultimate resolution enabled by supportive others. Conventionally, such a lack of trust would be an issue to resolve, yet *Push* endorses Precious' mistrust by cataloging the failures of the so-called 'helping' institutions (school, hospital, social services, etc.) around her. Some of these seem fairly routine, but others verge on becoming their own traumas: Precious ends up in a violent homeless shelter with a newborn baby after the maternity ward nurses refuse to help her find a safer place to go; she is almost pulled out of the literacy class and put on workfare because her standardized test scores do not improve rapidly enough; Medicare seems to obstruct, rather than provide, the medical care she increasingly needs. Trust, this novel insists, is simply uncalled for.

The novel's ambivalence about transcendent recovery collects most densely around Ms. Rain, the inspirational literacy teacher who routinely goes beyond her classroom responsibilities to advocate tirelessly on her students' behalf, wresting resources out of those inept and often callous institutions. Precious *does* trust Ms. Rain, and so takes seriously her teacher's faith that writing one's own story is a necessary step for posttraumatic flourishing. When Precious is overwhelmed by despair, Ms. Rain responds with confidence:

> If you just sit there the river gonna rise up drown you! Writing could be the boat carry you to the other side. One time in your journal you told me you had never really told your story. I think telling your story git you over that river, Precious.[37]

At key moments of crisis, Ms. Rain's advice is always to write, and to write completely. Yet the students alternately embrace and resist her advice. The book of "Life Stories" that the class compiles marks some willingness to "speak out," yet it is also filled with narratorial refusals. Rita's Life Story, for example, focuses on the early happiness she experienced in the years before her mother's murder. When Ms. Rain intimates that Rita's narrative avoids the real issues, Rita argues strongly for the value of refusals:

> Ms Rain . . . ask me to write more . . . about my life now. Just talk some more in the tape recorder and she transcribe it. What life? Foster care, rape, drugs, prostitution, HIV, jail, rehab. Everybody like to hear that story. Tell us more tell us more more MORE . . . But I tell you what *I* want, it's *my* book . . . [38]

Given her fervent commitment to her students' literacy, Ms. Rain's willingness to bypass the pedagogic utility of the "Life Stories" collection by offering to transcribe the additional text herself is surprising, registering her equally fervent belief that narration is salvation. More acquiescent than many of her classmates, Precious documents in her journal her worn-down agreement to follow Rain's advice and "push," to write the story she does not want to write. Strikingly, though, *Push* does not move on to offer us that story, nor does Precious appear to have crossed any psychic river in the following journal entry. The text thus leaves this question open—how much does the production of narrative actually help one let go of the past?

What's more, the text begins to question the basic premise of the narrative promise: should one let go of one's past? For Precious, the aftereffects of incest manifest most concretely in the two children she has conceived in the course of her father's brutal rapes. *Push* always contextualizes the children by their origins—they are the product of incest and neglect, and this, as Precious frequently reminds us, is just not the same as having a child with a boy you like. Yet at the novel's start, the children are surprisingly abstract: Precious has had almost no contact with her first child, a girl with Down's Syndrome who was born when Precious was twelve, and has initially given little thought to the second child with whom she is pregnant. Her pregnancy does not escape the attention of school administrators, though, who place her on suspension. This initially appears to be a disaster, yet Precious' pursuit of "an alternative" takes her to the all-important literacy class (p. 16). In this move, *Push* begins to interrogate the utility of incest's damaging impact, which it pursues through the figure of the new baby. Spending the last few months of her pregnancy in the literacy class, Precious builds confidence and a sense of purpose that grows as the child is born. She is horrified, then, when the hospital social worker suggests she should give both children up for adoption, and even more upset to find that Ms. Rain is in agreement.

Through their ensuing debate, *Push* lays out the core question—what to do with the lingering impact of incest? When Precious cites an obligation to the child, Ms. Rain argues that Precious' obligation is to herself, to her education, to "make something of her life" (p. 71). Ms. Rain's pressure is aligned with a commitment to writing, but more generally with her belief that Precious can, if she chooses, leave her victimization behind: "You could get your G.E.D. and go to college. You could do anything Precious but you gotta believe it" (p. 75). Their discussion takes place in the pages of Precious' journal, where Ms. Rain's exhortations skip fluently over Precious' labored objections. Hopelessly losing, Precious abandons their written argument but keeps her son; the wordlessness of the victory sets it beyond the pale of narrative resolution.

At this point, *Push* appears to offer a new model of recovery, one that does not deny the past yet draws upon the empowerment of the present to convert damage into strength. And yet this transformation is short-lived: *Push* refuses to let Precious recover. At the peak of her literary and familial successes, Precious discovers that her father has infected her with HIV. In the novel's setting of the late 1980s, this is a death sentence, especially for an impoverished black woman (a group with an especially high mortality rate). Undermining Precious' new identity as a survivor with terrible literality, the diagnosis prompts a textual reorientation toward her ability to make use of damage itself.

Push gives us two final passages, each of which conjures up transcendence only to reject it in favor of a salvation paradoxically rooted in devastation. The first is from Precious' journal:

> It's Sunday, no school, meetings. I'm in dayroom at Advancement House, sitting on a big leather stool holdin' Abdul. The sun is coming

through the window splashing down on him, on the pages of his book. It's called *The Black BC's*. I love to hold him on my lap, open up the world to him. When the sun shine on him like this, he is an angel child. And my heart fill. Hurt. One year? Five? Ten years? Maybe more if I take care of myself. Maybe a cure. Who knows, who is working on shit like that? Look his nose is so shiny, his eyes shiny. He my shiny brown boy. In his beauty I see my own. He pulling on my earring, want me to stop daydreaming and read him a story before nap time. I do.[39]

Precious' "hurt" first prompts a hope she is too savvy to sustain, then replaces it with identification. It is through this child, the mark of the incest, that she can see herself with love, something she has struggled to do throughout *Push*. Finally, though, her salvation is located precisely in the place of deepest damage. It is the HIV, and her awareness of her impending death, that fulfills the promise that transcendence could not: only now can she hold her attention on the present moment.

The focusing power of HIV is echoed in the second ending, Precious' contribution to the "Life Stories" collection with which the novel concludes. Her poem describes the limits of her life, limits which point also to the inadequacy of any liberal model of agency as simple freedom ("I'm not really free / baby, Mama, HIV") as well as the things that bring her happiness (her child's cleverness, the flight paths of birds, her new literacy), then ends by weighing advice from different sources:

PLAY THE HAND YOU GOT
housemother say.
HOLD FAST TO DREAMS
Langston say.
GET UP OFF YOUR KNEES
Farrakhan say.
CHANGE
Alice Walker
say.
Rain fall down
wheels turn round
DON'T ALWAYS RHYME
Ms Rain say
walk on
go into the poem
the HEART of it
beating
like
a clock
a virus tick
tock.[40]

Moving through these strategies, Precious comes to Ms. Rain's guidance, with its merging of literary and survival skills. Yet in her final segue, Precious disregards Ms. Rain's advice: moving from life to death, Precious turns to the virus for both rhythm and rhyme. *Push* ends thus, calling on damage to equip her not for transcendent survival, but for agency within a world of ongoing trauma.

Push's representation of HIV as simultaneously a fatal crisis and a fruitful temporality highlights the limits of dichotomous models of agency and powerlessness. The binary of innocence and guilt comes under suspicion too. In refusing to transcend the impact of abuse by recovering a whole, unharmed Precious, *Push* foregoes the traditional appeal to innocence—yet given Precious' social location and the historic difficulty of securing innocent status for victims who deviate from a white, middle-class norm, we should not be too quick to presume such an appeal would have been successful.[41] In her work on trauma within lesbian culture, Ann Cvetkovich observes similar refusals of transcendence, a phenomenon she identifies as a "queer healing practice" that inverts homophobic cultural "repudiation and shame" via a queer modality of creative reclamation.[42] Such dynamics are also at work for Precious, especially given the sexualized demonization of hegemonic representations of young impoverished black women. There is undoubtedly an antinormative energy—a queer energy, in a broader sense—to this use of damage as a site of agency. Even in the hands of putatively mainstream writers like Kathryn Harrison (the author of *The Kiss*, the text to which I turn next) the willingness to make use of damage pulls us away from conventional positioning of female innocence or purity. It forces both text and audience onto unfamiliar territory, dangerous but promising, in which suffering still matters but no longer indexes helplessness.

"THAT I MIGHT DESIRE TO BE CONSUMED"[43]: SELF-SHATTERING

Push's critique of transcendent recovery begins in Precious' surprise discovery of something of value—her child—amid the devastation of incest, but goes further to assert that even a damaging thing she does not value—her HIV infection—can be put to use. In turning to Kathryn Harrison's *The Kiss*, we encounter a text that goes still further: it raises the excruciating possibility that damage might be so potent as to inspire consent to one's own abuse. Telling the story of the sexual relationship between the narrator and the father whom she had barely known in childhood, *The Kiss* insists, disconcertingly, that this sexual relationship can be understood only by focusing on the ambiguity (not the absence) of the daughter's consent. The text sets that ambiguity against its firm clarity on two points: the incest was and is deeply painful and damaging to the narrator, and she was and is able to make powerful use of it. Despite the apparent passivity of her acquiescence to her father's sexual demands, the narrator uses the incest to claim an agency of calculated brutality, the cruelties of which she is willing to inflict on herself as well as others.

As a prelude to this brutal agency, *The Kiss* works hard to establish its narrator's victimhood, telling story after story of her suffering at the hands of various family members—her mother and maternal grandparents as well as her father. The incest itself takes place in canonical scenes that evoke conventional childhood incest: after her father unexpectedly pushes his tongue into her mouth in their first farewell kiss, for example, the narrator retreats into isolation and then denial as she realizes that no one will believe or understand; on the night she first lies in bed with him and kisses him back, she rises from sleep to sit on the floor of the shower under hot water that fails to wash away the emotional "dislocation" of the experience.[44] The iteration of these classic childhood scenes within Harrison's memoir registers the horror of incest, as do her catalogs of the manipulations by which her father and her past conspire to make the incestuous relationship irresistible.

It is this last point, of course, that is chillingly unfamiliar: *The Kiss* tells a story of quasi-consensual incest, undertaken at the father's insistence but with the young woman's fraught acquiescence. Over and over, the narrator describes herself in thrall to her father, always emphasizing the ambiguity of her own agency, stressing again and again the conceptual inadequacy of the consent/refusal binary:

> The kiss is the point at which I begin, slowly, inexorably, to fall asleep, to surrender volition, to become paralyzed. It's the drug my father administers in order that he might consume me. That I might desire to be consumed. [45]

And again:

> As frightened as I am to be with my father, I can't not see him. My need for him is inexorable. I can't arrest it any more than I could stop myself from falling if, having stepped from a rooftop into the air, I remembered, too late, the fact of gravity.[46]

Marking so carefully the interrelation of his compulsion and her compliance, demonstrating her control in the precision of her prose (notice, for example, how the commas of that last sentence slow but cannot stop its grave conclusion), the narrator pointedly offers no direct explanation for her seemingly inexplicable actions. Instead, she traces their multiple determinants, parsing out the needs and desires of her young adulthood. At times the narrator suggests relatively direct reasons for her acquiescence, such as the relief of yielding to her father's remarkable powers of persuasion. More often, though, she supplies indirect explanations in the stories she tells of her childhood: the crushing experience of her father utterly ignoring her on one of only two visits of her childhood, which underpins her resultant excitement at now capturing his attention; the abandonment of losing her special closeness with her grandfather once he perceived her to be sexualized by adolescence, which frames her desperate conviction that sex should not obstruct this new paternal relationship; her feeling of perpetual otherness within the ordered world of her maternal grandparents' home and the pleasure of discovering herself like her father, which leaves her unwilling to upset that likeness by refusing to share his desires.

These childhood stories are collectively suggestive, but stop well short of explaining the daughter's enthrallment. Given the text's overt display of narratorial competence, this registers as a refusal rather than a failure of explanation. Hanging within the memoir, the unanswered question of "Why would she tolerate the incest?" shifts to the related "What is she getting out of it?"—or, to put it most clearly, "How is she making use of the experience of incest?" *The Kiss* thus pushes its narrative (and its readers) into a profoundly uncomfortable search for incest's usefulness, a search encouraged by the seemingly endless series of motivations the narrator tacitly identifies. Among these possibilities, however, one dominates. *The Kiss* suggests that the narrator allows the incest because it enables her to redefine the terms of her relationship to her mother: in the reflected glare of the incest, the mother's emotional abuse finally becomes visible. Ostensibly an account of paternal incest, this short volume devotes most of its pages to maternal manipulation and abandonment. As the vignettes of the girl's childhood grow chilling, the narrator's own fury and desperation crystallize upon the page to make the unexpected 'solution' of incest appear discomfitingly logical. Having sex with her father has many indeterminate effects, but it is, she is sure, the very worst thing she can do to her mother.

Were it cast conventionally, this underlying account of maternal abuse could have reinstated the narrator as an innocent victim, thus invoking a familiar framework in which even the unfamiliar adult incest would be comprehensible as a dire manifestation of damage, a terrible experience to be transcended in survival. And yet *The Kiss* actively averts such a reading: it invokes the helplessness of innocence not to exculpate its victim, but rather to clarify the agency of guilt. At one point, reflecting on her mother's relationship to her own controlling mother, the narrator says "She'll never escape her mother . . . My grandmother has her in a death grip," and goes on to speculate with barely-muted pleasure: "Is this because my mother is not as ruthless as I am?"[47] This valuable ruthlessness is new, stemming from the devastation of the incest. For all the narrator's musing about her father's spellbinding power, she offers a more detailed portrayal of her history of reflexive submission to her mother. The narrator describes at length her youthful feelings of abandonment when her mother "fled into sleep," and yet the few scenes of maternal engagement are infinitely worse. One of the most disconcerting reads as itself a sexual violation:

She wants me to get a diaphragm . . . but I can't be fitted for one.

"Not without breaking her hymen," the doctor says after he examines me. "You don't want to do that, do you?"

My mother, standing near the window, hesitates. I sit up on my elbows. "Yes," she says.

He uses a series of graduated green plastic penises . . . One after the other he inserts them . . . until the second to last one comes out smeared with blood. This doctor deflowers me in front of my mother . . .

I lie on the table, a paper sheet over my knees, my hands over my eyes.[48]

This scene performs multiple functions within the text, but I want to focus us on its demonstration of the perils of helplessness. Having refused a model of complete innocence, *The Kiss* cannot mobilize helplessness into the conventional effect. Instead, it cites the girl's helplessness as the precondition of her desperate agency: offering this scene in lieu of narrating the intercourse between father and daughter, *The Kiss* demonstrates exactly why the narrator is willing to risk her own destruction in order to wrest free of her mother. While readers may well recoil from that choice and the damage it inevitably inflicts, *The Kiss* insists that we see its value for the narrator. In refusing to cast the incest as a victim's mistake, the text steps away from a conventional testimonial stance that would interpellate our empathetic understanding; instead, *The Kiss* insists that its narrator's interpretive authority exceeds our own.

Narrating scene after painful scene in which first the girl and then the young woman lies passively before one or the other of her parents, *The Kiss* goes further to suggest that, for this daughter at least, the utility of incest lies precisely in its patent abusiveness. In an unexpected reworking of classic misogynist mother–blame, the narrator uses paternal incest to mark the harm of her mother's actions. It is the incest that reveals the victimization inherent in the girl's helplessness, allowing her to understand and react to her mother's manipulations as abuse—even as she simultaneously undoes the interpretive framework of victimhood by incorporating agency within its founding helplessness. Note, for example, her turn to the potency of victim–blame in adopting the role of the "seductive daughter." After a lifetime of painful longing for her mother, the narrator takes up this guilty role to dislodge her mother from the position of she-who-is-desired; she does this not directly, but by ending the intermittent sexual relationship between her parents. "I have taken her husband," the narrator gloats, relishing not only her newfound power to punish but—more importantly—the promise implicit in her father's sudden disinterest in her mother. The rewriting of the relation between mother and father suggests that the devastating mix of desire and subjection that constitutes her own relationships might be less permanent than she fears: if the father can be dis-enthralled, perhaps so too can the daughter (p. 143). No longer static, victimhood need not demand transcendence. Instead, it can be put to use.

And what is that use? *The Kiss* charts the ways in which the incestuous relationship offers its narrator a new, more intimate connection to her mother: "Through my father I have begun at last to penetrate my mother" (p. 140). The sexual imagery of the verb can be no accident. As her refusal to grant her family members names of their own suggests, the narrator plays with a psychoanalytic frame in which circulating sexual desire constitutes familiality and helplessness alike; by enacting the forbidden sexual relation, she thus rewrites the structure of both family and victimhood. Stressing most clearly this final point—that the very fact of the incest reconstructs her relationship to her mother—the narrator of *The Kiss* emphasizes that her passive acquiescence is inextricably linked to her determined ruthlessness. The incest ends, strikingly enough, when her mother dies (of cancer, although the text takes seriously the mother's insistence that the incest is literally killing her) and the daughter finds herself no longer in need of incest's potent familial reconfiguration.

Ultimately, *The Kiss* suggests, the unthinkable maneuver worked. The text ends with a dream of the dead mother's return, in which the narrator finally achieves the much-longed-for maternal connection:

> My mother and I . . . look into each other's eyes more deeply than we ever did in life, and for much longer. As we look, all that we have ever felt but have never said is manifest. Her youth and selfishness and misery, my youth and selfishness and misery. Our loneliness. The ways we betrayed one another.
>
> In this dream, I feel that at last she knows me, and I her. I feel us stop hoping for a different daughter and a different mother.[49]

Repeatedly in *The Kiss*, the narrator has used the term "betrayal" to describe what it is she does to her mother by acquiescing to the sexual relationship her father desires. Given the ways in which she has suffered as her mother's victim, and given the efficacy with which she uses the incest to shift the dynamics of that maternal abuse, we might expect to hear not of betrayal but rather revenge. "Betrayal," though, offers a final repudiation of both transcendence and sentiment. There is no other daughter, no other mother, to be recuperated as whole and healthy, nor is there a void that the readers could fill with our own support. The "knowing" of that final sentence is the agency of damage—the combined helplessness and potency whose final triumph is the abandonment of hope.

"THE STRANGE FECUNDITY OF THAT WRECKAGE":[50] AGENTIAL DAMAGE

The damage-wielding narrators of *Push*, *The Kiss*, and other postconventional incest narratives offer a profoundly dystopic vision of empowerment.

This agency is high cost and highly circumscribed, and yet it is unquestionably potent. Within the diagesis of these narratives, postconventional victims exert partial but measurable control, exploiting the impact of abuse to their own ends; within the narrator–addressee relation, they reclaim the narrative authority conventionally passed to an interpellated readership who would usher the disoriented victim along the path to transcendent recovery. As both characters and narrators, these victims act for themselves, finding power precisely in their willingness to violate the expectations of innocent victimhood, including the expectation that victims should and will heal by transcending their abuse. Whereas the conventional incest narratives captivate readers by relying upon them to hold out hope for the victim's recovery, accounts like *Push* and *The Kiss* command their readers' anxious attention—we wait nervously to see how their improvised scenes will unfold, wondering how far these impure victims might be willing to go and what they will find upon arrival.

In light of recent feminist debates over agency—how do we imagine it, without falling back on the premise of the liberal subject?—the always already corrupted agency of postconventional victimhood is especially welcome. For all that these debates are prompted by poststructuralism, they invoke a too-simple binary between power and helplessness; in taking the two states to be mutually exclusive, theorists can easily slip into seeing only pure power as 'true' agency, a one-drop model of corruption in which agency can never exceed its own limitations. By insisting upon partiality and impurity, postconventional incest narratives actively dismantle the binary paradigm. These texts posit an agential subjectivity that is not nullified by victimization—an agency that operates not only within but through discursive and material constraints, even in the fraught realm of sexual violence.

RIVERS, AGAIN—TO WHERE DO WE CROSS?

And what of politics, of the feminist public created through the conventional incest narratives? When postconventional incest narratives such as *Push* and *The Kiss* do not script a sentimental response—when they no longer fuse the reader–narrator bond with victim's helplessness and the reader's need to support her—do they even remain testimonial, let alone political? Or, to ask this another way: if testimonial politics unfolds within the victim–addressee dyad, does the emergence of victim agency preclude the cultivation of an agential audience?

These questions are linked to the practices of sentimentality as well as testimony, to the longstanding presumption that structural injustices such as white supremacy and patriarchy can be revealed and fought via affect. Politics, here, emerges from the solidarity produced in the empathetic recognition of suffering. In its nineteenth-century abolitionist practice, as many theorists have argued, sentimentality often undermined its own goals: the textual display of the slaves' suffering, narrated by and addressed to a sympathetic white audience, paradoxically argues for the subaltern protagonists' humanity through the very representation that flattens them into passive objects-to-be-saved.[51] It might seem that the sentimental practice of conventional incest narratives eludes this problem by consolidating the narrator and protagonist, thus shifting the textual representation of suffering; in autobiography, we might hear the victim's voice. And yet by pinning themselves rhetorically to the project of testimonial address—that which impels the author to write, the reader to respond—sentimental autobiographies ventriloquize victimhood. Setting paradigmatically helpless victimhood against the therapeutic and political potency of testimony and the response it elicits, conventional narrators invoke experience but mute the authority it might confer. What's more, I would argue, the readership is ultimately drawn into this reification of female suffering—for readers are, by these very practices, bound not just to the narrators but also to their helplessness. The feminist public constituted through the conventional address may not, ultimately, excise the pure political agency with which we routinely credit it. That is not to say that this public has not had important political effects—it has—but rather that it is more complex, less transcendent, than we generally recognize.

Postconventional testimony takes place in the wake of these sentimental dynamics. It struggles to represent incest and victimization differently, attempting to narrate its stories through an address that does not reify vulnerability into helplessness. I say 'struggles' because, as Michael Warner reminds us in *Publics and Counter-Publics*, one cannot simply alter public discourse through sheer force of will or art.[52] The postconventional incest texts are necessarily haunted by their conventional predecessors, always bound to the rhetoric of helplessness and the sentimental public summoned by over a century of 'women's writing.' They cannot transcend that past. And yet this is, quite precisely, the discomfiting maneuver of postconventionality: to wring agency from a problematic, even violent, past. The political imperatives of texts like *Push* and *The Kiss* take form through a pentimento effect; their portrayals of victimhood are drawn atop the sentimental images of convention.[53] As readers, we approach these texts looking for sentiment, poised to offer empathy and guidance. Postconventional narratives play upon those expectations, soliciting and then rejecting readerly support. They thus trigger the familiar testimonial imperative—"Reader, you must act!"—but are not satisfied by the ritualized response of empathetic support.

In her incisive analysis of the politics of American sentimentality, Berlant follows the image of 'river crossing' through key texts, including Harriet Beecher Stowe's *Uncle Tom's Cabin* and Toni Morrison's *Beloved*. In Stowe's sentimental novel, she argues, readers cannot help but urge Eliza forward in her perilous crossing of the Ohio—we experience Eliza's flight from slavery as impelled by the readers' desire, and imagine her transit as "sublime" escape.[54] Morrison's postsentimental novel, in contrast, "shows that when you cross the Ohio you do not transcend it but take it with you": the events that follow Sethe's crossing are repeatedly interrupted by water, both literal and figurative, as the far shore fails to be the promised land of safety.[55] I would propose we read the metaphoric river of *Push* ("Telling your story git you over that river, Precious") as a similar exploration of trauma, empathy, and consequence—and of the potency of breaking not with the past, but with the conventional expectation that the past will be left behind. Within the unfolding crises of the novel, Precious' river passage appears as a matter of utmost urgency; by refusing to narrate that journey, *Push* interrupts the circuit of readerly urging and relief. The feminist public thus summoned is a thwarted one. We cannot soothe ourselves by pushing Precious into safety, nor are we bound together by the mutual accomplishment of delivering the plot to its generic transcendent end. For all the suffering they document, conventional incest narratives can palliate; postconventional incest narratives identify themselves by withholding comfort.

Herein, I would argue, lies their new mode of testimonial politics. In representing suffering but rejecting transcendence, texts such as *Push* and *The Kiss* address a public who must act, then leave that imperative unfulfilled. Unraveling the tightly woven representation of helplessness, damage, and recovery, these postconventional feminist narratives insist upon the agency made possible by 'unresolved' trauma—a challenge thrown out to their public, whom they abandon in a tumult of emotional and political irresolution.

NOTES

1. Margaret Randall, preface to *She Who Was Lost Is Remembered*, ed., Louise Wisechild (Seattle: Seal Press, 1991), xi–xiii.
2. Darlene Dralus and Jen Shelton, "What Is the Subject? Speaking, Silencing, (Self) Censorship," *Tulsa Studies in Women's Literature* 14 (1995): 19–37.
3. Sapphire, *Push: A Novel* (New York: Knopf, 1996); Kathryn Harrison, *The Kiss* (New York: Random House, 1997); Dorothy Allison, *Bastard Out of Carolina* (New York: Plume, 1992); Carolivia Herron, *Thereafter Johnnie* (New York: Random House, 1991).
4. Renee Heberle, "Deconstructive Strategies and the Movement Against Sexual Violence," *Hypatia* 11, 4 (1996): 63–76; Sharon Marcus, "Fighting Bodies, Fighting Words: A Theory and Politics of Rape Prevention," in *Feminists Theorize The Political*, eds. Judith Butler and Joan W. Scott (New York: Routledge, 1992), 385–403.
5. Marcus, ibid., 388–89.
6. Louise Thornton, preface to *I Never Told Anyone: Writings by Women Survivors of Child Sexual Assault*, eds. Ellen Bass and Louise Thornton (New York: Harper, 1983), 15–22.
7. For feminist discussion of such perspectives, see Louise Armstrong, *Kiss Daddy Goodnight: A Speak-Out on Incest* (New York: Pocket Books, 1978); Sandra Butler, *Conspiracy of Silence: The Trauma of Incest* (Volcano, CA: Volcano Press, 1978); Judith Lewis Herman (with Lisa Hirschman), *Father–Daughter Incest* (Cambridge, MA: Harvard University Press, 1981).

8. For examples of this political emphasis, see Armstrong, Butler, and Herman, op. cit. For later critiques of the stress on damage, see Sharon Lamb, ed., *New Versions of Victims: Feminists Struggle with the Concept* (New York: NYU Press, 1999); Janice Haaken, *Pillar of Salt: Gender, Memory, and the Perils of Looking Back* (New Brunswick, NJ: Rutgers University Press, 1998); Louise Armstrong, *Rocking the Cradle of Sexual Politics: What Happened When Women Said Incest* (Reading, MA: Addison-Wesley, 1994).

9. See, for example, Butler's *Conspiracy of Silence*, op. cit.

10. See Judith Herman, *Trauma and Recovery* (New York: Basic Books, 1992); Cathy Caruth, ed., *Trauma: Explorations in Memory* (Baltimore, MD: Johns Hopkins University Press, 1995); Shoshana Felman and Dori Laub, eds., *Testimony: Crises of Witnessing in Literature, Psychoanalysis, and History* (New York: Routledge, 1992).

11. Toni A. H. McNaron, and Yarrow Morgan, eds., *Voices in the Night: Women Speaking About Incest* (Minneapolis, MN: Cleis Press, 1982), 11.

12. Nikki Craft, "Drifting from the Mainstream: A Chronicle of Early Anti-Rape Organizing," in *Fight Back: Feminist Resistance to Male Violence*, eds. Frédérique Delacoste and Felice Newman (Minneapolis, MN: Cleis Press, 1981), 110–111.

13. My analysis here is influenced by Michael Warner's treatment of the reflexive relations between texts and their publics; his analyses of how one might (or might not) call a non-extant public into being are particularly helpful. Michael Warner, *Publics and Counterpublics* (New York: Zone Books, 2005).

14. Randall, Margaret, *This is About Incest* (Ithaca, NY: Firebrand Books, 1987), 14.

15. Ellen Bass, "In the truth itself, there is healing, " Introduction to Bass and Thornton, op. cit., 38.

16. The necessity of the reader's response is, for example, at the heart of the distinction Vikki Bell draws between witnessing, which produces politics, and confession, which produces oppression and voyeurism. Vikki Bell, *Interrogating Incest: Feminism, Foucault, and the Law* (New York: Routledge, 1993).

17. Christine Courtois, *Healing the Incest Wound: Adult Survivors in Therapy* (New York: Norton, 1988), xvi.

18. Sheila L. Sisk and Charlotte Foster Hoffman, *Inside Scars: Incest Recovery As Told By a Survivor and Her Therapist* (Gainesville, FL: Pandora Press, 1987), 204.

19. Ellen Bass and Laura Davis, *The Courage to Heal: A Guide for Women Survivors of Child Sexual Abuse* (New York: Harper, 1988), 23.

20. Randall, *She Who Was Lost*, op. cit., xi-xiii (emphasis added).

21. Some feminist incest writers contested this conclusion. See, for example, Louise Armstrong, *Kiss Daddy Goodnight: Ten Years Later* (New York: Pocket Books, 1987). The dominant rhetoric of feminist incest literature, however, casts individual recovery as a crucial political task.

22. Lauren Berlant, *The Female Complaint: The Unfinished Business of Sentimentality in American Culture* (Durham, NC: Duke University Press, 2008), 41–42. See also Lauren Berlant, "The Subject of True Feeling: Pain, Privacy, and Politics," in *Cultural Studies and Political Theory*, ed. Jodi Dean (Ithaca: Cornell University Press, 2000), 42–62.

23. For a particularly vivid definition of the distinction between 'victims' and 'survivors,' see Rosaria Champagne, *The Politics of Survivorship: Incest, Women's Literature, and Feminist Theory* (New York: New York University Press, 1996), 2–3.

24. Sentimental dynamics are also affected by the twentieth century shift from fiction to autobiography, an issue I take up later in this chapter. For a

discussion of a rare autobiography within the abolitionist canon, see Franny Nudelman, "Harriet Jacobs and the Sentimental Politics of Female Suffering," *ELH* 59 (1992): 939–964.

25. Sapphire, *Black Wings and Blind Angels: Poems* (New York: Vintage, 2000), 125.
26. Ibid.
27. Ibid.
28. Elly Danica, *Don't: A Woman's Word* (San Francisco, CA: Cleis Press, 1988), 14.
29. Ibid.
30. Carol Rambo Ronai, "Multiple Reflections of Child Sex Abuse: An Argument for a Layered Account," *Journal of Contemporary Ethnography* 23, 4 (1995): 395–426, 411.
31. Judith Butler, "Afterward: After Loss, What Then?" in *Loss: The Politics of Mourning*, ed. David Eng and David Kazanjian, (Berkeley, CA: University of California Press, 2003), 467–473, 467.
32. Push, op. cit., 99.
33. Laura Brown, "Not Outside the Range: One Feminist Perspective on Psychic Trauma," in *Caruth*, op. cit. 100–112.
34. Alice Walker, *The Color Purple* (New York: Pocket Books, 1982).
35. Push, op. cit., 4.
36. For a conventional accounting of the healing power of narrative, see Laura Milner, "On Writing, Healing, and Wholeness," *Intertexts* 8 (2003): 23–35.
37. Push, op. cit., 99.
38. Ibid., np.
39. Ibid., 142.
40. Ibid., np.
41. Esther Madriz, *Nothing Bad Happens to Good Girls: Fear of Crime in Women's Lives* (Berkeley, CA: University of California Press, 1997).
42. Ann Cvetkovich, *An Archive of Feelings: Trauma, Sexuality, and Lesbian Public Cultures* (Durham, NC: Duke University Press, 2003), 88. See also Didier Eribon, *Insult and the Making of the Gay Self*, trans., Michael Lucey (Durham, NC: Duke University Press, 2004).
43. Harrison, op. cit., 70.
44. Ibid., 71–75; 123–124.
45. Ibid., 70.
46. Ibid., 119–120.
47. Ibid., 142.
48. Ibid., 42–43.
49. Ibid., 206–207.
50. Butler, "After Loss," op. cit., 469.
51. For an excellent overview of feminist analyses of the mechanisms of sentimental politics, see Shirley Samuel's introduction to her edited volume on the subject. Shirley Samuels, *The Culture of Sentiment: Race, Gender, and Sentimentality in 19th Century America* (New York: Oxford University Press, 1992), 3–8. Also see Berlant, op. cit.
52. Warner, op. cit., 125–130.
53. In its standard use, 'pentimento' describes the traces, within a painting, of the artist's earlier vision(s), sometimes visible and sometimes effaced by the final work. My own usage is much looser, of course, in its description of readers' ability to see the conventional images over and against which the postconventional ones are drawn.
54. Berlant, "Poor Eliza," op. cit., 44–46.
55. Ibid., 66–67.

5   Fighting Rape

Nicola Gavey

> Rape exists because our experience and deployment of our bodies is the effect of interpretations, representations, and fantasies which often position us in ways amenable to the realization of the rape script: as paralyzed, as incapable of physical violence, as fearful.
>
> Sharon Marcus [1]

According to this poststructuralist claim, rape is not an inevitable outcome of sexual difference. Rather it is made possible through what Sharon Marcus refers to as "the language of rape"[2] or what I have described as the "cultural scaffolding of rape"[3]: the dominant discourses of sex and gender that position men as normatively and naturally both sexually driven and aggressive, and women as sexually passive and vulnerable.[4] For Marcus, it is the "gendered grammar of violence"[5]—which not only constructs women as the objects of (men's) violence, but also as the *subjects* of fear—that is of critical importance in sustaining rape. Any analysis of rape or strategy for preventing rape that accepts these gendered patterns as real (in an uncomplicated sense) and inevitable is therefore brought into question. This is because such analyses are trading in representations that can be seen as helping to constitute and reinforce the very dynamics of male power and female powerlessness that makes rape possible in the first place.

An increasing number of feminist theorists have found this kind of poststructuralist framework useful for theorizing the possibilities for preventing rape and other gendered forms of sexual violence and victimization.[6] Yet although these ideas have acceptance within an academic niche of feminist theory they remain provocative in relation to more mainstream responses to sexual violence. One of the dominant tropes of mainstream rape crisis and support services, for instance, centers on recognizing and addressing the trauma of rape. Implicitly, if not always explicitly, rape is imbued with dreadful power to harm. And the categories of 'victim' and 'abuser' are still generally rendered in ways that emphasize the vulnerability and fragility of the victim, and the aggressive power of the abuser.[7] In contrast to conventional assertions of the horrors of rape, women's vulnerability to rape, and men's danger, the poststructuralist argument put forth by Marcus suggests that such portrayals risk becoming part of the problem.[8] What truth there is to them is regarded as contingent upon particular cultural and historical formations. As suggested by the framework of Foucault's power/knowledge (*pouvoir/savoir*) nexus, our capacities *to be able* are completely intertwined with the kinds of norms and models for being and acting that are provided within our cultures.[9] The discourses and bodies of knowledge which elaborate these norms thus enable and constrain the range of desires, actions, and identities available to us as gendered beings. In the case of rape, the truths propagated within such knowledge can be said to play a constitutive role in shaping the possibilities for gendered action that create the cultural conditions of possibility for rape.

Accordingly, in order to stop rape, we would need to sidestep assertions of its overwhelming horror and of women's vulnerability. This is not to deny the truth of these assertions, when applied in specific circumstances, but to refuse them as generalized truth claims that take on an over-determining power.[10] The task, instead, would be to reject and break the shackles of conventional femininity which prevent women from directly fighting back against both the possibility and actuality of rape (as well, of course, as to undermine the cultural formation of masculinities that are too easily capable of sexual violence). Marcus calls for "a politics of fantasy and representation,"[11] suggesting that we should be looking to strategies that "enable women to sabotage men's power to rape, which will empower women to take the ability to rape completely out of men's hands."[12] On the way to eradicating the rape script, we could rewrite it, "perhaps by refusing to take it seriously and treating it as a farce, perhaps by resisting the physical passivity which it directs us to adopt."[13] With stirring words Marcus concludes that, "to construct a society in which we would know no fear, we may first have to frighten rape culture to death."[14] Self-defense is her key suggestion for the practical steps necessary to help make all this happen, through its potential to transform women into "subjects of violence and objects of fear."[15]

Marcus is not alone among feminist theorists in advocating a less cautious position on the role of (women's) violence in combating rape.[16] In her articulation of a "physical feminism" inspired by the integration of feminism and self-defense, Martha McCaughey has developed the most detailed and compelling argument for "women's self-defense training as a means of subverting the embodied ethos of rape culture."[17] She claims that it "metamorphoses the female body";[18] and in doing so undermines traditional gender ideology and the social order of female subordination. McCaughey, who conducted ethnographic research on women's self-defense, argues that its powerful effects go beyond enhancing women's courage and ability to fight back. She found they extended to "a new aesthetics of existence"[19] that was more confident and assertive in everyday life. In her 2001 book, *Rethinking Rape*, Ann Cahill provides enthusiastic endorsement of McCaughey's promotion of self-defense. While acknowledging it is not the only strategy, she concludes by suggesting that "self-defense training does hold the potential to undermine some of the most crucial and embodied tenets of a rape culture, and as such should become a central concern of feminist theory and practice."[20] The value of self-defense within this feminist vision for eliminating rape is not as a technique to enable individual (self) protection, but as a means to cultural transformation, to disrupt what we take to be the normal and natural forms of feminine and masculine embodiment.

Marcus's argument—and those like hers—illuminates some of the weaknesses of second-wave feminist theory. It draws attention to the ways in which women's agency and modes of resistance can appear to be foreclosed by models that posit rigid (and implicitly inherent or otherwise fixed) gender binaries as explanatory causes of women's exploitation and oppression. Marcus and Cahill in particular provide a way forward that is presented as a novel contrast to the deficiencies of the earlier feminist analyses of rape.[21] For instance, within theories like Susan Brownmiller's[22] classic feminist analysis, Marcus identifies a tendency to treat "violence as a self-explanatory first cause," endowing "it with an invulnerable and terrifying facticity which stymies our ability to challenge and demystify rape:"[23]

> In its efforts to convey the horror and iniquity of rape, such a view often concurs with masculinist culture in its designation of rape as a fate worse than, or tantamount to, death; the apocalyptic tone which it adopts and the metaphysical status which it assigns to rape implies that rape can only be feared or legally repaired, not fought.[24]

In short, Marcus and others have been calling for feminism to adopt a new militancy in fighting rape; and for women to be willing where necessary to take direct violent action (including, but perhaps not limited to, self-defense).

Primed by such feminist poststructuralist critiques of (other, earlier) feminist positions on rape, those of us without first hand experience of the early (1970s) grassroots feminist anti-rape activism might never have envisaged it as a site of militant praxis. Maria Bevacqua, however, suggests that poststructuralist feminists like Marcus misrepresent the anti-rape movement,[25] and that although well-intentioned, sometimes perpetuate an inaccurate understanding of history.[26] Indeed my own presumptions about the nature of early feminist responses to rape were overturned while I was doing archival research in the Schlesinger Library on the History of Women in America. In reading documents from the early 1970s I discovered records showing a rich body of feminist anti-rape praxis, in which I was surprised to encounter numerous examples of women's fighting response to male sexual aggression and rape. Many of the materials—the notes, clippings, pamphlets, posters, newsletters, feminist newspapers, and so on were originally collected by Susan Brownmiller, and at the time I was there in 2005 had recently been donated to the library. Others, including limited circulation radical periodicals, organization minutes, photographs, and so on were found in other collections within the library. My original purpose in looking through these archives was to examine the ways in which notions of trauma and the psychological impact of rape were represented in the early anti-rape movement. While reading through the boxes and boxes of papers, however, I couldn't help but be struck by this rather unexpected dimension of women's staunch and aggressive response to rape. I became captivated by the militancy running through so much of the material—in particular the strong self-defense theme as well as a more general fighting spirit.

Even Susan Brownmiller, it seemed, was not so prone within her own life to being completely stymied by endowing violence "with an invulnerable and terrifying facticity" as suggested by Marcus.[27] (While handing out leaflets for a rape conference on the streets of New York in 1971, Brownmiller was goosed[28] by a passing stranger; she responded by kicking him and, in doing so, sprained her ankle. After this sexually aggressive attack and her not entirely successful retaliation, Brownmiller was reported to be "learning how to kick," and saying "'I intend to become quite proficient!'"[29])

The juxtaposition between some of our poststructuralist representations of 'feminist' theories about rape and the praxis evident from the archival records of the early 1970s feminist activism was striking. It was also provocative and inspiring. Was it the kind of approach, I wondered, that Marcus might have imagined as strategies for rewriting the language of rape? And, what does the prior existence, and subsequent demise, of this kind of activism mean for how we read the transformative potential of the more contemporary visions for eliminating rape that are informed by poststructuralist critiques?[30] In this chapter I will consider these questions as I document some examples of the fighting spirit within feminist anti-rape activism in US urban centers at the time.[31]

A FIGHTING RESPONSE

> . . . we may first have to frighten rape culture to death.
>
> Sharon Marcus (1992)[32]

Just what Marcus means by this, and how it could be achieved are questions that might stretch our political imagination. It is interesting to counterpose Marcus's bold conclusion here with elements of the early feminist anti-rape activism. Rape was still routinely minimized, and rape-supportive views were boldly proclaimed within mainstream society in the early 1970s. Activists in the early days of the anti-rape movement therefore had to first draw attention to rape as a social problem and counter outright sexist victim-blaming discourse on rape. Their feminist analysis of and denouncement of what would later become referred to as "rape myths" could be straightforward and forceful.[33] In 1969 the Cambridge group Female Liberation distributed leaflets in Harvard Square to highlight the issue of "sex crimes" against women:

> The guilt is not on women for denying normal outlets to men. The guilt is on society for permitting the objectification of women and the cultivation in man of an attitude of brutality toward women. It is "manly" to "treat 'em rough."

With aggressive rhetoric characteristic of this group they went on to demand that:[34]

> This whole mystique must be destroyed. We must learn to fight back. It must become as dangerous to attack a woman as to attack another man. We will not be raped! We will not be slashed! We will not be "treated rough" by any man, "brute" or pervert. We will not be leered at, smirked at, or whistled at by men enjoying their private fantasies of rape and dismemberment.
>   WATCH OUT. MAYBE YOU'LL FINALLY MEET A *REAL* CASTRATING FEMALE.[35]

The castration theme was taken up again by Dana Densmore, one of the authors in this Boston group that later went on to become the radical Cell 16. In noting that women who have experienced rape can experience a "second rape" when going through the criminal justice system, Densmore suggested castration as a more appropriate punishment for rapists: "Ideally rapists should be castrated on the spot by their women victims." However she noted the problems:

> If the woman is overpowered enough to be actually raped, she is unlikely to be in a position to perform the castration. This problem may be met with rape squads, groups of women who collectively avenge rapes. However, it should be recognized that this is a very dangerous business, which could easily flair into an all-out war as men form counter gangs to fight the rape squads.[36]

This kind of aggressively uncompromising proposal was fully in keeping with the militancy of Cell 16. It should be noted that both the tenor and substance of their agenda were not characteristic of all feminist activism at the time, which included work in other political spheres directed at legislative and criminal justice reform, and so on. Nevertheless, such *sentiments* appear not to have been solely confined to these radical edges of the women's movement: one of Bettye Lane's photographs from this era shows a woman at the 1974 National Organization for Women (NOW) congress in Philadelphia with the slogan "castrate rapists" prominently attached to the back of her shirt;[37] and psychology professor Phyllis Chesler was reported as recommending "castration as a fitting punishment" for rape.[38]

Fighting responses that stopped short of castration were widely celebrated in feminist media at the time. One particularly arresting poster-style image, published by *No More Fun and Games: A Journal of Female Liberation* in 1971, showed a powerful-looking woman attacking a man in a self-defense type movement. Her foot is placed in the region of his groin, and he is shown to be falling backwards with a look of shock and pain.

In this Betsy Warrior image, the sketched figures are sandwiched between the words "DISARM RAPISTS" and "SMASH SEXISM."[39] Other outlets offered defiant vignettes of women's resistance to sexual harassment and violence. Under the heading "I'd rather fight", for instance, *It Aint Me Babe* published eight feisty accounts that countered representations of women's passive vulnerability:

> Mary: . . . i just slugged him as hard as i could, and when he turned his face to me, he looked shocked and his jaw was hanging down funny to the left of his face . . .

> R: i had a lot of hassle last week, so now i carry a little medicine bottle of ammonia. i'll just throw it in some guy's eyes if he bugs me. [40]

As with other works from this period, the fighting attitude displayed in these extracts resonates with the vision Marcus was to deliver some two decades later; and her aspiration for women to become subjects of violence rather than objects of (men's) violence and subjects of fear.

FIGHTING WITH HUMOR

> . . . allow us to rewrite the script, perhaps by refusing to take it seriously and treating it as a farce . . .
>
> Sharon Marcus [41]

Another dimension to this fighting response within some of the more radical expressions of the anti-rape movement was a rebellious humor that stretched into a kind of retaliation fantasy catharsis.[42] An aggressively humorous piece headed up "Another rape squad," "A play" accompanied another discussion protesting the courtroom treatment of women who have been raped—this time in the feminist newspaper *It Aint Me Babe*:

> *She:* "I've been raped."
> *He:* "Have you ever been fucked before?"
> *She:* "Yeah."
> *He:* "Then it wasn't rape."
> *She:* "But he pointed a gun at me and said . . ."
> *He:* "Sure, so what? How many guys have you slept with?"
> *She:* "What has that got to do with it?"
> *He:* "If you like it, what are you bitching about?"
> *She:* "I didn't like it, I hated it."
> *He:* "Well, you can't expect to get a good lay every time."
>   She throws him on the ground, rips off his pants, and rams a coke bottle up his ass.[43]

The staunch style of this play exposes the misogynist cultural (in the first act) and legal (in the second act) supports for rape; and highlights the extent to which at least some feminists in the early stages of the anti-rape movement were avidly refusing the kind of victim framework that has since been attributed to feminism.[44] Other writing from the time revealed a raw fury, as evident in this Jayne West poem below, which was illustrated by several photos of women in self-defense poses:

> i stand upon the hillside,
> and taste the morning air—
> i know i am a woman
> but frankly
>   i don't care.
>
> i'll kick up my heels and run to town
> and buy myself a bow
> and shoot the first man who laughs at me
> i'll shoot him in the toe.
>
> he'll dance and jump and grab his foot—
> and swear and yell catcalls
> i'll stick my tongue out at him
> and kick him in the balls.
>
> then he'll be furious and even a little mad
> he'll clutch his balls screaming all the while
> i'll chop out his liver
> and squeeze out the bile.[45]

Although not explicitly addressed to sexual violence, it seems predicated on a refusal of the kinds of restrictions and caution adopted by women in anticipation of the threat of sexual violence and as such is another demonstration of an aggressive refusal of passive victimization.

VIGILANTE ACTION

> . . . we can locally interfere with [the rape script] by realizing that men elaborate masculine power in relation to imagined feminine powerlessness; since we are solicited to help create this power, we can act to destroy it.
>
> Sharon Marcus [46]

The fighting spirit of the anti-rape movement was not limited only to angry rhetoric and acerbic humor, but also found expression in more militant

calls to underground forms of collective action against male sexual violence. It is difficult to ascertain the full extent and nature of such actions
because, as Bevacqua notes, although guerrilla activities have sometimes
been romanticized by feminists, few records remain.[47] Nevertheless, newspaper clippings within Susan Brownmiller's papers point to the existence
of vigilante operations targeting male sexual aggressors. The formation
of vigilante groups announced in the Berkeley-based women's liberation
newspaper *It Aint Me Babe* called:

> Attention All Women Hitchhikers!! This is to announce the forma-
> tion of Women's Anti-Rape Squads—groups of feminists dedicated to
> avenging the rapes or other kinds of harassment perpetrated on our
> sisters by male supremacists. If you need help with a problem in this
> area write to us c/o It Aint Me Babe.[48]

A few months later this same feminist newspaper reprinted a *San Francisco
Chronicle* article under the heading "DISARM RAPISTS"—the article
contained the addresses of two men charged with kidnapping, rape, rob-
bery, and oral copulation. Alongside was written:

> Attention anti rape squads. Above article taken from the San Francisco
> Chronicle contains the addresses of two rapists.[49]

Staunch responses to sexual harassment and violence were also found
in more mainstream feminist sites where women's fighting responses—
both individual and collective—were celebrated. A NOW newsletter, for
instance, published the news of a young "night shift billing clerk for a local
trucking firm", who:

> says she has only one regret about the way she handled a would-be
> attacker. "I should have beat him to a pulp," Ms. Peterson said. The
> man grabbed her as she walked from a bus stop and told her: "Don't
> yell or I'll kill you." Ms. Peterson began screaming and tossed her
> attacker to the ground. When he started to run, she grabbed him
> and told him what she thought of him. "But you couldn't put what
> I said in the paper," she said. The attacker, struggling to get away,
> told her, "I'm sory, [sic] lady. I'll never do it again." He then slipped
> loose and ran.[50]

Another woman told her story of surviving an attempted rape when she was
seventeen, in the New York City-based newspaper *Woman's World*. She was
saved any similar regret because as he proceeded to "violate" her she:

> suddenly became so enraged, I let out with a blood-curdling scream
> which startled even me. It so scared him, he took off like a shot!

> I took off after him and as I ran and ran, my anger intensified as
> well as my strength. I was ferocious. When I came up behind him, I
> remember leaping fiercely and coming down hard on his shoulder. For-
> tunately, he was a little guy and was knocked for a loop. Once he hit
> the sidewalk, I proceeded to kick him in his precious organ.[51]

This mood for celebrating women's refusal of passivity can be seen again
in the *Majority Report* newsletter's publication of a detailed account of a
feminist forum on the "verbal rapist," which considered the question of
"whether we should retaliate against him." As well as "talks on the psychology and politics of the street pig," it was reported that participants offered
"numerous" suggestions for how to deal with the problem, including:

> A small thin woman [who] startled the audience with the information
> that she habitually deals with obscene comments by punching the of-
> fenders in the face, they are too surprised to hit back, she said.

And another woman who:

> suggested that the zap group of women, instead of trying to get the
> man convicted under the law, merely beat the stuffings out of him and
> announce the reason for the action anonymously to the press.[52]

By 1972 the establishment of "anti-rape squads and counseling services"
was being reported in mainstream media across the United States. As well
as supporting "victims," many of these groups taught self-defense, and
their activities reportedly ranged to "tracking down a rapist and 'attacking' him":

> The Los Angeles anti-rape squad has a special plan for dealing with
> rapists. They say they will track down the man, jump him, shave his
> head, pour dye on him, take photographs and use them on a poster
> saying, "This man rapes women."[53]

Such rape squads had come to the attention of *Time* magazine by 1973,
which reported that:

> As part of their prevention efforts, some squads have adopted near-
> vigilante tactics. In East Lansing, Mich., members of the rape crisis
> center are said to have scrawled "rapist" on a suspect's car, spray-
> painted the word in red across a front porch, and make late-night
> warning telephone calls.[54]

According to another report, a group of six women in Florida attacked a
man working in his front yard and wounded him with a knife before police
arrived to arrest him for sexual battery:

"It appears to be an action carried out by women vigilantes," according to Sgt Robert Shape. "They took things into their own hands."[55]

Notably, I encountered no report from this period of any woman or groups of women *actually* castrating a man as retaliation for rape—suggesting perhaps that it was either the symbolic power of these such calls (discussed previously) that functioned as the political intervention *or* that no woman was willing to translate this theory into action.[56]

Less violent forms of collective vigilante action to stop rape were also advocated. Barbara Sutton, for instance, proposed that groups of four to eight women could patrol the streets together at night. They could enjoy both the freedom and exercise of an evening walk, she suggested, as well as protect and escort other women, intervening if necessary should they come across a man attacking a woman.[57] In a different vein, Germaine Greer warned men via the pages of *Playboy* magazine to beware of humiliating, albeit non-violent, forms of retaliatory guerrilla action that were brewing:

> Our weapons may be little more than ridicule and boycott, but we will use them. Women are sick to their souls of being fucked over. Now that sex has become political, the petty rapist had better watch his ass; he won't be getting away with it too much longer. How would you feel if a video tape of your last fuck were playing at the Feminist Guerrilla cinema? We didn't start this war, but we intend to bring it to an honorable settlement, which means we have to make a show of strength sometime.[58]

SELF-DEFENSE

> Self-defense, then, has a number of components that can tear down rape culture. The first potential impact on rape culture is that men may actually become too afraid to pounce.
>
> Martha McCaughey (1997)[59]

Probably the most prominent articulation of a fighting spirit within the early 1970s material I examined was the call to self-defense. Advocates wrote encouraging and optimistic accounts of the benefits of self-defense for individual women. It was presented as a form of training that would help women become less fearful, and more able to fight back to protect themselves against a sexual attack (by a man). It was also presented as a path to more radical social change, disrupting the cultural dynamics that make rape possible—and in this way it was a strategy that shared much in common with the argument for self-defense put forward by Marcus and McCaughey.

Free self-defense instruction for "females" of all ages was one of two key demands identified as essential for "female liberation" by the Boston group Female Liberation circa 1969 (the other was free full-time childcare).

It was advocated as necessary for basic freedom and equality, as well as for enabling women to, for example, "resist a brutal husband":

> It is an absolute step in eradicating male supremacy and dominance. We have no freedom over our own bodies now; we are "passive." We will not acquire that freedom until we develop the reflexes necessary to defend our bodies.[60]

Self-defense in the form of martial arts training became a prominent theme in the later issues of *No More Fun and Games: A Journal of Female Liberation*, published by Cell 16 in Boston between 1968 and 1973.[61] In addition to several articles, photographs of women in self-defense poses are scattered through the pages (even where there is no connection with the nearby text!). Jayne West, a Cell 16 member and a black belt in Tae Kwon Do, took up teaching this Korean martial art to women after a young college student was raped nearby. As she said, "the commonality of this woman's experience was the straw which broke this camel's back. I quit wasting my teaching skills on teaching men . . . and started teaching those who most need to know Tae Kwon Do—US—Women."[62] West was critical of some other forms of self-defense taught to women, including those offered under the auspices of "the Female Liberation Movement" that provide "self-defense tricks (a bag of a few what-to-do-ifs)."[63] Instead, she promoted a more disciplined and demanding process designed to enable a woman "to fight actively for her beliefs."[64] According to West, "if we are to be liberated and build a human society, we must be strong, healthy individuals who are capable of taking an active energetic part in this world."[65]

In a detailed paper on self-defense tips for women, Mary Ann Manhart concluded by urging her readers to toughen up to the possibility of acting violently.[66] Although she put it rather differently, her advice encouraged women to take up a position as subjects of violence and objects of fear, in much the same way as Marcus advocated:

> *When your body and life are at stake:* The belief that non-violent reactions are superior (i.e., women are superior) may well turn you into a victim, or get you killed. Try to rid yourself of masochistic reactions beforehand. Let's destroy ideas such as: male equals violence and "macho" is good; it's fun and exciting to be slapped around, seduced, carted off, and raped. Get rid of ideas such as: You will become "hard," unfeminine, a killing machine, just like men, that you want to be a "real woman," whether in the classical or Freudian sense, a nice girl, passive, protected by men, led, the receiver.[67]

Manhart's advice extended to instructions on a range of legal and illegal weapons, including a variety of different types of guns.

It is difficult to know how widely endorsed self-defense training was within the early anti-rape movement. Densmore has since emphasized that many women at the time were repelled by Cell 16's promotion of martial arts and training women to fight back—the very idea of it "offended and alarmed many women."[68] Nevertheless, records seem to suggest once again that it was not only those at the more radical end of women's movement who thought self-defense was a good idea; with women from NOW, for example, suggesting that "self-defense should be taught to girls when they are young."[69] By 1974 a diverse range of feminist groups (including NOW) joined together in support of Joanne Little, an imprisoned black woman who, acting in self-defense, had killed the jailor who had raped her. This campaign, according to Winifred Breines, represented a political milestone for feminists and other social justice activists working "across race" for race and gender justice.[70]

An intersection between the promotion of self-defense and the provision of support services for women who had been raped existed in a way that is not widely evident today. Symbolic of this connection, for instance, was the cover image of a 1972 booklet on "How to start a rape crisis centre": a sketch of a woman in a self-defense pose[71]—which today would strike us as a jarring and unlikely association. Following through on this theme, was the inclusion of a detailed section on self-defense in the 1972 newsletter from the Rape Crisis Center of Washington D.C. Also included was an attachment on "protection tactics," including advice on the use of a wide range of weapons, and the encouragement that "we must learn to fight back."[72]

These early calls for women to fight back consistently attributed women's lack of fighting ability to the gendered patterns in which girls were brought up. In an article on "Fighting back," for example, Cate Stadelman noted that:

> Most women have no experience in physical combat of any sort. The typical little girl spends much more time in flinching and crying than in striking back. As a result, little girls and grown women find themselves physically unable to deliver an effective blow when they need to. In addition to the physical inability caused by this blank in our experience, is the more crucial effect of our inability to seriously imagine ourselves slugging someone in the face.
>
> This repugnance toward fighting is not natural, not healthy, and not unalterable.[73]

Similarly, in a humorous critique of the circumstances enabling women's domination, Ann Sheldon suggested that what "dooms" women:

> is no lack of the means to be deadly but, rather, the conditioning process of centuries, instilling in women not only their passivity but a muddled conviction of their own virtue in not resisting. But it is error—unexamined and unreasoned—to halt [sic] that passivity is in any way virtue or true gentleness or true femininity.

Sheldon went on to argue for self-defense, including the use of weapons, and women's preparedness to be violent, as the solution to stopping rape.[74]

In going beyond this social constructionist orientation, Densmore advocated that we unhinge our assumptions about which sexed bodies are vulnerable and which are capable of physically exploiting such vulnerability:

> We have always known how vulnerable men's groins are: there is no part of women that is anywhere near as vulnerable, as painful or disabling when injured. And yet very few women have ever made use of this knowledge, either in a struggle or in making their assessment of their own helplessness before a man.
>
> It is as if they abide by a code of honor: because they do not have this vulnerability, it would be unfair to use it against men. Women abide by this code even when men are using crude muscle strength against a weakness (lack of crude muscle strength) which only women have.[75]

As Marcus would later observe, within the "gendered grammar of violence" "the male body . . . benefits from an enforced ignorance concerning its own vulnerability."[76] In drawing attention to the vulnerability of male genitalia, and suggesting women's capacity to take advantage of this point of sexual difference, Densmore and Marcus both make the simple, yet provocatively transgressive, point that the possibility of rape depends on certain cultural fictions that can be rewritten in ways that might work to disrupt the conditions of possibility for rape.

One woman learning self-defense in the early 1970s reflected on how the changes brought about by self-defense for women could ultimately subvert the gendered distribution of fear, making rape considerably more difficult to accomplish:

> As a woman in a society where you can't walk down a street without intimidating hassles or rapes, we have no choice but to learn how to defend ourselves in order to live with any kind of freedom of movement. Self-defense can be one of the basic ways women can learn to be strong and aggressive. Developing this self-reliance is vital for women to be able to lead their everyday lives free from dependencies or restrictions, and lead to a situation where rapists will be afraid of women. [. . . .] Eventually, when all women know self-defense, when it's taught in the schools, we will walk the street without fear. Rape will be something very difficult to do under such conditions, and women will be stronger in dozens of other ways as well.[77]
>
> Self-defense is a very serious commitment which requires lots of discipline. It's a lot more than simply getting your body in shape which could end up being a temporary whim. It's something that can bring radical changes not only in individual women, but also lend important strength to all women collectively.[78]

Writing nearly thirty years later, Ann Cahill also proposes that women's self-defense would lead to a world in which women were confident and able to "fend off sexual attacks." In such a world she imagines that:

> women could roam the streets at any time at night. They could walk through bars alone or with each other without the fear or discomfort of being harassed by male strangers. They would not fear their husbands, boyfriends, lovers, brothers, or friends, as those relationships would be founded on a mutual recognition of physical and emotional strength. Knowing themselves, individually and collectively, in a distinctly embodied way, to be deserving of this kind of freedom and security would also result in a confidence that, were they to be attacked, their experience would not be met with suspicion or dismissal.[79]

The hypothetical subject of such radical transformation is shaped by and embodies the oppressive constraints of dominant discourses, yet is not fully determined by these. The promise of women's self-defense is that it recognizes cultural constraints *as well as* "the possibility for disloyalty, for change, for transformation."[80] Although packaged in poststructuralist terms, the basis of Cahill's twenty-first century version of this argument bears strong resemblance to the sorts of optimistic testimonials about the transformative power of self-defense written by women in the early 1970s.

FIGHTING BODIES, FIGHTING WORDS?[81]

Although the tone of the early anti-rape movement was likely to have been more diverse and multidimensional than I am representing here, radical fighting edges are prominent in records of the time. Scrutinizing this praxis from a more contemporary perspective reveals a number of theoretical contradictions and tensions. But there are two main, interconnected, threads running through this early 1970s feminist anti-rape activism that I would like to highlight. One is simply a tone that I would describe as an 'attitude of refusal.' There is a rhetorical style to this activism that celebrates the *possibility* of women taking up positions as subjects of violence and refusing positions as subjects of fear, or merely passive objects of (men's) violence. The other thread is the more direct encouragement of women *actually* gaining and deploying self-defense and/or (other) forms of aggressive physical engagement in response to the threat of sexual violence.

What interests me in particular about this early activism are the insights it might generate in relation to contemplating the political efficacy of putting into practice the 'fighting' response against rape envisaged by Marcus and others. Despite the oppositional tone of the notion of *fighting* rape, it has an (admittedly ambitious) deconstructive logic of aspiring to reconfigure contemporary relations of gendered power and embodiment.

I do not think it is fruitful to debate whether or not some of the early activism *was* "postructuralist," *driven by* a deconstructive logic similar to that outlined by Marcus and others. Indeed I think it is difficult, if not impossible, to compare these two bodies of work in this way—not only because both more recent feminist poststructuralist writings and, in particular, earlier feminist anti-rape praxis are internally diverse, but because both tend to end up being more concerned with theorizing towards political ends than with theoretical purity for its own sake (which leads to complicated theoretical contradictions and compromises within the contributions from each era). I would suggest, however, that at least some elements of the early activism seem to embody some of the deconstructive impulse behind the poststructuralist-informed recommendations for preventing rape. Both the early feminist activists' and the more recent feminist theorists' advocacy of self-defense and a more general fighting spirit share an emphasis on the potential to reconfigure the gendered matrix of (male)-aggressive-agent/(female)-passive-victim that is seen to underpin and propel the possibility of rape. Both (at least in part) seem based on the belief that it is possible to rescript individual gendered responses in relation to sexual violence; and, moreover, both are focused beyond the limited goal of individual change and self-protection to the ways in which destabilizing these binary adhesions (e.g., male = agentic, aggressive; female = vulnerable, passive) would lead to more profound cultural transformation that could dismantle the cultural conditions of possibility for rape (and all forms of gender-based violence against women).

The whole mood of the struggle against rape has changed dramatically since these early days of the anti-rape movement; as have the cultural contexts in which this struggle took place. By and large, we have moved away from staunch and aggressive street politics. In their place we are more likely to provide somber demonstrations of the traumatic personal impact of rape and sexual abuse (as in clothesline projects[82]) and rational calculations of the high individual, social, and economic costs of sexual violence. Not only has the public face of anti-rape activism changed, but so too has the form of prevention strategies designed to prompt changes in individuals' attitudes, behaviors, and skills. Self-defense is still taught, but not with the same prominent and explicit connection to rape prevention; and most rape prevention programs do not offer self-defense training.[83] Such interventions have instead often become institutionalized in the form of rape prevention education programs that target knowledge and attitudes for change—seeking in particular to reduce people's adherence to rape myths.[84] At best, these are limited strategies for change, and even advocates acknowledge they are not the complete answer for preventing rape.[85]

The dramatic shift in the tone of (feminist) efforts to stop rape is unquestionably the result of a complex constellation of forces affecting the dynamics of all social change movements in places like the United States and New Zealand over the past three to four decades. And of course the particular mix of factors will be different in different sociogeographical contexts. More conciliatory modes of political expression have arguably become more usual than boldly oppositional tactics in campaigns targeted toward social justice agendas. The reasons for this are complex, reflecting trends within broader society as well as within feminist politics. In the US context it has been claimed that radical feminism receded during the early 1970s, to be replaced by cultural feminism. With this shift, according to Alice Echols, "the movement turned its attention away from opposing male supremacy to creating a female counterculture . . . where 'male' values would be exorcized and 'female' values nurtured."[86] This move arguably militated against the ongoing development of aggressive fighting responses to rape (which could be denigrated from a cultural feminist perspective as 'male' tactics).[87] Echols has suggested—in relation to feminism more generally—that the demise of radical feminism left activism to liberal feminists. In relation to an issue like rape where there is wide societal support—at least at face value—for change, the adoption and institutionalization of some liberal changes (by state and other formal institutions) has arguably had the effect of co-opting and domesticating the more radical impulses of activists.[88] It is also possible that the intensity of backlash responses to feminism has led some activists to adopt strategies less likely to ignite angry defensive reactions, in the hope that this might be more likely to foster change (allowing at least small gains to be made in the short term). Beyond the influence of this ascendance of liberal and cultural feminisms (in the United States at least), and these kinds of pragmatic considerations, however, are wider sociocultural and socioeconomic forces. The heightened individualism of neoliberalism, for instance, has provided a hospitable ground for a kind of 'psychologization' that shifts the analytic lens away from these broader social explanations for social problems.

The role of these dynamics in shaping the broader political landscape on which struggles for social justice take place is key. But my focus here is on changes that relate to specifics of the struggle against rape. The reasons for the demise of a more militant response against rape and the apparent sidelining of self-defense *as a form of rape prevention* are also no doubt multiple and complex. It seems plausible, however, that one factor has to do with the dramatic shift in our understandings of rape that have occurred since the 1970s. At that time 'rape' still evoked the image of a violent and dangerous man grabbing a woman in a dark street, or breaking into her home at night. This paradigmatic 'real' rape nearly always involved a stranger.[89] Feminist anti-rape activists were well aware that women were also raped by acquaintances and intimates. As Dana Densmore noted as early as 1973: rather than "calling street rapes 'rare by comparison,' one might be specific and characterize private rapes as 'extremely common.'"[90] Yet in this period of intense transition in the understandings of what rape *is*, attention seems to have been more often focussed on rapes by strangers. Mainstream media sources, in particular, represented violent sexual attacks in the public domain as an omnipresent danger for women; with a link between rape and murder often emphasized in sensational fashion.[91]

By the early 1980s, however, dominant representations of rape were shifting.[92] A vocabulary of new terms—'acquaintance rape,' 'date rape,' 'marital rape'—had become widely adopted; and new research showed that most rapes were committed by men in intimate or social relationships with the women they raped. By the 1990s attention to the problem of date rape had grown to such an extent that it had replaced stranger rape as the main focus for rape prevention. This changed the shape of rape prevention as the supposed dynamics of rape by an acquaintance frequently became configured in terms of the pitfalls of miscommunication. As well as being aware of the problem of rape and sexual coercion by men like husbands and boyfriends, early feminists were also aware of the risk of minimization brought about by a miscommunication paradigm for making sense of sexual coercion and violence. As Densmore maintained: "The commonness of private rapes (and the extent to which women are forced to accept them as 'misunderstandings' or, in the case of regular sexual partners and sometimes dates, 'his right') makes them extremely serious." Nevertheless, by contrast to "street rapes" ("violent forcible rapes by strangers anywhere"), she concluded such rapes tended to be "less traumatic, as well as usually less dangerous": "On the street one's life is at stake,"[93] a perception that probably explains why this particular danger was the focus (implicit or explicit) of much of the activism at the time.

ELIMINATING RAPE IN THE 2000S

The problem we face in seeking to eliminate rape has changed since the early 1970s, both in terms of our understanding of what rape *is* and in terms of the extent to which the dominant cultural milieu is rape supportive. Our notion of what rape is has shifted and expanded, so that the paradigmatic rape is no longer a violent stranger attack but coercive acquaintance rape. The broader milieu still clearly tolerates rape, but in a much less overt and stringent fashion than it did previously. So, in this contemporary context, what should we make of the call to self-defense and a more general fighting response to rape, (re)issued by feminist theorists like Marcus, McCaughey, and Cahill?

To my mind, the arguments in favour of what McCaughey calls physical feminism are compelling. Self-defense training for women is the practical core of her recommendations, and there are at least two ways we can think about such 'training' working toward rape prevention. One is a very direct skills-based, individual risk-reduction strategy: with self-defense training, girls and women will be taught a form of embodiment (including, but not limited to, skill and demeanor) that gives them a better chance of being able to fight off a rapist. Although there has been little systematic research evaluating the effectiveness of self-defense training in protecting women from rape,[94] there is strong evidence that when women who do employ fighting forms of resistance to an attempted rape they are less likely to be raped.[95] It is, nevertheless, a strategy that has evoked some degree of cautiousness within more contemporary anti-rape circles due to concerns that it may be seen as unreasonably imputing responsibility for rape (and rape prevention) onto women. Even staunch advocates of the promotion of self-defense and more general resistance strategies for women have been careful to emphasise that this should not be the conclusion.[96]

In a recent critique of feminist poststructuralist approaches to rape, such as Marcus', Carine Mardorossian argues that they share more in common with "backlashers" than they do with feminist activists.[97] In suggesting that they make "women's behavior and identity the site of rape prevention," she argued that they are not only victim-blaming, but unrealistic: "social inscriptions—that is, our physical situatedness in time and space, in history and culture—do not simply evaporate because we are made aware of them."[98] I agree with this point about the complexity of change; however, what I think Mardorossian is missing here is the second, more radical, promise of self-defense (in the widest sense);[99] and it is an angle that I think has been emphasized by Marcus, McCaughey, and Cahill, as well as by many early anti-rape movement activists. That is, the broader and more profound cultural implications of self-defense's disruption to the rigidly gendered "grammar of violence" that makes women automatically subjects of fear and objects of violence. Changing men's behavior is of course critical to stopping rape, yet women and feminists are limited in what they can do to directly bring this about. Another attractive element to this approach therefore is the expectation that men's behavior would be required to change in response to the challenge posed by women's collective refusal of passive vulnerability.

Martha McCaughey's vision for physical feminism is quite broad. Her agenda for shaking up conventional notions of femininity embraces the hope that women would no longer be so constrained by imperatives around passivity, politeness, and deference to men. Nevertheless, despite McCaughey's far-reaching aspirations for it, it is possible that the specific notion of self-defense automatically cues people into considering implicitly conventional (that is, limited) preconceptions about what rape might *be* like. For instance, in fantasizing about the implications for the relative (im)possibility of rape if men were to experience physical and social harm should they try to force sex on a woman, Ann Cahill uses terms such as "sexual attacks"[100] and "violent assault."[101] Too easy a conflation between rape and the language of attack and assault is pertinent in the way that it suggests an apparent reliance on a particular set of expectations about how rape is accomplished. Contrary to her assertion that "it is difficult to imagine a victim of rape, for example, describing her assailant as a sexual partner,"[102] women's accounts of their experiences of sex, sexual coercion, and rape show clearly that this is not at all impossible.[103] For some women, the "assailant" is her sexual partner before he rapes her, and while this act is certainly likely to complicate that relationship it does not automatically erase it.[104] In a situation initially perceived by a woman as a willing social or sexual encounter it may be incredibly difficult to pinpoint the moment at which her experience becomes one of being under attack—when it turns from some form of acceptable seduction into annoyingly persistent persuasion into attempted forced sex into rape.

In a recent review of the empirical research on rape avoidance, Sarah Ullman notes that it would seem that women are less likely to resist rape committed by a known man than they are to resist attacks by strangers.[105] One possible reason for this is that the moment of threat might look very different when the rapist is a man that the woman knows, especially when she is in a heterosexual relationship or some other potentially intimate context with him. Among women I have interviewed about their experiences of rape, for instance, several described the rape as taking them by surprise. In these cases it was not an encounter that resembled the typical script involving an apparent threat of danger leading up to what would tend to be described as an 'attack.'[106] As I have argued elsewhere, then, one limitation with a focus on self-defense and other forms of directly, physically *fighting* rape is that they tend to implicitly rest upon a somewhat restricted notion of how the moment of danger might present itself in rape.[107]

Although McCaughey's primary interest is in self-defense, which lies at the heart of her articulation of physical feminism, the ambit of physical feminism could—and should—be more inventive in envisaging a more diverse array of ways and means of heightening agentic physicality for women (at the same time—as with any feminist anti-rape praxis—as endorsing and elaborating critiques of cultural practices that condone, and indeed valorize some forms of, masculine aggression and sexual entitlement). Moreover, as I have suggested previously, it needs to be supplemented by, at the very least, cultural interventions directed at *rethinking sex*, so as to disrupt the gendered patterns of heterosex that continue to provide the cultural scaffolding for rape.[108] Not only do women need to be enabled to physically fight back when the situation calls for it; but also to be able to refuse passive submission in response to a man's pursuit of sex that is not wanted. To this end our standard scripts for heterosexual sex need to be overhauled so that it is clearer that the man who keeps pursuing an unwilling woman risks entering the territory of sexual coercion and potentially rape. The abundance of sexual imperatives (expressed in a vocabulary of needs, rights, and entitlements) circulating in our increasingly sexualized western societies warrant unpacking to expose the ways in which new and subtle dynamics for the sexual coercion of women are set up. We also need to be alert to the ways in which forms of oppression have mutated, and consider what the implications might be for sexual violence and coercion. What, for instance, might be the (regressive?) implications of new, sexualized, forms of femininity that are arguably just repackaged sex-objects-with-a-twist; where that twist is particularly insidious as women (and increasingly girls) are sold the notion that it is the cool and 'empowered' *choice* to take up this position.[109]

In recognition of the dynamics of a form of rape that is more likely to be conducted by sexual partners than strangers, some theorists have recently approached rape prevention by completely circumventing notions of self-defense. Moira Carmody and Kerry Carrington, for instance, have developed a model for rape prevention that applies entirely within the domain of sexuality. Rape prevention programs, they argue, should be about the promotion of "ethical sexual conduct."[110] While this innovative approach seems more responsive to the circumstances in which most sexual violence against women takes place (that is, within (hetero)sexual relationships or encounters that have the potential to be sexual), it is theoretically possible for it to be taken up in ways that are insufficiently attentive to the embodied differences between women and men entering this domain, and the ways in which this stacks the odds for who plays fair and who gets hurt. This is where the promise of physical feminism remains so important, through its potential to reconfigure the gendered identities and power relations that are brought to the intimate realm of sex. The underpinnings of this approach—which are informed by a blend of poststructuralist and radical feminist insights—lend it ambitious aspirations beyond simply the individualistic goal of helping women to resist rape. Rather, the nature of relations between women and men, as well as the balance of power between the sexes, would be transformed, as men would be enticed and/or incited to change in response.

Both feminist anti-rape activists of the 1970s and later poststructuralist theorists have advocated the benefits of a fighting response toward eliminating rape. The promotion of self-defense for women has been a key recommendation within both bodies of work; a recommendation that both is driven by and seeks to establish in women an 'attitude of refusal' toward rape, as well as a psychological-physical capability to fight it in practice. Within this vision, self-defense promises cultural transformation toward reconfiguring the embodiment of conventional femininity so that women are no longer disabled from acting aggressively and expressing physical and other forms of defiance. At the same time, it is assumed that such changes within the matrix of gender would force reconfigurations of masculinity, hopefully weakening the hold of those modes of masculinity that celebrate the sexual objectification (or 'derivatization,' to use Ann Cahill's concept)[111] of women and other forms of male sexual entitlement and the glorification of men's aggressive physical prowess. To the extent that it works to these ends, self-defense and broader more diverse outgrowths of physical feminism are valuable, possibly even essential, tools in fighting rape. But in looking back and revisiting the fighting words—and call to fighting bodies—of the original second-wave feminist struggles against rape, we can see that not only is this vision not new, but we could say it has been tried and that it faltered. I would like to think that the examples presented in this chapter furnish a more concrete set of ideas about what fighting praxis might look like to help us figure out what the realization of a 'fighting' theory of rape prevention means. In moving forward to consider the political value of this approach I think it will be helpful to recognize the early activism and interrogate why it was not as successful as we would want. We can then ask whether this was due to inherent limitations in the general approach and/or whether there are ways that it could be resurrected, modified, and nuanced as one (of several) viable strategies for eliminating rape in the current socio-political context.

ACKNOWLEDGEMENT

I am grateful for a Fulbright New Century Scholar award, a Royal Society of New Zealand Marsden grant, and a University of Auckland Research Committee grant, for funding that supported this work. I would also like to thank staff at the Schlesinger Library, for their assistance, and Victoria Grace and Renée Heberle for very helpful comments on an earlier draft.

NOTES

1. Sharon Marcus, "Fighting Bodies, Fighting Words: A Theory and Politics of Rape Prevention," in *Feminists Theorize the Political*, eds. Judith Butler and Joan W. Scott (New York: Routledge, 1992), 385–403, 400.
2. Ibid., 390.
3. Nicola Gavey, *Just Sex? The Cultural Scaffolding of Rape* (New York: Routledge, 2005).
4. It is highly significant that this 'language of rape' is also 'raced' as Marcus points out. Yet in considering the relationship between this dimension of the language of rape and the material realities of rape there is the need for a more multilayered, delicate, and complicated argument that takes account of ethics and politics at the historical intersections between rape and racial oppression and violence.
5. Marcus, op. cit., 392.
6. See, for examples of related social constructionist work, Ann J. Cahill, *Rethinking Rape* (Ithaca: Cornell University Press, 2001); Renee Heberle, "Deconstructive Strategies and the Movement Against Sexual Violence," *Hypatia* 11, 4 (1996): 63–76; Sharon Lamb, *New Versions of Victims: Feminists Struggle with the Concept* (New York: New York University Press, 1999); Jeanne Marecek, "Trauma Talk in Feminist Clinical Practice," in *New Versions of Victims: Feminist Struggles with the Concept*, ed. Sharon Lamb (New York: New York University Press, 1999), 158–182; Martha McCaughey, *Real Knockouts: The Physical Feminism of Women's Self-Defense* (New York: New York University Press, 1997); Paula Reavey and Sam Warner, eds., *New Feminist Stories of Child Sexual Abuse: Sexual Scripts and Dangerous Dialogues* (New York: Routledge, 2003).
7. Despite moves within official discourse to increasingly gender neutralize the categories of victim and perpetrator, I would argue that with reference to

sexual violence they are still coded as female and male, respectively, in the public imagination.

8. See, for instance, Heberle, op. cit., for an insightful discussion of this issue. See also, Nicola Gavey, "Writing the Effects of Sexual Abuse: Interrogating the Possibilities and Pitfalls of Using Clinical Psychology Expertise for a Critical Justice Agenda," in *New Feminist Stories of Child Sexual Abuse: Sexual Scripts and Dangerous Dialogues*, eds. Paula Reavey and Sam Warner (New York: Routledge, 2003), 187–209; Marecek, op. cit.

9. For a useful discussion, see Gayatri Chakravorty Spivak, *Outside in the Teaching Machine* (New York: Routledge, 1993).

10. By this I mean power to authorize and shape particular singularized forms of personal experience and social action, which works at the same time to de-legitimate or exclude other possibilities for experience and action.

11. Marcus, op. cit., 400.

12. Marcus, op. cit., 388.

13. Marcus, op. cit., 392. In relation to this point about the possibility for treating rape as a farce, see Helliwell's claim that the Gerai people of Indonesian Borneo find rape impossible to imagine, in part because the penis is not inscribed with phallic power as it is in the West. Gerai men and women, according to her account, are shocked at the notion that it would be possible for "a penis to be taken into a vagina" if the woman didn't want this to happen. Her argument is a thought-provoking analysis of the cultural inscription of bodies necessary to make rape possible. See Christine Helliwell, "'It's Only a Penis': Rape, Feminism, and Difference," *Signs: Journal of Women in Culture and Society* 25, 3 (2000): 789–816.

14. Marcus, op. cit., 401.

15. Marcus, op. cit., 398.

16. See, in particular, Pamela Haag, "'Putting Your Body on the Line': The Question of Violence, Victims, and the Legacies of Second-Wave Feminism," *differences* 8, 2 (1996): 23–67.

17. McCaughey, 1997, op. cit., xii.

18. McCaughey, op. cit., 188.

19. McCaughey, op. cit., 116. Similarly, see Jocelyn Hollander's claim that self-defense classes are "life transforming" (225). Jocelyn A. Hollander, "'I Can Take Care of Myself': The Impact of Self-Defense Training on Women's Lives," *Violence Against Women* 10, 3 (2004): 205–235.

20. Cahill, 2001, op. cit., 207. Strong support for women's self-defense has also been expressed by influential psychology rape researchers over the past decade—although not explicitly based on the theoretical framework I am discussing here. In particular, see Patricia D. Rozee and Mary P. Koss, "Rape: A Century of Resistance,"*Psychology of Women Quarterly* 25, 4 (2001): 295–311; Sarah E. Ullman, "A 10-Year Update of 'Review and Critique of Empirical Studies of Rape Avoidance,'" *Criminal Justice and Behavior* 34, 3 (2007): 411–29.

21. For a similar progress narrative that is critical of similar features attributed to the early feminist antiviolence work, see Nadya Burton, "Resistance to Prevention: Reconsidering Feminist Antiviolence Rhetoric," in *Violence Against Women: Philosophical Perspectives*, eds. Stanley G. French, Wanda Teays, and Laura Martha Purdy (Ithaca, NY: Cornell University Press, 1998), 182–200. Although her argument is nuanced in parts, she makes such misleading claims as: "the early feminist anti-violence rhetoric propagated insupportable notions of resistance as ineffective and dangerous" (187).

Although it is beyond the scope of my discussion in this chapter, it should be noted that there are some connections (as well as important differences) between these poststructuralist feminist analyses and the (in my view, highly problematic) positions taken up by 'postfeminist' backlash critics such as Camille Paglia and Katie Roiphe. See Chris Atmore, "Victims, Backlash, and Radical Feminist Theory (or, the Morning after They Stole Feminism's Fire)," in *New Versions of Victims: Feminists Struggle with the Concept*, ed. Sharon Lamb (New York: New York University Press, 1999), 183–211.

22. Susan Brownmiller, *Against Our Will: Men, Women and Rape* (Harmondsworth, UK: Penguin Books, 1975).
23. Marcus, op. cit., 387; see also, Cahill, 2001, op. cit.
24. Marcus, op. cit., 387
25. Maria Bevacqua, *Rape on the Public Agenda: Feminism and the Politics of Sexual Assault* (Boston: Northeastern University Press, 2000).
26. See also Pamela Haag's charge that Marcus overstates the essentialism, and ignores the "aggressive tack" of the early feminist work (Haag, op. cit, n8, p. 63). (To be fair, I would say that this kind of misrepresentation of the early anti-rape movement, and the lack of attention to the flavour of more grass-roots dimensions of it, are not peculiar to feminist poststructuralist writers.)
27. Marcus, op. cit., 387.
28. 'Goosing' refers to the act of poking or digging a person in a "sensitive spot," especially "between the buttocks with an upward thrust of a finger or hand from the rear" (*Webster's Unabridged*, accessed via the web June 5, 2007).
29. "Learning to fuck back," *Central N.J. NOW Newsletter*, [Special Issue on Rape] May 1971, p. 9, [Authorship ambiguous.] Susan Brownmiller Papers, Schlesinger Library, Radcliffe Institute, Harvard University, Carton 6, Folder, "Rape research women fight back" (accessed March 29, 2005).
30. Marcus's key text published in 1992, and McCaughey's book published in 1997, are not particularly recent, but they form key parts of a larger body of poststructuralist-informed work on rape prevention that has a consistent flavor and maintains contemporary influence.
31. I would like to emphasize that this chapter does not aim to provide a historical analysis that represents *the* nature of this movement; my research has not been exhaustive enough to allow me to make any such claims. Rather my interest has arisen from the serendipitous observation of a fighting spirit within the early anti-rape movement; my point is to illuminate this in relation to more contemporary theorizations of rape prevention.
32. Marcus, op. cit., 400–401.
33. Martha R. Burt, "Cultural Myths and Supports for Rape," *Journal of Personality & Social Psychology* 38:2 (1980): 217–30. See Gavey, 2005, for further discussion of rape supportive discourse around this time.
34. Most of the authors going under the name of Female Liberation here later went on to become key members of Cell 16, which was probably the most militant of the influential US feminist groups of this period (see Dana Densmore, "A Year of Living Dangerously: 1968," in *Feminist Memoir Project, Voices from Women's Liberation*, eds. Rachel Blau DuPlessis and Ann Snitow (New York: Three Rivers Press, 1998); Alice Echols, *Daring to be Bad: Radical Feminism in America 1967–1975* (Minneapolis, MN: University of Minnesota Press, 1989).
35. Female Liberation (Roxanne Dunbar, Dana Densmore, Jayne West, Abby Rockefeller, Sandy Barnett), "More Slain Girls", *Female Liberation Newsletter*, vol. 1, no. 1: 9–10. [no date, but circa approx 1969] Annie Popkin Papers, Schlesinger Library, Radcliffe College, [Box 3: Folder: "Women–Female Liberation (once Cell 16) [1969–71, nd]"]. [Accessed April 19, 2005] (NB: a similar version is also published in *No More Fun & Games: A Journal of Female Liberation*, Issue 3 [1969].)

36. Dana Densmore, "On Rape," *No More Fun and Games: A Journal of Female Liberation*, no. 6 (1973a): 57–84. p. 83.
37. Bettye Lane Photographs, Schlesinger Library, Radcliffe College, (accessed March 11, 2005).
    Some writers were even more militant, calling for death, rather than castration. Catherine Henry, for instance, insisted that a revolution was necessary to eliminate rape, and that "fighting squads must be organized to prepare for the armed offensive." Once accomplished, she proposed, "Rapists and all others who appropriate women for the satisfaction of lust will be put up against the wall and shot. The only solution is execution, not castration. If rape does not demand the reward of death, what crime is great enough?" See Catherine Henry, "How to eliminate rape (and other crimes against women)" in "Women Speak out Against Rape," In *Woman's World*, vol. 1, April 15, p. 5. Susan Brownmiller Papers, Schlesinger Library, Radcliffe Institute, Harvard University, Carton 7, un-marked manilla envelope (accessed March 21, 2005) (I would note that her analysis was also anti-gay.)
38. Maryanne McNellis, "Rape Victims Tell Libbers what it's Like," *Sunday News*, April 18, 1971: 36, Susan Brownmiller Papers, Schlesinger Library, Radcliffe Institute, Harvard University, Carton 7, un-marked manilla envelope (accessed March 22, 2005)
39. Betsy Warrior, "Disarm rapists, Smash Sexism" [poster image]. *No More Fun & Games: A Journal of Female Liberation*, Issue 5, July, p. 19, 1971. (Note that the text of this poster evokes one of the other striking themes running through the activism of this period—the "gender analysis" that saw sexual violence as inextricably related to patriarchal power and women's oppression.)
40. "I'd rather fight." *It Aint Me Babe*, vol. 1, no. 15, p. 13, October 8, 1970, Susan Brownmiller Papers, Schlesinger Library, Radcliffe Institute, Harvard University, Carton 6, Folder, "Rape research articles—general" (accessed March 30, 2005).
41. Marcus, 1996, op. cit., 392.
42. I realize that this kind of writing might not be seen as 'humorous' by everyone, and I agree it is in questionable taste. However, I think there is something to be gained from recognizing such representations *as humor*. Doing so points to the irony in which feminist 'over-zealousness' and 'heaviness' are themselves portrayed in the mainstream media as funny; and how such humor relies on overplaying the earnestness and underplaying the pleasure-in-humor working in this kind of feminism. (For a discussion of "the Humorless Feminist," see Chris Atmore, "Feminism's Restless Undead: The Radical/Lesbian/Victim Theorist and Conflicts over Sexual Violence against Children and Women," in *New Feminist Stories of Child Sexual Abuse: Sexual Scripts and Dangerous Dialogues*, eds. Paula Reavey and Sam Warner (New York: Routledge, 2003), 15–33.
43. "Rape in the courtroom" and "Another Rape Squad, A Play" in *It Aint Me Babe*, vol. 2, no. 1, April 1971, p. 2. Susan Brownmiller Papers, Schlesinger Library, Radcliffe Institute, Harvard University, Carton 6, Folder, "Rape research women fight back" (accessed March 29, 2005). (The accompanying article also contained a description of a recent case, with political analysis and a call to protest at the particular judge's courtroom.)
44. See Chris Atmore's, 1999, op. cit., work for a discussion of what she refers to as the "media feminists'" (aka backlash proponents) characterizations of "victim feminism" in relation to sexual violence; see also Gavey, 2005, op. cit.
45. West, Jayne, [no title], *No More Fun and Games: A Journal of Female Liberation*, 5 (July 1971): 51–52, 51. (These verses constitute about one third of the full poem.)

46. Marcus, 1992, op. cit., 392.

47. Bevacqua, 2000, op. cit.

48. "Community Services" section, *It Aint Me Babe*, Sept 4–17, 1970, vol. 1, no. 13: 19 Susan Brownmiller Papers, Schlesinger Library, Radcliffe Institute, Harvard University, Carton 7, un-named Folder (accessed March 16, 2005).

49. "Disarm Rapists", *It Aint Me Babe*, Dec. 1, 1970, Vol.1, No. 17:2. Susan Brownmiller Papers, Schlesinger Library, Radcliffe Institute, Harvard University, Carton 6, Folder, "Rape research articles—general" (accessed March 30, 2005).

50. "A news item from about one year ago," *NOW Newsletter,* National Organization for Women, Central New Jersey, Chapter, Dec. 1971: 14. Susan Brownmiller Papers, Schlesinger Library, Radcliffe Institute, Harvard University, Carton 6, Folder, "Rape research articles—general" (accessed March 30, 2005).

51. Patricia Lawrence, "The Police took his Side," in "Women Speak out Against Rape," in *Woman's World*, vol. 1, April 15, pp. 5, 11. (p. 5) Susan Brownmiller Papers, Schlesinger Library, Radcliffe Institute, Harvard University, Carton 7, un-marked manilla envelope (accessed March 21, 2005). (Note that Lawrence writes of having been treated as pathological and as a criminal by those on the scene. She concluded her piece calling for "CASTRATION FOR RAPE." [p. 11])

52. "The Verbal Rapist," in *Majority Report,* vol. 1, no. 5: 4 (Newsletter published by Focas, New York), Susan Brownmiller Papers, Schlesinger Library, Radcliffe Institute, Harvard University, Carton 6, Folder, "Rape research women fight back" (accessed March 29, 2005).

53. Marsha Dubrow, "Women Organize to Combat Rapists and Counsel Victims", in *The Washington Post*, December 21, 1972: G1. Susan Brownmiller Papers, Schlesinger Library, Radcliffe Institute, Harvard University, Carton 6, Folder, "Rape research women fight back" (accessed March 29, 2005).

54. "Women Against Rape", *Time*, April 23, 1973, Susan Brownmiller Papers, Schlesinger Library, Radcliffe Institute, Harvard University, Carton 6, Folder, "Rape research women fight back" (accessed March 25, 2005).

55. "6 Women Attack Man Identified as a Rapist", newspaper clipping, July 21, 1975 [newspaper unidentified], Susan Brownmiller Papers, Schlesinger Library, Radcliffe Institute, Harvard University, Carton 6, Folder, "Rape research articles—general" (accessed April 1, 2005).

56. It has been suggested to me that the idea of castration as a political tool arises from Susan Brownmiller's (op. cit.) argument that "men's structural capacity to rape" is key in explaining rape. I am not convinced, however, that the political salience of castration is necessarily always tied to explanations that rest on biological notions of sexual difference. It seems to me that the *idea* of castration works also at the symbolic level—not only threatening the anatomical apparatus involved in (most) rapes, but perhaps more potently operating as a violent affront to the cultural edifice of masculinity and male dominance through targeting that symbolic site of male power that also happens to be an obvious (but disavowed) site of men's vulnerability.

57. Barbara Sutton, "Women Will Stop Rape," in Women Against Rape, *Stop Rape* [Handbook], 1971: 43–46; Susan Brownmiller Papers, Schlesinger Library, Radcliffe Institute, Harvard University, Carton 7, un-named Folder (accessed March 17, 2005). (Another suggestion recommended by Sutton, in addition to the ubiquitous call for self-defense, was the formation of guerrilla theatre groups.)

58. Germaine Greer, "Seduction is a four-letter word," *Playboy*, January (1973): 80–82, 164, 178, 224, 226, 228. (p. 228) Susan Brownmiller Papers,

Schlesinger Library, Radcliffe Institute, Harvard University, Carton 6, Folder, "Rape research articles—general" (accessed April 1, 2005).

59. McCaughey, op. cit., 179.

60. "Female Liberation" Unpublished document, Contact details: Female Liberation Office, Somerville, MA [2 pages] [no date, circa 1969, from postmark]. Annie Popkin Papers, Schlesinger Library, Radcliffe College. [Box 3: Folder: "Women–Female Liberation (once Cell 16) [1969–71, nd]"] (Accessed April 19, 2005).

61. Green Lion Press website, https://www.greenlion.com/cgi-bin/SoftCart.100. exe/nmfg.html?E+scstore (accessed June 8, 2007). (For discussion of Cell 16's staunch commitment to martial arts training see: Densmore, 1998, op. cit.)

62. Jayne West, "Tae Kwon Do," *No More Fun and Games: A Journal of Female Liberation*, 5 (1971): 16–18, 16.

63. West, 1971, ibid., 16.

64. Ibid., 17.

65. Ibid., 18.

66. It is notable that self-defense was promoted from a range of points of view in relation to 'violence'—some being noncommittal, others keen to distinguish it from 'violence' (e.g., Marian Copeland and Suzanne Mottahedeh, "Learning to cope with physical threat," in *Central N.J. NOW Newsletter*, Special Issue on Rape (May 1971): 8. Susan Brownmiller Papers, Schlesinger Library, Radcliffe Institute, Harvard University, Carton 6, Folder, "Rape research women fight back," (accessed March 29, 2005); and others that could be read as embracing the necessity of violence (e.g., Pat Galligan, "Violence and Self-Defense," *No More Fun and Games: A Journal of Female Liberation*, 4 (1970): 99–100; Mary Ann Manhart, "Self-defense," unpublished document. 8 pages [no date], Susan Brownmiller Papers, Schlesinger Library, Radcliffe Institute, Harvard University, Carton 6, Folder "Rape research women fight back," (accessed March 29, 2005); Sheldon, Ann, "Rape: A Solution," *Women: A Journal of Liberation* 3, 1 (Special Issue on Sexuality; 1972): 22–23. Susan Brownmiller Papers, Schlesinger Library, Radcliffe Institute, Harvard University, Carton 6, Folder, "Rape research articles—general" (accessed April 1, 2005); Note that Manhart was a member of the New York Radical Feminists, who organized a rape conference in 1971; this document may have been notes for a self-defense workshop at the conference—for a similar, although considerably revised, version see: Mary Ann Manhart, "Report from the Workshop on Self-Defense," in *Rape: The First Sourcebook for Women*, ed. New York Radical Feminists, Noreen Connell and Cassandra Wilson (New York: Plume/New American Library, 1974), 215–225.

67. Manhart, n.d., ibid., 8.

68. Densmore, 1998, op. cit.

69. Barbara Kross, quoted in: Mary Vespa, "Rape: It's Still 'Let the Woman Beware,'" *Newsday*, July 26, 1973: 4A–5A, 19A, Susan Brownmiller Papers, Schlesinger Library, Radcliffe Institute, Harvard University, Carton 6, Folder, "Rape research articles—general" (accessed April 1, 2005). (See also the *Central N.J. NOW Newsletter*, [Special Issue on Rape] May 1971, which reported on a New York Radical Feminists self-defense workshop, and other fighting responses, Susan Brownmiller Papers, Schlesinger Library, Radcliffe Institute, Harvard University, Carton 6, Folder, "Rape research women fight back" [accessed March 29, 2005]).

70. Winifred Breines, *The Trouble between Us: An Uneasy History of White and Black Women in the Feminist Movement* (New York: Oxford University Press, 2006).

71. The Rape Center Women, "How to start a rape crisis center," [Booklet] Washington, DC, August 1972, Susan Brownmiller Papers, Schlesinger Library, Radcliffe Institute, Harvard University, Carton 7, un-named folder (accessed March 16, 2005). (Note also that New York Radical Feminists, 1974, advised that many rape crisis centers provide martial arts courses: New York Radical Feminists, *Rape: The First Sourcebook for Women*, ed. Noreen Connell and Cassandra Wilson, (New York: Plume/New American Library, 1974), 214.

72. "Protection Tactics," 3-page attachment to *Rape Crisis Center Newsletter*, July/August 1972, Rape Crisis Center, Washington D.C. (p. 1) Susan Brownmiller Papers, Schlesinger Library, Radcliffe Institute, Harvard University, Carton 6, Folder "Rape research women fight back" (accessed March 29, 2005).

73. Stadelman, Cate, "Fighting Back", in Women Against Rape, *Stop Rape*, [booklet] 1971: 13–34 (p. 13), Susan Brownmiller Papers, Schlesinger Library, Radcliffe Institute, Harvard University, Carton 7, un-named Folder (accessed March 17, 2005).

74. Sheldon, op. cit., 23.

75. Dana Densmore, "On Self Defense," *No More Fun and Games: A Journal of Female Liberation*, 6 (1973b): 148–80.

76. Marcus, op. cit., 395 (Marcus also criticized police manuals "that often neglect to mention male genitalia when they designate the vulnerable points of a potential rapist's body, thus perpetuating the myth of the unassailably powerful penis.")

77. "Effects of self-defense," in *Rape Crisis Center Newsletter*, July/August 1972, Rape Crisis Center, Washington D.C. (p. 3) Susan Brownmiller Papers, Schlesinger Library, Radcliffe Institute, Harvard University, Carton 6, Folder "Rape research women fight back" (accessed March 29 2005).

78. "Effects of self-defense," ibid., 4.

79. Cahill, op. cit., 206.

80. Cahill, 2001, op. cit., 205.

81. The phrase in this heading is taken from the title of Marcus' 1992 article.

82. Clothesline Projects involve the public display of a collection of t-shirts on which women have written expressions of their feelings about their personal experience of (sexual) violence; and are designed to bear witness to violence against women (including sexual violence).

83. Ullman, op. cit. Note that in Carmody and Carrington's discussion of preventing sexual violence (situated in the Australian context), self-defense is not specifically mentioned among a fairly long list of activities attributed to feminist efforts to reduce violence against women (Moira Carmody and Kerry Carrington, "Preventing Sexual Violence?" *Australian and New Zealand Journal of Criminology* 33, 3 [2000]: 341–61.) Interestingly, although Campbell et al.'s survey of US rape crisis centers found that over one third offered self-defense programs for women, this activity was barely discussed in the paper and appeared not to be recognized as having the kind of radical potential for change that both poststructuralist and (some) early anti-rape feminists have seen for it. It was coded under "victim services" as a "risk reduction program," rather than as a social change activity directed to the primary prevention of rape. See Rebecca Campbell, Charlene K. Baker, and Terri L. Mazurek, "Remaining Radical? Organizational Predictors of Rape Crisis Centers' Social Change Initiatives," *American Journal of Community Psychology* 26, 3 (1998): 457–483.

   (See Ullman for an argument, based on analysis of empirical research on rape avoidance, that there is a need to teach women self-defense and other resistance strategies.)

84. For example, Kimberly A. Lonsway et al., "Beyond "No Means No"— Outcomes of an Intensive Program to Train Peer Facilitators for Campus Acquaintance Rape Education," *Journal of Interpersonal Violence* 13, 1 (1998): 73–92. (Note the explicit specific focus on acquaintance rape, which is not unusual.)

85. At worst, beyond the issue of what appears to be the limited effectiveness of most such programs (for example, Bachar and Koss concluded that "current preventive interventions are largely ineffective" [137]; Karen Bachar and Mary P. Koss, "From Prevalence to Prevention: Closing the Gap between What We Know About Rape and What We Do," in *Sourcebook on Violence against Women*, eds. Claire M Renzetti, Jeffrey L Edleson and Raquel Kennedy Bergen [Thousand Oaks, CA: Sage, 2001], 117–142), it has been noted that the logic behind some program aims is counter-productive. McCaughey, op. cit., has noted that some rape prevention education programs appear to measure success by the extent to which they instill a sense of vulnerability in women (on the reasoning that this should lead to less risk-taking behavior). Gidycz, et al., 2006, for instance, noted of their program: "In accordance with the health belief model, women are reminded again in the self-defense course that all women were at risk of experiencing sexual victimization" (Christine A. Gidycz et al., "The Evaluation of a Sexual Assault Self-Defense and Risk-Reduction Program for College Women: A Prospective Study," *Psychology of Women Quarterly* 30, 2 [2006]: 173–86, 176). McCaughey argued that such approaches (albeit this one in relation to a program that includes a two and one half hour self-defense course), buy into a problematic acceptance of restrictions in women's basic freedoms in the name of risk reduction.

86. Echols, op. cit., 5. (Echols made the point that within the terminology of the late 1980s, the radical feminism of the early 1970s would typically have been social constructionist, as opposed to a more essentialist bent within the later cultural feminism. Although I am reluctant to label the early feminist anti-rape activism within a typology of feminisms—for the reason that many of my sources are rescued fragment traces that do not readily invite a confident categorization—this is consistent with my observation that threads within the early 1970s analyses of rape would share much in common with later poststructuralist analyses.)

87. See also McCaughey, op. cit., for a discussion of late 1970s cultural feminist opposition to celebrations of women who fought back against violence, by killing abusive men, on the grounds that it "glorified violence" (180).

88. Sometimes this occurs in a fairly direct way when the State funds or partly funds nongovernmental agencies, through the inclusion of 'gag clauses' in contracts, which inhibits certain kinds of critical social commentary. (Field-notes, 2006, New Zealand.) For a discussion of the institutionalization (and arguable de-radicalization) of the anti-rape movement in the United States, see Campbell et al., op. cit.

89. See Susan Estrich, *Real Rape* (Cambridge, MA: Harvard University Press, 1987).

90. Dana Densmore, "On Rape," *No More Fun and Games: A Journal of Female Liberation* 6 (1973a): 57–84, 74. (See also: Dana Densmore, "The Dating Fraud," *No More Fun and Games: A Journal of Female Liberation* 5 (1971): 4–15.)

91. This claim is based on my reading of newspaper clippings in Susan Brownmiller's papers.

92. See Gavey, 2005, op. cit.

93. Densmore, 1973a, op. cit., 75.

94. Hollander, op. cit.; Ullman, 2007, op. cit. (See Gidycz et al., op. cit., for a discussion of the difficulties inherent in the attempt to systematically evaluate the efficacy of rape prevention programs, including those involving self-defense.)

95. Ullman, 2007, op. cit.

96. For example, Patricia McDaniel, "Self-Defense Training and Women's Fear of Crime," *Women's Studies International Forum* 16, 1 (1993): 37–46; Sarah E. Ullman and Raymond A. Knight, "The Efficacy of Women's Resistance Strategies in Rape Situations," *Psychology of Women Quarterly* 17, 1 (1993): 23–38.

97. Carine M. Mardorossian, "Toward a New Feminist Theory of Rape," *Signs: Journal of Women in Culture and Society* 27, 3 (2002): 743–75, 755. (Note, however, that she describes these approaches as "postmodern" rather than poststructuralist.)

98. Mardorossian, 2002, ibid., 755.

99. Interestingly, Bevacqua made a similar point, claiming that self-defense "transcends the differences between radical and liberal anti-rape organizers," and that it rests on liberal strategies of promoting individual change "one woman at a time" (op. cit., 69).

100. Cahill, op. cit., 205.

101. Cahill, op. cit., 207.

102. Cahill, op. cit., 140.

103. See for example, Gavey, 2005.

104. See for example, Gavey, 2007.

105. Ullman, 2007, op. cit.

106. Nicola Gavey, "Rape, Trauma, and Meaning," in *Global empowerment of women: Responses to globalization and politicized religions,* ed. Carolyn M. Elliott (New York: Routledge, 2007), 233–246. (As part a research project on "Rape narratives", I carried out interviews with twenty-five women about their experiences of rape [twenty-two in New Zealand, and three in the Boston area of the United States]. The majority of participants were recruited in response to a suburban newspaper article.) (See also Rozee and Koss, op. cit., who note, on the basis of reading several hundred rape narratives, that women often experience a long period of uncertainty, during which they are shocked by the man's behavior but unsure what is happening.)

107. See Gavey, 2005, op. cit.

108. Gavey, 2005, op. cit.

109. For an engaging discussion of these issues in relation to recent shifts in images of women in advertising, see: Rosalind Gill, "Supersexualize Me! Advertising and 'the Midriffs,'" in *Mainstreaming Sex: The Sexualisation of Culture,* eds. Feona Attwood, Rosalind Brunt, and Rinella Cere (London: I.B. Taurus, 2009), forthcoming.

110. Carmody and Carrington, op. cit., 355. (See also Carmody, Moira, "Ethical Erotics: Reconceptualizing Anti-Rape Education," *Sexualities* 8 (2005): 465–480.)

111. Ann Cahill, "Sexual Violence and Objectification," in this volume.

6 Rethinking the Social Contract
Masochism and Masculinist Violence

Renée J. Heberle

Attention to male masochism heightened at the turn of the twentieth century as it was named as both a symptom of and an explanation for a historical crisis in masculinist subjectivity and liberal politics. In this chapter I will explore the hermeneutic value of masochism as it informs the cultural logic of liberalism. I use sexual violence as a marker, or point of reference, for thinking about the contemporary condition of gendered relations of power supported by this logic. I turn to Friedrich Nietzsche for an elaboration of how masochistic desire, not named as such by Nietzsche, but certainly, I will argue, recognizable in his theory, is imbricated in masculinist, twentieth century, political subjectivity. Through this reading of Nietzsche I suggest that sexual violence can be interpreted as a reactive response to the radical decentering of the subject of power in modernity rather than a proactive behavior of an always already coherent and self-authorizing figure of dominance. The paradoxes of liberal, modern subjectivity should be taken into account as we struggle with ending sexual violence. Otherwise, we risk investing masculine norms with a coherence and solidity they do not possess. We will thus miss opportunities to subvert and perhaps transform those norms into something that we experience as more liveable.

Western feminists have typically theorized sexual violence as an effect of relations of dominance and submission between men and women. As it became clear that appealing to the abstract equality and rights ostensibly available through the terms of the liberal polity was not lessening the levels of domestic violence, sexual assault or rape, sophisticated critiques of the terms on which liberalism sustains gendered relations of dominance emerged. In discussions of the modern liberal polity, feminist critics argue that the terms of the social contract are devised in such a way as to allow men to 'legitimately' victimize women. Carole Pateman's work, *The Sexual Contract*,[1] laid some of the groundwork for feminists who would show how the origin stories of the liberal social contract and the habits of the liberal polity allow for violence against women to be legitimated, normalized, and/or rendered invisible.[2] Concepts central to the success of the social contract such as privacy, property, and individuality, have been shown by feminists to be infused with masculinist assumptions about human nature, the terms of action in the public sphere, and the difference that sexual difference makes in human capacities and desires.³ The project of these critiques is to show how apparently benign liberal concepts sustain and even rely upon a relationship of domination wherein man is always already the authorized subject of power and woman is rendered the subordinate figure.

Pateman elaborates on how, within the sphere of civil society, women contract into relationships of dominance and submission such as husband/ wife, patriarchal father/surrogate mother, or john/prostitute. Thus, in Pateman's reading of John Locke, the social contract is essentially different for men from how it is for women, constitutive of right, justice, and even freedom for the former, while obscuring the reality of the relations of dominance and submission experienced by the latter. The abstract concept of contract and individuality displaces the concrete conditions of submission and sexual difference in assessments of justice. Pateman argues that there is a logic of dominance and submission always already there as an underside and precondition of the social contract. Following Pateman, one might argue that the social contract itself exists among and for the dominant (male) figures of a social order, while the terms of the sexual contract hold (socially-conditioned female) subordinate figures in thrall—all in the name of freedom and individuality.

In the best tradition of critical and feminist theorizing, Pateman's analysis exposes a dirty secret of liberalism, that is, that it is founded upon, indeed cannot do without, a space of violence that is constituted on ethical terms as private, thus properly immune to state intervention, and whose inhabitants (wives, daughters, prostitutes) are assumed to be consenting to their own undoing as subjects in the interest of the patriarchal order. As a response to the question why the liberal polity does not respond adequately to, or indeed inhibits, efforts to eliminate sexual violence, Pateman offers an immanent critique that exposes the relations dominance effectively obscured by the apparently equalizing force of the social contract. She argues "Rather than undermining subordination, contract theorists justified modern civil subjection."⁴

However, Pateman's critique fails to take seriously the paradox immanent to the social contract itself: that it assumes a self-willed submission to authority on the part of all of its participants. While there are different layers of contract, that which constitutes the state/individual relation and those formed between 'consenting' individuals (and enforced by the state), contract itself is a paradoxical relationship with respect to the coherence of and freedom assumed by those subjects who sign on. As noted previously, feminists have pointed to the intrinsically masculinist character of the notion of contract. It suggests a formal and abstract relationship governed by an abstract authority (the rule of law) rather than the embedded and concrete relationships historically identified with the feminine character.⁵ But the normative masculinism of the social contract should not lead us to assume its solidity or the coherence of the selves that enter into it. In fact, I would argue that normative masculinity, whose needs for order and control are expressed through the modern contract, is a far more fragile and uncertain construct. Furthermore, the contract to which the liberal self consents expresses a paradox with respect to freedom. This paradox is illustrated in the following quotation from John Locke's Second Treatise:

> No body can give more power than he has himself; and he that cannot take his own life, cannot give another power over it . . . This is the perfect condition of slavery, which is nothing else, but the state of war continued between a lawful conqueror and a captive: *for if once compact enter between them, and make an agreement for a limited power on the one side, and obedience on the other, the state of war and slavery ceases, as long as the compact endures*: for, as has been said, no man can, by agreement, pass over to another that which he hath not in himself, a power over his own life.[6]

This is, on the face of it and in opposition to Monarchist patriarchalism, a revolutionary argument for the natural right to self-determination. Locke emphasizes that suicide, assuming the 'right' to end one's life, or giving oneself into total bondage as a self-willed (or imposed) slavery, are the limits of contract—the subject does not 'own' himself, but only certain properties of the self, and therefore may give of himself, or has a right to dispose of himself only to a certain point. Looking at the logic of this claim about contract slightly differently one could further argue that Locke's definition of bondage and therefore his notion of freedom is quite narrow. We cannot give over the entirety of our self, but what would be bondage differs from drudgery, and more importantly, it transforms, qualitatively, into a 'free' relationship between presumably reasonable individuals with the moment of contract, activated by the consent of the two parties. In other words, the modern individual is one who wills himself into conditions of submission as a means by which to control the contingencies of the state of nature. The liberal subject wills his personal submission in the name of controlling not only the external world but the vagaries of the self.

In the *Second Treatise* it is initially self-love that Locke references as the problem to be solved with the social contract. Individual men will have a vested interest and therefore not be the best judges in their own cases, overstepping appropriate responses. Later in the text it is "evil and degenerate men" that threaten a community of men who otherwise reasonably adhere to the laws of nature.[7] The social contract, thus, is a response to the basic untrustworthiness of the self and others when not subject to the authority of the rule of law as implemented by the state.

As Pateman identifies the terms of women's positioning within the sexual contract, she assumes the self-identity and self-assuredness of those who are 'legitimately' included within the terms of the social contract. For Pateman, the social contract is a rational working out, among men, shared access to women. It constitutes a transition from the prerogative of the Monarch in his access to women to men peacefully sharing access to dominance over women, or what Pateman identifies as "sex right." It is thus an overcoming of arbitrary violence between ruler and ruled as men progressively define legitimate (legal) against illegitimate (illegal) force through relations of contract and reference to the rule of law. It is this arrangement that allows for the privatization of violence against women and its consequent invisibility in the political realm. Violence among men is rendered illegitimate and turned over to the state as an institutional source of rationally adjudicated punishment. Violence against women, however, remains within the terms of the civil contracts between men and women that constitute marriage and therefore remains beyond the reach of state sanction. Men will punish other men for violence against or theft of property (including women and children) but not for violence against that property that is legitimately theirs and thereby subject only to their private will.

That men will their submission to the rule of law and to the state as the legitimate agent of violent enforcement (punishment) is the paradox of the 'freedom' allegedly won through the revolutionary movement into a social contract. It is these paradoxes and dilemmas of modern forms of individual 'freedom' under the terms of the social contract that feminism is missing as it seeks to conceptualize the terms on which sexual violence becomes possible, even apparently inevitable, as a 'fact' of gendered life under its terms. In what follows, relying on Friedrich Nietzsche's approach to 'contract' in *On the Genealogy of Morals*, I explore further how these paradoxes might inform feminist theorizing about the terms on which sexual violence remains not only possible in conditions of modern liberalism, but a 'normal' part of gendered life.

Feminist discussions about the culture of sexuality and male aggression have moved the theorizing of sexual violence forward, and are especially important when related to strategies of adjudication of sexual violence as a legal harm that demands legal remedies. I want to take a step back, however, and in light of what I have suggested earlier about the paradoxes immanent to modern liberal subjectivity, take contemporary theorizing about the self, about power, and about sexuality into account in furthering the discussion. I think looking at the self in relationship to sexuality through the lens of masochistic logic, defined quite broadly for my purposes as constituting oneself as a victim as a means to the end of staying in control of the self and others, can capture the paradoxes immanent to modern masculinist subjectivity as it emerges within the terms of the social contract. It can help us see how the propensity to sexual violence is embedded in, not incidental to, its terms. In other words, I think the masculine subject of the social contract signs on as a potential victim of his own or others' actions. There is, thus, a simultaneously preemptive and reactive quality to the violence enacted by this subject, particularly to that violence which is related to sexual difference, that which is constituted as the core of the modern self.

The complexity of the dynamics of sexual violence are in part accounted for by the apparent satisfaction the liberal subject finds in identifying as a victim even while he is lashing out at those who potentially threaten his stability or the stability of his environment.[8]

In the next section I discuss contemporary cultural analyses of masochism. Then I explore Friedrich Nietzsche's *On the Genealogy of Morals*, reading it as a classic argument about and parody of masculine subjectivity. While he is only occasionally interested in gender or sexuality, per se, his thinking about the reactive qualities of punishment can help us think through the way the subject who contracts into the social order is living out a masochistic subjectivity that, as Nick Mansfield has suggested,[9] not only becomes indifferent to the suffering it imposes but justifies it through asserting its own victim status.

ON MASOCHISM

What if, as Nietzsche argues in *On the Genealogy of Morals*,[10] the terms of the modern contract itself is constituted not by proactive dominant figures, but by reactive, self-identified victims? Can we still explain, as does Pateman, how sexual violence is built into its terms? As I will discuss, Nietzsche's narrative about the moment of 'contracting in' to the political order offers an alternative to the classical narrative about political subjectivity offered by Locke and criticized by feminists for its exclusions. I want to reconsider the logic of the social contract and masculinity as a masochistic logic. This will allow us to take the diffusion of power and self in modernity into account as we theorize sexual violence. Interpreting the logic of contract and masculinity *as masochistic* tells a story that takes the paradoxes immanent to those forms into account. I think it can offer insight into the reactive quality of the sexual and sexualized violence and suggest to us why they are so brutally common in what John Keane has aptly named late modern 'uncivil' society.[11] Thinking male violence through a Nietzschean lens contributes to a description of it that captures its traumatic, destructive, self-defeating, grindingly familiar, quality. Furthermore, it can bring discussions of male violence and contemporary feminist thinking about power and sexuality together. Acts of sexual violence are not only the seamy underside of liberal contractual relations, they are an acting out of the terms of identity and power that I argue are inherent in relationships and social dynamics shaped by the terms of the social contract.

I elaborate first on why I turn to masochism as a descriptive term for the dynamic that drives sexual violence. Masochism was first named by Richard von Krafft-Ebing in 1890. He described it as, "a peculiar perversion of the psychical *vita sexualis* in which the individual affected, in sexual feeling and thought, is controlled by the idea of being completely and unconditionally subject to the will of a person of the opposite sex; of being treated by the person as by a master, humiliated and abused."[12] Krafft-Ebing named his pathology after Leopold von Sacher-Masoch, a celebrated historian and novelist from Galicia in central Europe. Krafft-Ebing ignored the political and cultural implications of Masoch's texts. He named masochism as a specifically sexual pathology to be cured. As I will discuss, subsequent work on masochism, including those who interpret Masoch's texts, has shown it to be more aptly understood as a strategy for negotiating the paradoxes of subjectivity and power in a then rapidly industrializing, and now increasingly fragmented social order in the modernizing West.

Masoch's most famous novel, *Venus in Furs*,[13] pulls together the iconography and contractual conditions of the masochistic scenario. A young, classically supersensual, bourgeois man, Severin, falls in love with a statue of Venus in a garden. This abstract, unrequitable love is soon transferred to a woman of flesh and blood, Wanda. Through a lengthy period of courtship and pleading Severin succeeds in persuading Wanda to become master to his slave identity, and to sign onto a contract, written by Severin, to which they will both adhere for one year. The classic instrument of punishment and torture, the whip, and the classic costume of woman's seductive power, furs, mediate their physical relationship.

When Krafft-Ebing named masochistic desire, it came into focus as alternatively an explanation for and a symptom of a felt crisis in modern, masculinist, liberal subjectivity at the turn of the twentieth century. However, it should be noted that in naming masochism as an individual pathology, Krafft-Ebing (and many of those who followed) was trying to tame a complex and perplexing logic of modern subjectivity and desire elaborated in Masoch's novels. Suzanne Stewart tries to capture the paradoxes of masochism by describing it as existing in the nexus of compulsion and consent. Whether by the schoolmaster or by the psyche, the masochistic individual is always already simultaneously a subject of compulsion and consent with neither trumping the other in time and space. The practicing masochist takes this logic to its performative heights. The practices of self-willed punishment, the phenomenon of men paying women to whip them into ecstasy which was becoming more common and visible in the nineteenth century, rendered transparent that the heroic individual of liberalism and capitalist initiative is in effect, constituted through the transformation of pain into pleasure through suspended desire.[14] Masochism as a practice and as a cultural trope muddled modern thinking, essential to the logic of the social contract, that self-preservation and aversion to suffering sustains the autonomous self in light of the withdrawal of God as a source of meaning in life.

The complexity of the novel *Venus in Furs* already shows masochism to be about more than alternative means to orgasm. In this text, masochism is shown to be about the self-willed suspension of pleasure. The pleasure of the masochist is not in the realization of orgasm (there is no reference to genitalia, bodies, or orgasmic moments in Venus, only images, yearning, longing, hopeful anticipation) but, more precisely, in the anticipation of pleasure that will be most intensely experienced through the experience of the most intense pain. No one has definitively claimed that the pleasure of masochism is in the anticipatory structure of the experience of the masochist or in the actual pain and suffering, but when desire takes this form it indicates that the proactive drive for self-preservation posited by liberal contract theory may not be separable from a form of reactive desire constituted through a perpetual sense of lack and dissatisfaction.

We can see in this dynamic the logic of liberal capitalism. As the master articulator of this logic, John Locke himself puts it, "the great Principle and Foundation of all Vertue and Worth, is placed in this, That a Man is able to deny himself his own Desires . . . "[15] Thus, masochism is not just about self-denial, it is about a self-denial that is rendered more heroic and pleasurable the more intense the experience of unsatisfied desire becomes. It implies that the more powerful the experience of lacking something, of not having, then the more powerful the Man.

In common with these studies of masochism, the target of critique in this chapter is the self-representation of the modern masculinist social contract. I think understanding the logic of the modern contract as masochistic offers an alternative explanation for sexual violence to that which assumes a seamlessly structured condition of the masculine self or of male dominance. I bring Nietzsche's critique, *On the Genealogy of Morals*, to bear as it reflects on the modern social contract through paradigmatically masochistic imagery and storytelling. I think Nietzsche best captures the logic of the violence of the masculinist subject as realized through extra-legal forms of sexualized and gendered punishment.

MASOCHISM AS PARODY/PARODYING MASOCHISM

Nietzsche's work illuminates the masochistic logic of the liberal contract and suggests him as a resource for thinking about specifically masculinist subjectivity. This is often missed in interpretations of his work as the mid-twentieth century association of masochism with femininity has been projected back onto his representations of women. For example, Nietzsche offers one of his more infamous commentaries on 'woman' in a section titled "On Little Old and Young Women" in *Thus Spoke Zarathustra*. Zarathustra meets a little old woman to whom he speaks of 'woman.' She responds with a little truth which she directs him to wrap up and hold still lest it speak too loudly. "'You are going to visit women? Do not forget the whip!'"[16] This phrase is commonly interpreted as yet another of Nietzsche's misogynist comments. However, the meaning of this phrase is not so clear. A famous picture of Nietzsche and Paul Ree, taken shortly before he wrote this section of Zarathustra, depicts him and Ree pulling a cart carrying Lou Salome who, in turn, wielded a small whip—adorned with flowers. Especially in light of the foregoing commentary Nietzsche offers on woman, this picture should indicate to us that the whip in the aphorism is for the woman to use against the man, in the service of the man's enjoyment as a disciplined child/slave.

While I do not want to make a definitive statement on Nietzsche's views about women in this context, I would suggest that Nietzsche is mocking male subjectivity as he comments on 'woman,' not affirming, and much less praising it.[17] Though Freud and others identified masochism with the feminine character, Nietzsche's work reflected on masochism as a symptom of masculinity. At the end of the nineteenth century, masochism was still primarily a male-identified phenomena. John Noyes shows this to be the case in his genealogy of masochism, as does Suzanne Stewart in her study of masochism in late nineteenth century literature.[18] Nick Mansfield argues that "Masochism is not implicitly masculine or implicitly feminine, but historically, it has been dominated by men. Indeed, the identification of masochism with femininity relies on a crude binarism that links masculinity with activity rather than passivity, a complete misunderstanding, . . . of the nature of masculine power."[19]

Of all of Nietzsche's work, *On The Genealogy of Morals* gives the clearest expression to, as well as being a parodic critique of, masochistic political subjectivity. While it is clearly a general attack on modern forms of political subjectivity, whether that subjectivity be democratic, socialist, or nationalist, *The Genealogy* can be a resource for understanding more specifically the modern *liberal* masculine subject of the social contract as constituted through the anticipation of victimization. Nietzsche observed the conditions of his time and directed his theoretical compass through interpreting political conditions and human behavior. The stability of the social order, contingent upon a coherent sense of self among citizens (men) within rapidly changing global conditions, was an explicit concern at the turn of the century. Given the paradoxical demands on the masculinist subject at the turn of the century—"to take on the burdens of imperial rule abroad, to submit to the governance of capitalist advancements in technology and production domestically, to live one's life as a Darwinian struggle of all against all while being the benevolent racist abroad and the Good Bourgeois Father at home"—a certain sense of crisis was inevitable.[20]

Nietzsche had a complex relationship to that sense of crisis. For him, the dissolution of the coherent sense of self was, in part, the reason for his "cheerfulness" as described in *The Gay Science.*[21] However, as becomes clear in the *Genealogy*, he also did not think that coherent self ever *actually* existed. The "doer behind the deed" was always already a necessary fiction. Thus, as theorized in the *Genealogy*, the terms of the modern contract turn on a completely different kind of self from that drawn in typical interpretations of liberal origin stories.

The first essay of the *Genealogy* describes Nietzsche's theory of *ressentiment*, the reactive quality of modern/civilized subjectivity. In this essay,

Nietzsche offers a parodic morality play. He presents the little lambs, the meek of the earth, as they become attached to their powerlessness vis-a-vis the birds of prey that threaten them in the name of *the good*. This is a classic representation of the reactive mentality that inspires the moral foundationalism of the self-conscious subject. As Nietzsche's lambs project evil onto the strength of the birds of prey, they project a malicious interior life and subjectivity onto those who are innately powerful and not particularly concerned with reflecting on or moralizing about that power. The lambs thus transvalue themselves into the good or moral subject. The lambs project evil onto the birds of prey; this act of saying 'no' to power of the self through the projection of power onto the other becomes the lambs' creative act, as it is the masochist's creative act. In developing a discussion of masochistic logic through Nietzsche, I am drawing together several arguments about the phenomenon as it has been named and historically contextualized by several contemporary literary and cultural theorists. The most important interventions for my purposes are those that look at masochism as a logic definitive of self/other relationships of desire. For example, in his reading of *Venus in Furs* Gilles Deleuze argues that masochistic desire is constituted through contract and not through an antithetical positioning vis-a-vis the sadistic moment. In the masochist's universe, the other enacts the projected desire of the masochist for internal discipline and coherence. S/he performs the position of dominance but does not represent it in any ontological sense. Like the masochist, the lambs come to articulate the terms of inclusion in the social contract specifically *through* the disavowal of power.

For Nietzsche, then, the self-conscious subject's sense of identity within the social is a reactive one. This subject, like the masochist, comes to desire his own victimization and that sense of victimization determines the terms on which otherness, as evil, can *be* in the world. The masochist may well control the terms of the social order (Deleuze), but this order serves the demands of the crisis-ridden subject whose sense of identity and self-assuredness is derived from his knowledge of otherness, of evil. Thus, as Mansfield argues, "Masochism presents a model of a power that can strengthen itself by self-renunciation, that can advance itself by acts of self-denial, even self-mutilation."[22]

It is in Essay II of the *Genealogy* that the violence of masochistic subjectivity becomes more clear. It is through Nietzsche's story, reflective of masochistic logic, that we can understand the potential for violence of the (masculinist) subject within a liberal order. Nietzsche's is not an argument against violence. His is an argument against reactive violence wherein the subject organizes the punishment of the other through his own identity as victim. Nietzsche addresses the actual physical violence and cruelty through which he claims the social contract is constituted. He describes the contract as steeped in blood, as indebted to cruelty, telling a story about the foundational, rather than the incidental, violence of contracting into a social order founded on the reactionary moral judgments described in Essay I.

In Essay II, Nietzsche describes the logic of various forms of punishment derived in the name of "good conscience." But first he turns to what he calls "prehistory." Before punishment was conceived as a consequence for a bad *choice* of behavior, it was driven by the belief that for every injury there existed an equivalent form of suffering that could be inflicted on the perpetrator. "And whence did this primeval, deeply rooted, perhaps by now ineradicable idea draw its power—this idea of an equivalence between injury and pain? I have already divulged it: in the contractual relationship between creditor and debtor, which is as old as the idea of 'legal subjects' and in turn points back to the fundamental forms of buying, selling, barter, trade, and traffic."[23] The capacity to make promises is contingent upon the development of memory. But where does the most effective form of memory come from? Not from the infliction of pain, but from the experience of pain. "If something is to stay in the memory it must be burned in: only that which never ceases to hurt stays in the memory . . . Man could never do without blood, torture, and sacrifices when he felt the need to create a memory for himself . . . "[24] The self-conscious subject is the subject with the capacity to make promises, or memory. Thus, the memory of pain is necessary to legitimate and sustain inclusion in the social contract. The masochistic twist Nietzsche suggests is that the subject comes to name and find meaning in his own suffering toward service of 'the good' and in the name of 'justice.'

For Nietzsche, the soul of self-conscious man is an effect of the turning inward of the aggressive instincts. "All instincts that do not discharge themselves outwardly turn inward—this is what I call the internalization of man." "The entire inner world, originally as thin as if it were stretched between two membranes, expanded and extended itself, acquired depth, breadth, and height, in the same measure as outward discharge was inhibited."[25]

It is in an explosive moment that the aggressive instincts, which represent for Nietzsche the potential for human freedom, turn inward and become reactive.[26] As man develops an inner-life, a depth, a soul, a conscience, the otherwise unbridled and unconscious (in the best way, for Nietzsche) tyrannical wills to power that drive the strong and proactive conquerors and founders of states are radically displaced:

> They do not know what guilt, responsibility, or consideration are, these born organizers; they exemplify that terrible artists' egoism that has the look of bronze and knows itself justified to all eternity in its 'work' like a mother in her child. It is not in them that the 'bad conscience' developed, that goes without saying—but it would not have developed without them, this ugly growth, it would be lacking if a tremendous quantity of freedom had not been expelled from the world, or at least from the visible world, and made as it were, latent under their hammer blows and artists' violence. This instinct for freedom forcibly made latent—we have seen it already—this instinct for freedom pushed back

and repressed, incarcerated within and finally able to discharge and vent itself only on itself: that, and that alone, is what the bad conscience is in its beginnings.[27]

Ressentiment is ultimately internalized and constitutive of the conscience of the aware, reasoning, self-conscious individuals. It is on the terms of this dynamic that we lose the potential to realize a free self and become bound to our suffering. "The suffering are one and all dreadfully eager and inventive in discovering occasion for painful affects; they enjoy being mistrustful and dwelling on nasty deeds and imaginary slights; . . . "[28] And as that self constituted through suffering becomes the predominant subject of history it searches out for purposes of punishment the causes of suffering— "making evildoers out of their friends, wives, children, and whoever else stands closest to them."[29] The priest, however, tells the suffering subject that he himself is responsible, thus, again, directing *ressentiment* inward and constituting the guilty conscience. In this way the "curative priest" exploits the bad instincts of all sufferers for the purpose of self-discipline, self-surveillance, and self-overcoming. Thus, for Nietzsche, the potential of slave morality is realized when the priest is no longer necessary; it is realized with the invention of the self-willed disappearing subject who punishes otherness as a means by which to find meaning in his own suffering.

For Nietzsche, the noble man is one who experiences pain but does not experience the need to find the 'cause' or to understand it, much less to imbue it with meaning in order to sustain a sense of self through the experience of suffering. The subject of ressentiment, on the other hand, is one who experiences suffering as identity, as a means to redemption, as a means to insight about humanity. The subject of *ressentiment* comes to desire suffering as the means to his self-knowledge. It is because of such subjects that social order, civilization, and ultimately, modernity becomes possible. The journey to self-knowledge, to reason, is constituted through pain which creates the most effective form of memory. It is this memory which makes a man able to keep promises. Thus, the modern subject is an effect of pain and becomes invested in pain as a means to identity, selfhood and belonging. Victimization becomes a source of legitimacy and recognition; from such a position, one can make demands on otherness and justify punishment if those demands are not met. The theory of the free-willing individual, she who could have done differently, justifies all manner of punishment. Contract, and the terms of punishment embedded in it, becomes a means by which the nay-saying, self-denying, subject of late modernity attempts to invent himself, to assert an identity. Modern man comes to desire the punishment and develops a guilt complex that is played out through masochistic performances and the masochistic logic of contract.

I should look briefly again at some of Nietzsche's discussions of gender identity and relationships in order to further see how his critique is specifically targeted at masculinity. In the *Gay Science* he discusses the terms of love available to men and to women. He says 'man's love' is constituted as being satisfied only with possession of the other while woman's love is only about giving herself. According to Nietzsche, a woman's love leads to her faithfulness and has no end, while a man's love always comes to an end with 'having.' Thus, the man's love is always in a state of suspension, of deferral, of lack, " . . . wanting to have always comes to an end with having." " . . . he will not readily concede that a woman should have nothing more to give him."[30] It is, thus, a masochistic love Nietzsche describes as 'man's love.'

If we look at the language used by men who commit battery against 'their women' today, this logic becomes brutally apparent. Women who leave abusive relationships are at the most risk of being murdered. The most common explanation by men who murder their lovers or wives, is that they could not stand the thought of someone else 'having her.' Thirty percent of men who murder women then kill themselves, a fact too often overlooked in discussions of male violence. Male violence can thus be read as a symptom of the futility of the desire for total possession that Nietzsche describes in *The Gay Science* as constitutive of masculinist subjectivity. The incapacity of masculinist subjects to finally experience the having, and the tortured sense of self that leaves them with, inspires a violence that, as has been repeatedly shown by feminists, is all about the desire to control. However, I would add that this desire to control is, importantly, inspired by lack, by a perpetual 'not having.' It is the violence of a dissolute self who takes out his perpetual dissatisfaction against the other.

With this in mind, we might reread the *Story of O*, a famous point of reference for discussions of women's masochistic desire, turning attention instead to the story of the male protagonist.[31] Typical interpretations of the *Story of O* assume masochism to be about the passive, specifically feminine desire for punishment and pain. Attention has focused on O, the female character about whose sexual adventures the (presumably) female narrator tells the reader. But what if we redirect our attention to the male character, Rene, assuming what we have discussed to be true of masochism? Rene brings O to Roissy, the place she will be trained to be the possessed object of male desire. But his desire for possession is not satisfied. So he then 'gives her' to Sir Stephen, his half-brother, in the name of bearing witness to a more successful form of possession. Rene then falls in love instead with Jacqueline, a model from O's commercial photography studio who becomes O's lover while ignoring Rene's advances.[32]

The Nietzsche quote offered previously suggests that the masochistic subject wills his own disappearance as he satisfies his desire to become victim. Could we then reinterpret Rene's actions, his giving over of O to others, his gradual disappearance from her life as lover, his experience of unrequited love as he courts O's friend and female lover, as masochistic, as his way of reinventing of himself as victim? The violence the women are subjected to in the name of absolute possession, then, become symptoms of his self-willed disappearance from the text.

MASOCHISM AS THE ART OF POWER

I want to now address more directly the political potential I find in this reading of Nietzsche and masochistic subjectivity for thinking about sexual violence. I therefore briefly discuss the conclusions of two recent studies of masochism by Nick Mansfield and David Savran. Both texts make sense of masochism as an accommodationist strategy of power.

Nick Mansfield reads texts of modernity and postmodernity for what they can tell us about the qualities and capacities of the masochistic subject of power. He says:

> The subjectivity of the male masochistic subject continually folds and refolds itself in a series of contradictory, decomposing states where it is always returning to itself in moments of semi-misrecognition. But while it is dispersing into these micropositions, the subject maintains a consistency of agency and intention that preserves a centered, authoritarian subjectivity. The subject splinters and preserves, fragments and controls itself at the same time. It is both active and passive, powerful and powerless, in the one act.[33]

This would counter theorizing like that of Robin West[34] who has argued that the essence of the masochistic subject is in his/her capacity for absolute trust in the other. West thinks this could be read as a freeing of the otherwise controlled and self-contained subject. She thus sees progressive potential in masochistic subjectivity for challenging assumptions about identity and power and suggests that masochism harbors the potential for realizing the progressive dissolution of the subject who relies on an authoritarian relationship to himself and to others for a sense of identity. From Mansfield's point of view, however, the masochistic subject derealizes the self, *but in the name of its own power.* He goes on:

> Masculinity imagines its own powerlessness. Power is reflected back at itself as victimization. . . . The other is annihilated at the moment when the subject projects suffering inwards. The suffering of others is not recognized because suffering is initiated and suffered first by the masochistic subject himself. The suffering of the other is derealized, and no amount of its representation can reinstall its meaning and weight within the consciousness of the subject, whether the sufferer is woman, the colonized, the indigene, the child, the beautiful, the handicapped, the criminal, or the dead.[35]

Thus, as Nietzsche also argues, the imperative to impute meaning to suffering *is* the condition of entry into subjectivity, but it simultaneously precludes attentiveness to otherness. It is a narcissistic suffering, fully self-absorbed, and cognizant of otherness only as threat. The masochist's other cannot suffer as does the masochistic subject; certainly the fantasized dominatrix of the masochistic imagination cannot suffer. For Mansfield, then, the ability to bear witness to the suffering of otherness, rather than to simply, and narcissistically, position oneself as sufferer, becomes a normative aspiration defeated by masochistic logic.

Mansfield's analysis suggests that the masochistic subject can defeat any and all resistance to its terms of existence. For Mansfield, masochism, as it expresses the intractable paradoxes of modern, masculinist, liberal subjectivity, finds a home in the aesthetic, thus allowing it to disavow through cultural politics its own hegemonic positioning in structural politics. His study of masochism suggests that it 'escapes' into the work of art, into literature, into the world of the sublime because it consists of paradoxes and performative contradictions of subjectivity that cannot be expressed elsewhere. This literary turn allows the impossibility of masochistic logic to survive in a place from which it can 'safely' reproduce the disavowals of power that keep power in place. Mansfield is most sharply critical of poststructuralist theorists who not only find the political in the aesthetic, but leave it there, failing to see that migration as a symptom of how power reproduces itself. He thus suggests that poststructuralism is complicit with masochistic logic as it agreeably disavows the centeredness of power and defers critique. Mansfield's reading of male subjectivity as masochistic also suggests to us why it is so hard to render sexual violence visible as a constant in the lives of women, girls, boys, and some men. Why are testimonials, speak outs, and the constant flow of human interest stories not enough to render a crisis mentality with respect to its magnitude? Part of the answer has to be that the violent terms on which heterosexual intimacy is founded is the great 'public secret' of the modern, civilized world, a claim that follows from Carol Pateman's analysis. But another part has to be that the paradoxical subjectivity that constitutes the structures of power renders the subject constitutionally unable to see the terms of his own violence as such. Victims need no rationalization for the reactive forms of violence they impose on those who threaten their coherence as selves.

Like Mansfield, David Savran, deploys masochism to explore the terms of survival of the masculinist political subject. He suggests that the backlash against feminism and other new social movements in other words, the phenomenon of the angry white male can be explained through the logic of masochism. More so than Mansfield, Savran's analysis emphasizes the ambivalences of modern, masochistic masculine subjectivity as an always already threatened cultural construction.

Savran offers a genealogy of masculinity as an identity under threat. However, among Savran's conclusions is that the male masochist "proves an intractable subject for all those systems designed for personal transformation, from psychoanalysis to meditation to twelve-step programs. He proves the extraordinary resilience of an oppressive cultural hegemony and of white men in retaining their enormous economic, political, and social power."[36] Now I do not know why, politically, Savran, in the particular historical moment with which he is concerned (the latter decades of the twentieth century) invests those systems oriented to therapeutic self-discipline he lists with any potential to challenge white male hegemony. Or, to put it another way, why would the intractability of male hegemony be proven through the 'failure' of those systems? Rather than being cures for male masochism, the application of those systems to masculinity, it seems to me, could be read as symptomatic of the disintegration of the liberal humanist subject as I have described him, a disintegration Nietzsche felt quite cheerful about as he wrote *The Gay Science*. "The whole pose of 'man against the world,' of man as a 'world-negating principle,' of man as the measure of the value of things, as judge of the world who in the end places existence itself upon his scales and finds it wanting—the monstrous insipidity of this pose has finally come home to us and we are sick of it. We laugh as soon as we encounter the juxtaposition of 'man and world.'"[37] Might we not find hope in the increasing application of therapeutic technologies to men *as men* for the very dissolution of masculinist hegemony? Could we not see this phenomenon as symptomatic of the increasing transparency of the paradoxes of liberal masculine subjectivity—as signaling not its intractability, but its very instability?

In any event, given the contingencies that Savran locates in the construction of masculinity, his pessimism, as indicated by his statement that "this book takes issue with those poststructuralist theorists for whom the disintegration of the liberal humanist subject offers radically subversive possibilities . . . [because] masochism functions precisely as a kind of decoy and the cultural texts constructing masochistic masculinities characteristically conclude with an almost magical restitution of phallic power"[38] seems appropriate only if one ignores the dynamic quality of gendered selves that are always under construction. Similarly, Nick Mansfield argues "masochism shows us that masculinity is capable of operating a power to which the deconstruction of binarism offers no challenge, a power that can even tolerate castration."[39] Each analysis ultimately suggests that sameness and indifference toward difference rules contemporary culture and successfully absorbs radical challenges (apparently without, I should note, resorting to violence). Thus, masochism is understood as an artifice of power, rather than the power of artifice, and offers a means by which to understand masculinist desire as it elides the politics (power) of its own positioning.

These discussions suggest we read the practices and assertions of victimization by men as a masochistic cover for their structural positioning as the dominant sex which allows them to control and victimize women and other marginal subjects with impunity. Both are concerned that white men, in particular, are successfully, through masochistic logic, displacing the real suffering of marginalized peoples. I agree that the terms on which suffering is represented are distorted, but think it is important to remember, following Nietzsche, that masochism is not just a cover for the otherwise coherent, systemic dominance of white male subjectivity. As Nietzsche famously asserts in the Genealogy, " . . . there is no 'being' behind doing, effecting, becoming; 'the doer' is merely a fiction added to the deed; the deed is everything."[40] Nietzsche offers a counter to the optimistic stories of contracting into the political order of things that suggests that the normative masculinity demanded by the terms of contract is a reactive and punitive formation, not an autonomous figure ultimately transparent to himself and his desires.

Further, I would suggest that contemporary manifestations of the masochistic logic of modern masculinist power signals its potential subversion. We might take note, as well, that simultaneously with the increasing transparency of this cultural logic (I am thinking, here, of the "angry white male" who expresses his political identity as victim primarily vis-a-vis affirmative action and feminism) over the last twenty years, incidences of sexual violence have increased. Following in a long tradition of theorizing about power and violence, including that of Hannah Arendt and Michel Foucault, I would suggest this violence, at this point in history, could be interpreted as signifying the limits and even the failures of masculinist power, not its continuing 'real' hegemony. Foucault teaches us that power, if thought as always circulating through and in relationships such as gender, does not consolidate and reconsolidate itself in the face of threats to its presence in any simple or straightforward fashion. It engenders the terms of its own resistance, and indeed the terms of its own undoing. And when it turns to force and violence the relationship of power is over and some other means of contracting into those authoritative norms that govern, in this case, masculinity, become necessary. As I suggested about the turn to therapeutic measures for healing masculinity, I think the increasing incidents of sexual violence show masculinity as such to not be so functional as Mansfield and Savran conclude.

I should also note that my argument is not that the cultural and structural power of men has no presence. However, I find in Nietzsche an image of masculinity as ontologically emasculated by the terms on which the social contract constructs the possibility of inclusion. We could thus see masculinist violence as symptomatic of threatened dissolution rather than as the effect of self-assured dominance. Sexual violence may be the effort masculinity makes to reassure itself of its solidity given its masochistic ontology. It is not then, signaling the 'real' power of masculinity as suggested by Mansfield and Savran's discussion, or, for that matter, an assertion of dominance and control as suggested by Carole Pateman.

SHE MADE ME DO IT

I have suggested that studies of men who commit sexual violence illuminate the reactive quality of that violence. Most feminist theories of sexual violence do not take the words of the masculinist perpetrator seriously as a means to understanding the dynamic of battery and rape. As suggested at the start of this chapter, they invest the perpetrator of violence with a self-authorizing position of dominance he himself may not phenomenologically experience. [41]

In contrast to the wealth of material about victims of sexual violence, there is relatively little work done on batterers and rapists themselves.[42] However, the research that has been conducted supports the counter-narrative I have offered with respect to masculinity and the dynamic of desire that inspires sexual violence. The explanations that batterers and rapists offer for their behavior are infused with the ressentiment Nietzsche describes. Thinking about the logic of masochism suggests a theory of the connection between sexual violence and the logic of the social order that acknowledges the fragmented, reactionary quality of the masculinist subject of modernity. However, it should also warn of the dangers we may face as that sense of dissolution becomes more transparent. As the terms on which normative masculinity is lived and understood as a structuring device for 'civilized' society are challenged, there is every reason to predict that reactive forms of violence will continue to escalate.

In suggesting that there are masochistic trends in the phenomenon of battering, I am not making the claim that men are 'really' victims. The evil other does not have to 'really' exist for Nietzsche's slaves to make their claims about suffering. The masculinist subject, like the masochist, invents his other that the terms of contract protects against. It is the figure of woman, or, indeed, any feminized other, that most threatens this condition of possibility for masculinity and becomes the target for reactive forms of punishment. The self-imagined victim is ultimately more dangerous than the noble actor in Nietzsche's narrative. The violence he inflicts is more intractable, founded as it is in his reactive identity which assumes the moral rightness of all actions taken in his defense.

If we listen to what they say about their violence we will find that men do not commit violence against women as assertions of dominance. This would help us account for the high percentage of batterers (approximately 30% according to a recent NIJ Study on Domestic Violence) who commit suicide upon killing their victims. And we might look again at the fact that women are in the most danger of suffering an acute battering incident when they try to leave the abuser or become pregnant.[43] Or we might note that the majority of batterers are what Neil Jacobson and John M. Gottman in their longitudinal study of two hundred relationships involving physical and emotional violence have termed "Pit Bulls."[44] In describing one such batterer, Jacobson and Gottman note: "Despite his obvious violence and cruelty, which we observed, he acted like a victim of battering, and we believe he really saw himself that way. Don told us that Martha was not afraid of him; on the contrary, she 'got off' on making him angry and the angrier he got the more antagonistic she became."[45]

Rapists commonly claim the victim of the assault is to blame, essentially for taking over the perpetrator's libido. Batterers say their victims deny them their rightful place as men. Adam Jukes notes that "our clients [batterers who present for treatment] are keen to present themselves in the best possible light as well as maintaining a consistent self-image. As often as not this invariably involves presenting themselves as victims, either of their childhood, their victims, uncontrollable impulses or toxic substances."[46] That the best positioning for the masculinist subject is that of victimization should tell us something about the terms on which the modern polity establishes the terms for legitimate self-representation.

Most research psychologists understandably interpret men's words as denial or as rationalizations for behavior they know is wrong. However, if we take men who commit rape and battery at their word (which does not mean taking their word as the truth), the explanations of men who commit sexual and sexualized forms of violence expose the fissures and contradictions in masculinity and should challenge feminists to take another look at the dynamics of masculinist violence in light of the politics of sexuality and identity. Batterers and rapists are not simply in denial about their own dominance and power when they claim victimization. The decentralization and diffusion of power in late modernity has had its effects. A phenomenological study of batterers' narratives, conducted in 1997, shows a central metaphor used by batterers to be that of the self as a dangerous space and as a locus of intense inner struggle. They describe the provocations of the women they have hit as appealing to the worst side of themselves, as always already threatening their sense of self-control. "The self [of the batterer] is passive and humiliated. Only when abused does it react. Violence becomes a way to empty the container, transforming the self's perception of its inner space into a dangerous and uncontrollable entity."[47] Thus, sexual violence is best understood as a reactive, or symptomatic, form of violence, rather than as a proactive act of dominance and control. It is a kind of punishment inspired by the perpetrators' projections of dangerousness onto the other of his desiring self.

Sexual violence is an acting out of failure. Violence may be the antithesis of power, as argued by Hannah Arendt and Michel Foucault, but it is also a strategy, or action, linked to the necessary failures of masculinity to master and control. To argue that batterers, rapists, and harassers 'suffer' the effects of fragmentation and uncertainty in modernity is not to excuse or rationalize their behavior. It is to understand the intractable and apparently inevitable quality of sexual violence under conditions of rigid gender expectations. This is why to theorize sexual violence we must turn to theories of sexuality and power that highlight the indeterminacy of gender. While it describes an empirical truth to say that men as such commit violence against women as such, it simply repeats that which we all already know, that boys will be boys and girls have to be careful. Instead, we might argue that sexual violence is an acting out of the failure to master and control, not a culmination of successful self-realization and power. This makes it all the more dangerous because of the dangers implicit for the self in the confession of failure. The tortured self-representations of male perpetrators (she made me do it) indicate a basic paradox: that in decentering their agency, they recenter their sense of self. They identify their masculinity with a suffering self while projecting blame onto the evil other that perpetually threatens that self. The feminine threat must be punished, not necessarily out of a righteous sense of dominance or prerogative as suggested by Pateman's critique of contract, but out of a reactive and persistent fear of self-dissolution. That dissolute masculinity is so dangerous suggests that the deconstruction of rigid forms of gender is the means by which we will get to the end of sexual violence. Theorizing political forms as if they only reinforce always already extant forms of dominance may simply rewrite the story of gender we are already living out, with all of its pain and unbearable violence. Subversive readings such as those offered by Nietzsche of what appear to be solid and unquestionable forms of rational understanding among subjects gendered as male are helpful, I think, in sustaining optimism about the end, literally, of gender.

NOTES

1. Carole Pateman, *The Sexual Contract* (Stanford, CA: Stanford University Press, 1988).
2. Wendy Brown, in a critical discussion of Pateman's work, suggests that Pateman invests too much energy criticizing a construct—the sexual contract—that is no longer particularly necessary to the legitimacy project of contemporary liberalism. Brown sets out to show "where male dominance lives" in contemporary liberalism as notions of contract recede in historical and discursive significance. While I agree for the most part that discussions of contracting into political society are no longer explicitly salient to liberalism's legitimacy project in the sense of the imperative to render it superior to other forms of governance, I do not think it is irrelevant to our self-understanding as specifically liberal subjects. We may be living through the hangover of the giddy days of contracting into political relations, but I think political subjectivity remains conditioned by the imperatives of contract in a number of ways. This is why I think it important to revisit, in a critical manner, origin stories about the terms on which individuals contract in and thus represent themselves in the public sphere. See Wendy Brown, *States of Injury: Power and Freedom in Late Modernity* (New York: Routlege, 1995).
3. See especially Martha Albertson Fineman and Roxanne Mytiuk, eds. *The Public Nature of Private Violence* (New York: Routledge, Press 1994) and Christine DiStefano and Nancy J. Hirschman, *Revisioning the Political: Feminist Reconstructions of Traditional Concepts in Western Political Theory* (Boulder, CO: Westview Press, 1994).
4. Pateman, op. cit., 44.
5. Nancy C. M. Hartsock, *Money, Sex, and Power: Toward a Feminist Historical Materialism* (New York: Longman Press, 1983).
6. John Locke, *The Second Treatise of Government*, ed. C.B. MacPherson (Indianapolis, IN: Hackett Publisher, 1980 [original publication 1689]), 18–19.

7. Locke says in chapter two, "That in the state of nature every one has the executive power of the law of nature, I doubt not but it will be objected, that it is unreasonable for men to be judges in their own cases, that self-love will make men partial to themselves and their friends: And on the other side, that ill nature, passion and revenge will carry them too far in punishing others; and hence nothing but confusion and disorder will follow, and that there God has certainly appointed government to restrain the partiality and violence of men." He says in chapter nine, "Of the Ends of Political Society and Government," "For in the state of nature, to omit the liberty he has of innocent delights, a man has two powers. The first is to do whatsoever he thinks fit for the preservation of himself and others within the permission of the law of nature: by which law, common to them all, he and the rest of mankind are one community, make up one society, distinct from all other creatures. And, were it not for the corruption and viciousness of degenerate men, there would be no need of any other; no necessity that men should separate from this great and natural community, and by positive agreement combine into smaller and divided associations."

8. I should note at this point that my discussion is specific to the dynamics of sexual violence as a traumatic experience inflicted on particular people (primarily, but not solely, women and girls) and within the terms of Western versions of liberal democratic life.

9. Nick Mansfield, *Masochism: The Art of Power* (Westport: Praeger Press, 1997).

10. Friedrich Nietzsche, *On the Genealogy of Morals*, trans. Walter Kaufman and R.J. Hollingdale (New York: Vintage Books 1967).

11. John Keane, *Violence and Democracy* (Cambridge UK: Cambridge University Press, 2004).

12. John Noyes, *The Mastery of Submission: Inventions of Masochism* (Ithaca, NY: Cornell University Press, 1997), 6.

13. Leopold Ritter von Sacher-Masoch, *Venus in Furs* (New York: Sylvan Press, 1947).

14. I am not, in this chapter, going to discuss the politics of what we might call the practice of sadomasochism. I think the project of interpreting the masochistic logic of modern political subjectivity is a different one from that of interpreting the politics of acting out masochism in a ritualized, staged, consensual manner. The acting out may, in its literalizing of an otherwise abstracted logic, effectively parody and subvert an otherwise unseen and unspoken social logic. The masochistic impulse of religious martyrdom, for example, is not named as such by its practitioners. Nonethless, certain forms of religiosity and masochism may have much in common.

15. David Savran, *Taking it Like a Man: White Masculinity, Masochism and Contemporary American Culture* (Princeton, NJ: Princeton University Press, 1998), 21.

16. Friedrich Nietzsche, *Thus Spoke Zarathustra: A Book for All and None*, trans. Walter Kaufman (New York: Viking Press, 1966), 67.

17. According to Deleuze, "The woman torturer of masochism cannot be sadistic precisely because she is in the masochistic situation, she is an integral part of it, a realization of the masochistic fantasy. She belongs in the masochistic world, not in the sense that she has the same tastes as her victim, but because her 'sadism' is of a kind never found in the sadist; it is as it were the double or the reflection of masochism." See Gilles Deleuze, *Masochism: Coldness and Cruelty* (Cambridge, MA: Zone Books 1989), 67.

18. Suzanne R. Stewart, *Sublime Surrender: Male Masochism at the fin-de-siecle* (Ithaca, NY: Cornell University Press, 1998).

19. Mansfield, op. cit., xxi.

20. Noyes, op. cit., 105–107.

21. In section 343 of *The Gay Science*, referring to the death of God in modernity, Nietzsche says, "This long plenitude and sequence of breakdown, destruction, ruin, and cataclysm that is now impending—who could guess enough of it today to be compelled to play the teacher and advance proclaimer of this monstrous logic of terror, the prophet of a gloom and an eclipse of the sun whose like has probably never yet occurred on earth? Even we born guessers of riddles who are, as it were, waiting on the mountains, posted between today and tomorrow, stretched in the contradiction between today and tomorrow, we firstlings and premature births of the coming century, . . . why is it that even we look forward to the approaching gloom . . . are we perhaps still too much under the impression of the initial consequences of this event—and these initial consequences, the consequences for ourselves, are quite the opposite of what one might perhaps expect: They are not at all sad and gloomy, but rather like a new and scarcely describable kind of light, happiness, relief, exhilaration, encouragement, dawn." See Friedrich Nietzsche, *The Gay Science with a Prelude of Songs and Appendix of Songs*, trans. Walter Kaufman (New York: Random House, 1974), 279–280.

22. Mansfield, op. cit., xi.

23. Nietzsche, op. cit., 63.

24. Ibid., 61.

25. Ibid., 84–85.

26. Robert Pippin reminds us of the possibility that Nietzsche's noble action is an action that is expressive, not necessarily comprehensible in terms of determinant causes or transparent intentions. Thus the expressive action of the noble man is not 'self' conscious in the traditional way we understand that term. It is not a choice, but an action embedded in the circumstances one finds oneself in, that perhaps can be explained in retrospect, but not judged as it becomes plain that the actor would not have been themselves if they had not done that particular deed.

27. Nietzsche, op. cit., 87.

28. Ibid., 127.

29. Ibid., 128.

30. Friedrich Nietzsche, *The Gay Science* (New York: Vintage Books, 1974), 320.

31. There has, in my opinion, been quite enough comment about O herself and why a woman would write about a woman who comes to desire her own oppression and violation. Jessican Benjamin worries about why we come to desire the dominant other through our development phases as gendered beings. She uses psychoanalysis as an alternative to "false consciousness" and/or internalized oppression. I am more interested in what the men want in the Castle of Roissy and what Rene wants in bringing O there. She is merely a sidenote, a body, a visible object of an inadequate, needy, uncertain masculine desire. The way the storyline treats the figure of O is exemplary of what Ann Cahill calls derivitization in her chapter in this volume.

32. It is important to note that I am referring to the novel and not the film in this discussion. The changes made in the film warrant a separate discussion in themselves. I will only briefly say here that the changes as I read them include a dash of female solidarity among the slaves at Roissy that is not in the book. Also, the movie ends suddenly with a signal as to the potential reversal of the master/slave relationship between Sir Stephen and O, a reversal which is not included in either of the alternative endings suggested in the book.

33. Mansfield, op. cit., 19.

34. Robin West, *Narrativity, Authority and Law* (Ann Arbor, MI: University of Michigan Press, 1994).
35. Mansfield, op. cit., 21
36. Savran, op. cit., 37.
37. Nietzsche, op. cit., 1974, 286.
38. Savran, op. cit., 37.
39. Mansfield, op. cit., 102.
40. Nietzsche, op. cit., 1989, 45.
41. I am not suggesting we 'sympathize' with the felt sense of crisis experienced by the male batterer or rapist as he describes his relationship to the victim. I am suggesting we should pay more attention to what they say about their crimes rather than rely on concepts of 'false consciousness' or 'denial' to interpret their words. Also, I am not trying to render perpetrators less than fully responsible for their actions by suggesting they are not ultimately acting as self-authorized or coherent subjects. I am suggesting that the paradigmatic model for understanding sexual violence, that of dominance and submission, does not capture the lived experience of perpetrators and victims of violence as they, themselves, describe it to psychoanalysts and researchers. If we are to deconstruct the terms on which violence is normalized in our society, we may want to shift our energies from insisting on the impenetrability of masculine power, to interrogating and exploiting the inconsistencies and historical variabilities of the masculine self.
42. Joanna Bourke, *Rape: A History from 1860 to the Present* (London: Virago Press, 2007) is a notable exception to this tendency.
43. Martha Mahoney, "Legal Images of Battered Women: Redefining Separation Assault" in *The Legal Response to Violence Against Women* (New York: Garland Publishers. 1997), 165–256.
44. Neil Jacobsen and John M. Gottman, *When Men Batter Women: New Insights Into Ending Abusive Relationships* (New York: Simon and Schuster, 1998).
45. Ibid., 116.
46. Adam Jukes, *Men Who Batter Women* (New York: Routledge, 1999), 135.
47. Zvi Eisikovits and Eli Buchbinder, "Talking Violent: a Phenomenological Study of Metaphors Battering Men Use," *Violence Against Women* 3, 5 (October 1997): 487.

7 Feminist Interrogations of Democracy, Sexual Violence, and the US Military

Meghana Nayak

In 2004, Seymour M. Hersh and others broke the Abu Ghraib prison abuse story, releasing descriptions and photographs of military personnel delighting in the sexual torture of Iraqi men. While pundits and the public alike called for then-Secretary of Defense Donald Rumsfeld's resignation and debated whether these abuses indicated an aberration from or the logical endpoint of military training, few were aware that the Department of Defense (DoD) was, at that very moment, in the process of crafting responses to ongoing relationship violence, sexual assault, and rape committed by US military personnel. Rather than dismiss the DoD's focus on sexual violence as hypocritical, I argue that these responses serve as a way for the military to entrench its importance and credibility. I further claim that the military's repertoire of responses should be interpreted in terms of how they shape how democracy is lived, understood, and practiced. I critique three specific areas in terms of how these efforts impact democratic life: (1) that they limit sociopolitical recognition rendering some people's experiences of sexual violence invisible and unimportant; (2) they reinforce a private/public divide, by legitimizing the military's public violence and dealing with the violence committed by military members through 'separate' rules and secrecy; and (3) they prevent dissent, by focusing on procedural mechanisms and circumscribing potentially critical discussions of militarization and its relationship to sexual violence.[1]

In effect, the issue of sexual violence can be deployed in ways that run counter to actually challenging its existence. For example, military policies treat sexual violence as an anomaly even while the military's very mission and presence relies on masculinist norms that perpetuate such violence. So, rather than assume all efforts to eradicate sexual violence are progressive and good, or expect the military to transform into a democratic space that can effectively tackle sexual violence, I want to shift the focus to why sexual violence occurs in the first place and to the varying effects of addressing sexual violence on democratic experiences and discourses. Indeed, supporting the military's efforts to address sexual violence only succeeds in propping up the military's supposedly honorable and necessary role in defending democracy. Instead, I critically assess the responses so as to reveal and challenge the type of military and masculinist ethos to which sexual violence is intrinsic as well as to question the role of the military in the democratic context.

The theoretical significance of my claims is three-fold: I open ways to explore how and why responses to sexual violence serve as ways to secure particular political agendas; I examine the implications that ensue when institutions, such as the military, that themselves sustain high levels of sexual violence, officially address such acts; and, I theorize democracy as a political project that can be reconstituted through political actors' reactions to violence. As to the first point, I claim that sexual violence has powerful political currency because of the success of advocates around the world in both documenting and holding accountable governments and individuals for such violence. The prolific scholarship on transnational advocacy networks shows how they have been able to press for policy changes, making sexual violence a necessary issue for many mainstream political actors to address if they are in the spotlight.[2] The issue of sexual violence is, in effect, a site for privileging and advocating ideas about what counts as sexual violence, why it occurs, and by and to whom, thereby allowing those responding, whether they are feminists, academics, the state, institutions and organizations, or social workers and advocates, to use the opportunity to advance particular political agendas and worldviews and to promote their own importance in improving people's lives.[3]

Regarding the second point, advocacy networks and the US Congress are pressing the military to increasingly institutionalize a set of official responses to sexual violence. As has been made clear by numerous feminist critiques of militarization, the military is complicit in perpetuating and relying upon sexual violence in both combat operations and the militarization of daily life and is committed to a violent, undemocratic political agenda. Thus, I seek to understand the effects when such an institution takes up sexual violence within its own ranks.[4]

As to the third point, feminist democracy theorists and those interested in the 'quality' of new, transitioning, postcolonial, and stable democracies, theorize democracy as a historically situated, socially constructed, immanently contested political project. As I will go on to discuss, this is why I focus on sociopolitical recognition, the politics of the private/public divide, and dissent, all of which get at the nuances of how democracy is 'lived' and articulated by various people in various ways. Accordingly, I ask: how are responses to undemocratic, violent acts shaping what democracy is and can be? Do responses to sexual violence increase recognition, confront the private/public divide, and encourage dissent in ways that invigorate democracy? Or, do they suture democracy to, perhaps, masculinist nationalism (the protection of the female body), neoliberalism (individual responsibility), national security (against the alleged criminal elements), or multiple other possibilities that simply reinforce power relationships? Do these responses challenge the underlying structures, discourses, and meanings that make sexual violence possible? Do they constitute democracy as a transformative political project for survivors of sexual violence, for gendered subjects who may be subject to the threat of various forms of such violence, for those who understand bodily integrity as crucial for democracy, or for those who see militarization and the military itself as a threat to democracy?

In the pages that follow and in order to address these issues, I first critically reposition and rethink democracy in terms of the themes mentioned previously: sociopolitical recognition, the public/private dyad, and dissent. I then trace the discourses and narratives that emerge in the texts of the Congressionally mandated DoD task force reports and related Congressional and DoD memos, statements, and policy changes. I also examine DoD reactions to specific incidents of sexual violence, and commentary and evidence gathered by organizations addressing military sexual violence. Here, the military will be understood as a constellation of actors, including the DoD, which formulates and coordinates policies, codes, and operations regarding security and warfare, and the component departments of the Army, Navy, Air Force, and the Marines, which are in turn responsible for implementing the DoD's directives through a chain-of-command system of training. After tracing how military responses to sexual violence shape sociopolitical recognition, the private/public divide, and dissent, I summarize and reflect on the implications of my claims.

CRITICALLY RETHINKING DEMOCRACY AS POLITICAL PROJECT

Mainstream democracy scholars seek to understand how well democracies evolve to meet a predefined set of conditions, including competition for electoral office, institutional arrangements and procedural mechanisms, economic growth, and liberal ideals such as individualism and civil/political rights. However, two sets of scholars, feminist democracy theorists and 'quality of democracy' scholars, offer ways to redefine democracy to be more in line with critical scholarship and lived experiences. Here I discuss and build on this scholarship to elucidate three particular themes of democracy.

The first set of scholars, feminist democracy theorists, generally interrogate how mainstream democracy studies pay insufficient attention to gender, much less sexual violence, at the cost of seeing how democracy is interpreted and contested via gendered identity and power relationships.[5] Feminist democratic theorists point out how misogyny and masculinity can be intrinsic to the terms of democracy's existence. Some, for example, have examined the interweaving of masculinist morale and national security, as well as the masculinist anxiety about and backlash against gender equality and parity, in new and 'established' democratic regimes.[6]

The second group of scholars is rooted in multiple disciplinary traditions and was galvanized by the 1980s and 1990s wave of democratization and negotiations with neoliberalism throughout Eastern Europe, Africa, Asia, and Latin America. These scholars specifically debate and grapple with human agency, participation, public discourses, and the quality of democratization in everyday life in "really existing democracies."[7] In particular, 'quality of democracy' scholars often explore the legitimacy and endurance of democracies in the face of various forms of violence, particularly that which is part of the legacy of prior authoritarian and colonial regimes. Accordingly, while many of these scholars do focus on procedural or liberal elements of democracy, a fair number examine how democracy can mask the persistence of violence, including sexual violence, in interpersonal interactions.[8] These two sets of scholars do not offer a sustained focus on or theory of sexual violence in the context of democracy. Thus, I leverage the work discussed thus far to inaugurate a more systematic, theoretical approach to better understand sexual violence in the context of democracy theory and the realities of democracies.

The first theme that emerges from this critical scholarship on democracy is sociopolitical recognition, which signals the ongoing inclusionary struggles to encompass multiple subjectivities and experiences in decision making at various levels. The circulating representations of and responses to people's subjective experiences and identities constitute whether various individuals and communities are recognized as 'mattering,' not only in terms of the rights discourse, identity politics, or raising awareness about issues, but also in terms of struggles regarding redistribution, decision making, responsibilities, and social justice. How do members of democratic societies represent themselves and each other? Are they, in their various relationships with civil society and the state, visible and valued by each other and through political discourses and decisions? Who receives privileges, and who is criminalized and marginalized?

Recognition is not limited to loyal citizen–subjects. Aihwa Ong challenges "how the universalistic criteria of democratic citizenship variously regulate different categories of subjects or how these subjects' location within the nation-state and within the global economy conditions the construction of their citizenship."[9] Indeed, countries use citizenship as a legal concept to regulate lives, resulting in the seepage of governmental discourses into people's lives and the creation of hierarchies of human value. Transitioning democracies, in resisting these tendencies, have turned to Truth and Reconciliation Commissions to lend nuance and complexity to the narrative of what democracy and citizenship mean and to challenge representations of some as disposable or of lesser value.

Embedded in the responses to sexual violence are assumptions about what counts as violence and whose suffering matters; I claim that these presumptions can shape sociopolitical recognition in certain ways. Do the responses highlight only certain experiences or demonize marginalized communities as the main perpetrators of sexual violence? Does the response to violence degrade the recognition of the survivor and obscure why the violence occurred?

The second theme is the private/public divide, or the presumption of mutually exclusive public and private spheres. Carole Pateman specifically points to creation of the private sphere in the social contract as a way to provide to men unlimited sexual access to women.[10] As such, feminist democracy theorists argue that the very division between public and private spheres serves patriarchal and racial power but at the same time is useful for feminists to be able to speak about and politicize the 'personal' and the 'private.'[11] To experience democracy as transformative requires a sustained critique of the private/public divide, to see, for instance, if it is indeed possible to "loosen citizenship from its almost exclusively public location . . . [to lodge] bodies in their physical and social particularities."[12]

This gets at the construction and deployment of the public sphere as the 'civilized' arena of debate, often for and by only certain political actors. So-called private experiences, such as sex, parenting, abortion, birth, suffering, disease, and death are simultaneously denied their place in public debates about rights (for example, the right to health care, reproductive rights, and sexual subjectivity) and subjected to intrusive disciplinary control by the state. And, it is not coincidental that the removal of public transparency of and deliberative discussion about financial transactions, industries, and social services is called privatization. As Coole notes, we cannot magically deconstruct the cartographic project of the public/private dyad, but we can politicize, challenge, and trace the dyad's effects so as to imagine and experiment with different discursive fields and spatializations.[13]

Do responses to sexual violence dictate that men must 'protect' women, or that violence should be resolved 'privately'? Perhaps some forms of violence, such as militarization, prison rape, and marital rape, are tolerated, but others, such as 'stranger in the alley' rape and heterosexual relationship abuse, are not. These presumptions are predicated upon and perpetuate the understanding that some things are private, to be left in the dark excesses, to not enter the public realm of (often controlled) discourse that in many ways pivots on normative, legal identifications of the offender and the victim. The public/private dyad is central to democracy as a disciplinary political project, as the division serves to regulate the boundaries between the acceptable and the unacceptable, and governs how we talk about certain forms of sexual violence while obscuring/ignoring the existence of others. Through responses to sexual violence, can we possibly challenge the political projects for which bodies are marshaled?

The third issue is dissent, or the questioning and challenging of whether political principles and practices are fair and just as well as the creating of space to voice such issues. Political theorists understand dissidence as political courage, disobedience, and resistance to and reimagining of power relationships.[14] Feminist democratic analysis illustrates the necessity of articulating and unmasking power relationships and of using oppositional, contestatory, performative political action to invigorate creativity, spontaneity, and intersubjective political relationships.[15] Quality of democracy scholars note that democracies are capable of silencing and condemning dissent, particularly when powerful sociopolitical forces label protest, contestation, opposition, or experiences of marginalized communities as unpatriotic and a disturbance to the political order, freedom, and the existence of democracy itself.

Often, political actors enact sexual violence as retribution against dissent, particularly in political conflicts, but they can also use the actual responses to sexual violence to suppress dissident politics. Political actors responding to sexual violence might blame dissident groups or marginalized communities for the existence of such violence, or they might try to penalize or criminalize men from marginalized communities for allegedly 'causing' sexual violence.[16] Do responses to sexual violence serve as a strategic way to shut down dissent? If those responding to sexual violence do so for politically expedient reasons, such as promoting their own importance and world view or criminalizing certain groups, then are they really meaningfully challenging the structures, practices, representations, and discourses that allow such violence to occur in the first place?

Also, while politico-legal institutionalized mechanisms have their place and appeal, they also problematically place an incredible emphasis on the power of the law and the state to protect the marginalized.[17] As such, it might be problematic to privilege such mechanisms over dissidence as a way to deal with sexual violence. When Nivedita Menon explores anti-rape laws in India, she discovers that:

> in the case of sexual violence, once 'rape' can be proved in legal terms, its harm is not in question . . . What if our struggle were rather to emancipate ourselves from the very meaning of rape? Does the ever-present threat of sexual violence flow from the locating of the 'female' self inside the sexually defined body of woman?[18]

In other words, advocates often focus on establishing rape as a crime and on creating legal mechanisms to help victims prove that such a crime occurred. While in many ways this is a crucial step, what goes unchallenged is why rape happens and whether we presume that it is always an eventuality for women, in particular. Anti-rape laws might simply confirm that rape will continue to occur, without an end in sight. Indeed, our responses often presume that the institutions that constrain our possibilities in the first place are the only ways through which we can address sexual violence, perhaps leading us to believe that there is nothing we can ultimately do about the meaning and existence of sexual violence. Heberle notes that our attempts to empathetically respond to sexual violence survivors by listening, describing, raising awareness, and—ultimately—pushing for legal intervention, focus on the ever-growing threat of sexual violence; but, this approach could very well confer totality and coherence onto the quite fragile, fractured, and illegitimate assemblage of masculinist dominance.[19] Might we imagine that sexual violence is actually possible to resist, through responses to sexual violence that help to radically push the limits of democracy, to recognize the limits of and subvert the political actors and structures that oppress, and to open and use some space for dissidence and contestation?

In posing these three indicators, it becomes clear that democracy could be a political project for achieving more peaceful, just, and progressive communities, particularly if multiple identities are recognized and valued, the public/private division is challenged, and dissent is encouraged. Or, it may inevitably be intertwined with neoliberal globalization, national security, economic growth, or militarization, all of which insist on the recognition of only certain experiences, rely upon the public/private divide, and find dissent threatening. Surely, both (and more) versions of democracy exist simultaneously. The focus of this chapter is how responses to sexual violence, in this case, those shaped by the US DoD, can matter for shaping democracy for different communities in various circumstances.

THE CONSTRUCTION OF OFFICIAL MILITARY RESPONSES TO SEXUAL VIOLENCE

As feminists have noted, militarization involves the increased influence of the DoD's decision makers in forming national policy; exceptional weight is accorded to the importance of the military in that an understanding of security as protection from those constructed as enemies and threats within and outside of national borders drives the organizing and diverting of corporate, media, governmental, and societal activity towards the expectation of militarist conflict as a way to solve problems.[20] In order to militarize, the military disciplines bodies to fight for and defend militarized national policy. It also uses sexual violence as a tool to break down the enemy, to punish resistance to the military's goals, and to assert the military's strength and disciplinary power, thus leading to the rape of local women and girls in international military bases and war zones and sexual torture and assault of male and female prisoners of war. Accordingly, my overarching claim is that military efforts to confront sexual violence are paradoxical given the central role that masculinity and violence play in the existence of the military. At the same time, it is important to not dismiss the military's responses to sexual violence, precisely so we can locate and trace how the responses themselves actually reveal the military's priorities, undergird the military's alleged role in 'defending' democracy, and deflect attention away from the reasons for sexual violence. In the pages that follow, I explore how the DoD, as an institution decidedly invested in US militarization, approaches the issue of military sexual violence.

When the DoD, research organizations, and Congress started to conduct task forces, commissions, panels, and reports on sexual violence in 1988, the documents produced strictly focused on incidents of military sexual violence and discrimination against US civilians and on those that took the form of relationship violence, assault in military academies, and attacks on US female soldiers in military theaters.[21] Several topics and issues related to sexual violence were and continue to be off the table, particularly regarding non-American victims. For the most part, these particular reports did not result in substantial criminal investigations or permanent changes in DoD policy.

During the 1980s and 1990s, sexual violence prevention advocates persistently pushed Congress to mandate the DoD to construct permanent, systematic policies regarding the specific types of violence Congress was willing to acknowledge. Congress finally started to respond by the 1990s and early 2000s with the formation of three task forces. But only some of the advocacy organizations that had testified before Congress served on or had consultative status on these task forces. Organizations such as Stop Military Rape, the Military Rape Crisis Center, and Survivors Take Action Against Abuse by Military Personnel, that held explicitly critical views of the military and militarization, either opted out of or were (and continue to be) actively left out of DoD policy making. Organizations, advocates, and experts with concerns about non-US victims/survivors of military sexual violence have had a difficult time even gaining access to Congress, relying instead on speak outs, academic journals, feminist and human rights organizations, and other sites geared towards not only documenting specific cases but also challenging militarization as such.

The formation of the first DoD official policy on relationship violence was founded in the work of The Miles Foundation, a nonprofit organization dedicated to assisting women and children affected by interpersonal violence in the military. This organization collects case histories, consults with media outlets, compiles and presents Congressional briefings, and works in a coalition of sexual violence prevention advocates. Their work eventually resulted in the January 1999 CBS 60 Minutes special, The War at Home, which aired findings about the astronomically rising rates of relationship violence in the military and the significantly higher rate (three to five times higher) of relationship violence among military couples than civilian ones.[22] In response to civilian lobbying about this issue, in October 1999, the Domestic Violence Provision (sec. 581) of the Congressional National Defense Authorization Act for Fiscal Year 2000 mandated that a task force be formed to provide recommendations to the DoD so as to encourage long term, strategic planning to eliminate this violence and to reassess old DoD methods and mechanisms, such as the decades-old Family Advocacy Program, of addressing sexual violence.

The task force, comprised twelve members of the DoD, the Department of Justice, and the Department of Health and Human Resources as well as twelve civilian advocates, such as the National Training Center on Domestic and Sexual Violence and the Battered Women's Justice Project/Domestic Violence Resource Network, submitted its first report in February 2001 to then-Secretary of Defense Donald Rumsfeld, with a follow-up report and final report issued in March 2003.[23] The task force report argues that relationship violence could occur at the hands of spouses, those who shared a child, and current/former intimate partners, referring all other cases to civilian services.[24] The definition is predicated on the assumption of relationship abuse between those of the opposite sex; while allowing that it can occur to men, the "Don't Ask Don't Tell" policy preempts any focus on sexual violence between same-sex partners. The report made 194 recommendations, setting in motion struggles over the definition of relationship abuse and violence. Further, the report included claims about the need for a 'culture' shift that held offenders accountable, requiring command awareness of mechanisms to address violence, jurisdictional issues on and off base, victim advocacy, early intervention, fatality rates, the importance of confidentiality and reporting mechanisms, and continual evaluation. Each year since, the National Defense Authorization Act, available on the DoD website, makes recommendations including, for example, adjustments to the definition of relationship violence, the improvement of forensic examinations of victims of violence, and the need to support the children of those murdered by relationship violence.

In 2003, military bases started to enforce civilian protective orders. However, victims still struggled with the lack of confidentiality, a limited form of which was granted to rape survivors on military bases. At the behest of civilian advocates who served on the task force, by June 2005 for sexual assault victims and by January 2006 for victims of relationship violence, the military instituted restricted reporting policy, which gives violence survivors two options: first, they can make an official report that will trigger a formal investigation; second, they can request confidential medical help and counseling but with no involvement or action taken by military commanders. But by 2006, Congress' Government Accountability Office noted that while the DoD had implemented 2/3 of the recommendations, it was falling short in monitoring command officials' compliance with reporting and confidentiality procedures, providing complete data on its Defense Incident-Based Reporting System and the Family Advocacy Program Central Registry, creating and training domestic violence response coordinator positions at military bases, and communicating policies effectively.[25]

Soon thereafter, stories emerged in 2004 about rampant sexual harassment and assault at the US Military Academy in West Point, NY, and the US Naval Academy in Annapolis, MD, surfaced. These cases followed the 2003 revelation that US Air Force Academy in Colorado Springs, Colorado reprimanded female cadets for reporting sexual assault. Although the DoD had issued reports on the care of sexual assault victims and the numbers of reported rapes and sexual assaults within the military, it had not ventured into constructing an official response to violence in military academies. Thus, advocacy groups successfully framed the 2004 scandal as one of many, including the 1991 Tailhook assaults and the 1997 Aberdeen training ground assaults, that would continue to plague military gatherings, associations, and academies, unless Congress acted. As such, Congress mandated a task force comprising military officials from the four branches of the armed forces and civilian representatives of advocacy groups, such as the Pennsylvania Coalition Against Rape. The task force issued a set of several recommendations for improving what it noted was a 'hostile' climate in military academies and a poor system for responding to assaults and harassment.[26]

The report suggests that sexual violence could be prevented if military academies could shift their cultures to incorporate and understand the 'value' of women. In other words, male members of the academies must recognize that women can and do provide "intellect, discipline, dedication, and leadership"; the report carefully comments that the "expansion of women's roles was a carefully crafted strategy based on operational requirements, not on equal opportunity or political correctness."[27] The idea is that so long as men believe that women do not 'belong' and contribute to the military, harassment and assault are more likely to happen. Another crucial step in the military's strategy, according to the report, is to revamp awareness by integrating classes on sexual harassment within the course curriculum, particularly in regularly scheduled classes and those addressing military leadership and ethics. As a result of the report's studies, the DoD launched specific pages and links on its website to reaffirm its commitment to encouraging the implementation of the recommendations.

Around the same time, in February 2004, as a response to several cases of sexual assault of service members in theaters of war and military bases abroad such as in Iraq and Kuwait, a January 25, 2004, Denver Post article on the lack of effective and thorough support for such victims, and pressure by organizations working with military families, then-Secretary of Defense Rumsfeld directed a review of the DoD's treatment and care of sexual assault victims. A few months later, the DoD Care for Victims of Sexual Assault Task Force, comprising members of DoD components and departments with limited consultation with civilian advocates such as the Rape, Abuse, and Incest National Network and the Miles Foundation, released a report of recommendations to rectify what it called an inconsistent and incomplete services for sexual assault victims.[28] Soon after the report was issued, the National Alliance to End Sexual Violence and the Miles Foundation submitted written testimony to the Total Force Subcommittee of the Armed Services Committee in the House of Representatives, noting that the report failed to thoroughly interrogate sexual assault prevention, perpetrator behavior, the problematic military cultural climate, and community safety.

As a result, in October 2004, the DoD Leadership Summit reached consensus on a response to the recommendations and the complaints; the DoD thus established the Pentagon's Joint Task Force for Sexual Assault Prevention and Response as a single point of accountability and promised to implement the recommendations, especially those suggesting sexual assault response coordinators and victim advocates for all armed services. For the first time, in 2005, Directive Type Memorandums were issued that included a checklist on how commanders could respond to and support victims.[29] Also, the DoD finally switched its characterization of sexual assault from "inappropriate behavior" to "criminal behavior."[30] But critiques of the task force's work include allegations by members of Congress, advocates, and academics alike, that the recommendations, while expressing the need for better services and training regarding sexual violence both before and during deployment, are vague and less detailed than other DoD reports[31] and pay very little attention to the role and accountability of perpetrators of violence.[32] Since the summit, the DoD has failed to attend to or resolve several of the issues raised in the task forces even while it consistently refers to the task force recommendations as the basis of its policy.

SOCIOPOLITICAL RECOGNITION

While the texts of the three reports and many of the subsequent DoD press releases and memos indicate a genuine desire to eliminate sexual violence, I claim that the military's responses limit sociopolitical recognition in several ways. First, sexual violence only matters to the extent that it interferes with the military's progress in being 'mission-ready' and that it draws attention to issues that are antithetical to the military's understanding of its own 'values.' Second, the actual experiences of all survivors of military violence are not represented, visible, and valued but rather downplayed and depoliticized, due to both DoD cover-ups and negligence. Third, the responses fail to thoroughly and diligently understand why sexual violence occurs, presuming that such violence is simply statistically higher within larger groups of men and pathologizing actual incidents as psychological disturbances.

As to the first point, the military regularly issues public statements, which clearly situate sexual violence as an offense to the institution of the military. As noted on the DoD Public Awareness page on the National Domestic Violence Hotline website:

> Domestic violence is a crime that ruins families, weakens communities and *undermines military readiness*. With this campaign, we are calling on our service men, women and their families to Take a Stand Against Domestic Violence. (emphasis added)[33]

And, then-Deputy Secretary of Defense Paul Wolfowitz noted, echoing and foreshadowing several DoD memos on the matter, "domestic violence is an offense against the institutional values of the military."[34] Also, as the DoD report on relationship violence declares in the introductory overview, "doing everything possible to prevent incidents of domestic violence within our military communities, and dealing effectively with both victims and offenders when incidents do occur, is not only the right thing to do, it is a military necessity."[35] Other comments speak to fears that reports of sexual violence will chip away at the faith Americans have in the military.

Furthermore, members of the DoD express disbelief as to whether there is even a significant problem.[36] And, the Fiscal Year 2007 National Defense Authorization Act comments:

> Crime rates committed by members of the armed forces are generally lower than those in the general public. Nevertheless, a number of high profile assaults have resulted in increased congressional oversight, scrutiny and legislative interest in the policies concerning the prevention, reporting and handling of these cases.[37]

In a 2004 House of Representatives Panel on the Prevention of Sexual Assault in the Military, Vic Snyder (D–AR) argued that the military usually "led the way on social change" but unfortunately not on the issue of sexual assault.[38] Indeed, those who can accept that sexual violence at the hands of military members is actually worthy of concern, to the point of supporting the task forces' activities, cannot imagine why it actually happens, since they see sexual violence as incompatible with, rather than as embedded within, the military.

Even the simple attempt to remove sexual assault victims from the proximity of the alleged offenders proves difficult in the war zone, because of the priority of military needs. As the report on the care of sexual assault victims comments: "One commander noted that the movement of one or both trained service members out of a unit supporting a critical warfighting mission could significantly erode its ability to accomplish it, particularly if either party performed a critical skill."[39] At the same time, often victims did not want to be relocated and were not consulted before doing so. And, in the end, as the report notes through its interviews, "[s]ome commands communicated, either directly or indirectly, that 'the mission' comes first."[40]

The military cannot 'see' how pervasive, traumatic, and endemic sexual violence is because of what it believes the military represents: honor, loyalty, protection of freedom and democracy. Indeed, the report on the military academies comments that aggressive peer loyalty can contribute to both incidents of sexual assault and lack of political will to report such violence. But at the same time it suggests that these institutions' cultures can be redefined according to the military's most highly trumpeted value, honor, which somehow would deter violence from happening.[41] The report also notes that these schools have higher standards of honor than others. Honor is never defined, but feminists understand 'honor' as a masculinist code which prompts killing and violence to defend and reclaim it, and military personnel to either laud or ignore their buddies' rapes and assaults against Americans and foreigners.[42]

This point brings us to the second issue—the devaluation of sexual violence victims and survivors. When certain groups of victims are simply not acknowledged, it not only highlights the hypocrisy of military 'honor' but severely delimits democratic possibilities of all people mattering. The preliminary and final reports of the task force on domestic violence, for example, did not go into depth about relationship violence fatalities. In turn, the military and Congress did not push the task force to do so even as relationship violence fatalities increased as soldiers returned from new wars in Afghanistan and Iraq. For example, in the summer of 2002, after the Domestic Violence Task Force issued its first report, four special operatives soldiers who had recently returned from a tour in Afghanistan murdered their civilian wives on the Fort Bragg, North Carolina, military base; two of the soldiers then committed suicide, and another woman murdered her soldier husband. Although refusing to explore the health effects of depleted uranium weapons, the DoD took an interest in the soldiers' health and speculated that the relationship violence in the Fort Bragg cases resulted from the violent side effects of the prophylactic Larium; the DoD accordingly sent an epidemiological team, the US Army Epidemiological Consultation (EPICON) to Fort Bragg.[43] EPICON found no links to Larium and declared the root causes to be "marital problems" and a flawed military mental health system.[44] While EPICON's report did acknowledge that the Army's attempts to address relationship violence were hampered by entrenched military attitudes, it did not address privacy and confidentiality protocols, even though the process of forming DoD policy was already in motion.[45]

Anthropology professor Catherine Lutz points out that the military, and some media, framed the male soldiers in the Fort Bragg cases as the ultimate victims, with the murdered wives as a "sign of [their] sacrifice and [their] pain."[46] Lutz suggests this "sacrificial logic" shifted the attention from the murders to the military's importance, particularly in the context of needing to boost military morale, to valorize soldiers, and to recruit larger numbers of soldiers.[47] As such, the actual suffering of violated bodies became something that paled in comparison to the centrality of the military in defending our freedom.

The US Army Investigator, Congress, and the DoD have also avoided thorough investigations of sexual violence against Iraqi and Afghani civilians and US female soldiers during wartime, the exception being the highly publicized Abu Ghraib case. The task forces and follow-up reports and memos failed to discuss the Abu Ghraib case or related examples of the use of military sexual torture and abuse of non-American prisoners, the numerous cases in which the DoD covered up murders of US female soldiers as due to combat-related injuries or suicide, despite sufficient evidence of sexual violence,[48] or the cases in which US service members involved in gang rapes and murders of Iraqi and Afghani civilians were declared "unfit" through DoD-ordered psychiatric exams and triaged into a federal trial and out of the military's hands.[49] The families of many of the US victims have allied with social justice organizations to bring attention to their relatives' cases and to the military's cover-ups or refusals to conduct thorough investigations.[50] Journalists such as Helen Benedict and Sara Corbett have been and are currently collecting and corroborating evidence of rampant rates of rape against female soldiers and non-American civilians in Afghanistan and Iraq.[51] Anti-war organizations are bringing Americans' attention to sexual violence against non-Americans. But, given these victims' glaring absence from the task forces' research, recommendations, and commentaries, it is clear that in the context of military responses to sexual violence, some victims are simply disposable.

Regarding the third point, understanding the cause of sexual violence is particularly important in recognizing and valuing the experiences of survivors. The military does not understand or seem to want to understand why sexual violence is occurring. All three task forces downplay the higher rates of sexual violence among military populations, thus minimizing the explanations we might find by comparing civilian and military sexual violence. At the same time, the report on violence in the military academies suggests that sexual violence is related to the culture of academic institutions, where the majority of students are young adult males exposed to casual attitudes towards sex, drugs, and alcohol.[52] And, according to a February 2008 talk at the Minnesota Advocates for Human Rights by Loretta Frederick and Connie Sponsler, affiliated with the Battered Women's Justice and involved in military-civilian collaboration on addressing sexual violence, relationship violence should also be understood in the context of concentrated populations of young men.[53] Sexual violence, then, is not represented as a highly pervasive problem in the military but as a phenomenon that is related to the demographics that just so happen to exist in the military. The report on the care of sexual assault victims provides more nuance regarding the causes of sexual violence but refers mainly to military workplace factors, or patterns and indicators within military climates, that would indicate increased likelihood of sexual violence incidents.[54] It does not, however, examine the military itself as a place that valorizes, specializes in, or trains in violence. The interpretation of research findings by both DoD and certain civilian advocates suggests that violence is incidental and is not related to what the young men are actually learning or being trained to do in terms of warfare. All they consider, then, are idiosyncratic behaviors, rather than investigating how sexual violence relates to the discipline, order, and violence that is so integral to war making.

Importantly, the military academies' report claims: "[p]ower is highly correlated with abuse. Experience in the military services has demonstrated that this phenomenon has no cultural, gender, or racial boundaries."[55] Recommendation 29C of this report suggests that the DoD "address the military ethos as it relates to the appropriate use of force and aggression within the profession of arms."[56] While the commentary seems to be a moment of progressive, self reflection by the military about how power and aggression do somehow matter for why sexual violence occurs, it focuses on aggression within the military rather than in relation to militarization. Thus, while admitting that the military is male dominated, there is no understanding that, more importantly, the military is masculinist. The military is not simply a profession of arms or a politically neutral institution that spreads and stands for 'good' values but is bound up with masculinity. As such, the nuances of how a masculinized, militarized environment creates the possibility of sexual violence are lost. And, given that the same report encourages more awareness and discussion on the value, importance, and capabilities of women in the military, the task force does seem to be aware that gendered ideas do play a role in incidents of sexual violence. Are the assumptions, statements, and contradictions discussed earlier indicative of the growing pains of a slowly evolving commitment to truly addressing sexual violence, or of the way the DoD will continue to gloss over, sidestep, and downplay the issues? Some advocacy groups might find promise in DoD narratives about sexual violence, but this might be because the recommendations echo their own understandings of sexual violence as pathological and incidental.

Even when the military acknowledges the abuse of power, the reports often slip into framing sexual violence as an isolated and solely psychological issue: a moment of disturbance, explosion, or insanity. All three reports place a large, explicit emphasis on mental health issues and psychological services and on defining sexual violence as a public health concern. This is not to say that mental and emotional health is irrelevant for offenders, survivors, families, and friends; rather, it is to point to the depoliticization of sexual violence in which many civilian advocates participate as well. Even with the potential to implement hundreds of recommendations, the DoD, among other things, focuses on the 'intention' and psychological state of the perpetrator rather than on the assault itself, attempts to portray a neutral stance while at the same time often questioning victim responsibility, reliability, and mental health, and consistently fails to rely upon existing procedures for long term treatment and handling of sexual assault victims.[57] Organizations and journalists are carefully watching as an increasing number of sexual violence cases come to light: will Congress and the DoD be able to recognize survivors and victims in ways that make bodily, family, and community security matter as much as national security does to US democracy? In the meantime, I claim that the discussion thus far illustrates the difficulty the military experiences in adequately responding to sexual violence because it, unsurprisingly, does not challenge the 'mission,' 'values,' and attitudes that are central to the military's existence.

THE PUBLIC/PRIVATE DIVIDE

My second claim is that the US military's responses to ongoing sexual violence help to keep a particular type of private/public divide intact. The military ensures that it responds in ways that legitimize the public violence of wars, at the behest of the state. At the same time, the military firmly holds together a private, secretive network of military academies, laws, regulations, and values that are not entirely subject to public debate and discussion. The military's responses to sexual violence allow little challenge to the military's perception that it is separate from the public; yet, they also show the military's need for public recognition and support for its public violence in war making.

Recall the claim in the previous section that the military responds to sexual violence in ways that valorize the military's own importance over the experiences and needs of victims and survivors. What it also does is create a division between the acceptable (public war) and unacceptable (certain forms of relationship and acquaintance rape and assault) forms of violence. The goal of labeling sexual violence (or at least the attention to it) as unacceptable, is not only to protect the image and representation of the military but also to allow the military to continue without interruption in its business of training people in warfare and potential attack on designated enemies. As noted in an interview with a Special Forces soldier, he "was once arrested for domestic violence, [and] told [the interviewers] that Memorial Day ceremonies always left him pondering why he would get medals for killing others in battle but would be arrested if he killed his wife."[58] Carol Cohn comments that technostrategic language that is purportedly integral for national security operations also dehumanizes both those who use the language and those who are the targets.[59] As such, soldiers come home to family members after experiencing a specific training to break down the natural aversion to killing. Dehumanizing military training may create good soldiers, but they then have problems readjusting to healthy intimate and interpersonal relationships. In effect, masculinity cultivated in a militarist context thrives in non-military spaces as well, particularly when military training does not differentiate between the types of interaction, level of aggression, or reactivity one must use in military and civilian spaces.

The report on the care of sexual assault victims mentions the context of the 'combat theater' numerous times but barely gets into what happens in the combat theater, as it not only wants to refrain from questioning the military's 'values' and importance but also the very activities in which the military engages. At the same time, the report implies that the public duties of the military are what might prevent adequate assistance for victims of sexual assault. As Finding 27 states:

> It is possible the unavailability and workload of investigative agents also may have been a reason why a number of sexual assaults reported in the combat theater were first investigated by the command rather than by investigative agencies with appropriate expertise . . . Some investigators acknowledged that current shortages in investigative resources within the combat theater might mean they would have to rely on 'reach back' capability. Furthermore, the focus of their efforts was on trying to gather intelligence and protect U.S. personnel from enemy forces.[60]

So, while the military has finally acknowledged that sexual violence is a crime, its more important role is the public violence of war. It thereby segregates the two types of violence.

One way the military attempts to control the type of attention sexual violence receives is to create separate rules about responding to it. These rules, even when subject to scrutiny of civilian advocates, remain under the control of the military, and, based on the task force reports, at most we know that the military does not even always abide by them. The task force reports do try to negotiate this issue. Despite noting that there is a perceived lack of privacy and confidentiality and a lack of education about the fairness and balance of the military justice system,[61] the task force report on the care of sexual assault victims expresses concern about the lack of comparability between civilian laws on sexual harassment, sexual misconduct, and sexual assault, and the Uniform Code of Military Justice, wherein sexual assault is not a specific offense but a catchall category.[62] And, the report on domestic violence reveals that the DoD issued an interim policy in 1997 to implement the Lautenberg Amendment to the Gun Control Act of 1968, which prevents the Armed Services from issuing firearms to or recruiting people convicted of relationship violence; the task force pushes for the creation of a permanent policy.[63] Also, Recommendation 16 of the report on sexual violence in military academies argues that Congress should revise current sexual misconduct statutes to more clearly address the wide range of sexual assault/harassment behaviors, including acquaintance and date rape. This move is important, as indicated by the attempts by US Representative Loretta Sanchez (D–CA), one of the leading advocates of rape prevention within the military, to replace the military's antiquated 1950s sexual assault laws within the Uniform Code of Military Justice with the type of language encompassed in federal and most state laws.

The DoD admits such change should be reviewed but persistently stalls, perhaps because it would set the precedent of chiseling away at the distinctness of military law. When certain cases of sexual violence either elicit too much media attention, as in the cases of US soldiers gang raping Iraqi girls, or prove to be daunting for the limited services on military installations, the military at its discretion sometimes pushes the cases into the civilian world, particularly if there is a high level of cooperation between a particularly military installation and local civilian authorities and advocates. At the same time, as acknowledged by a recent April 9, 2008, Senate Committee on Foreign Relations statement about sexually assaulted Americans in war zones, the DoD has not been able to clearly resolve the conflict over civilian jurisdiction, allowing many military offenders to avoid trial. In other words, we simply do not know enough about military rules and definitions, since they are perpetually under revision and consideration, making public accountability difficult.

The DoD also uses different rules of confidentiality and privacy from those used in the civilian world. In fact, the latest DoD Report on Sexual

Assault in the Military for Fiscal Year 2007 raises the problem that civilian mandatory rape reporting laws in some states pose for the military's ability to protect the privacy, confidentiality, and safety of victims who are left without a choice about the restricted reporting mechanisms described earlier.[64] Rather than putting the needs of the victim first, the military is attempting to work around its own confidentiality rules, secrecy of the military, the military structure of obedience and duty, and the real possibility of retribution against victims in a military climate. Advocates Frederick and Sponsler applaud the restricted reporting option, noting that the extensive control the DoD exercises over all aspects of military personnel's lives is conducive to guaranteeing some type of action in cases of relationship violence.[65] While Frederick and Sponsler acknowledge that action is dependent on the "command discretion," wherein it is against military law for any civilian to have any influence, these advocates accept that the military is a "great place" for an intervention because of military "ownership" of military bodies and activities.[66]

This commentary is fascinating, as is that by other advocates, particularly those approving of the fact that the restricted reporting policy came from the 'top down,' i.e. from the Pentagon's Joint Task Force on Sexual Assault Prevention and Response.[67]

The idea that the military would respect and prevent the suffering of the people it 'owns' is at least somewhat belied by the discussion about sociopolitical recognition. Further, the military's continued segregation from the public, civil sphere and its possession and ownership of bodies does not actually challenge the existence of violence but simply attempts to manage Congressional and public scrutiny about it.

The military, although it collaborates with civilian advocates on these task forces, does not respond to actual incidents of sexual violence in ways that are transparent or in line with civilian laws and policies. The rationale is that doing so would damage the essence of the military structure. The control over men and women's bodies, to the point of attempting to control how someone might report an assault, is not about responding to sexual violence but about demonstrating the military's perceived right to possess every element of soldiers' intimate lives.

It is not surprising to anyone who has studied the military that it pivots on the control of bodies. After all, the military officially discourages sex between soldiers yet encourages male virility through distribution of condoms and pornography and cultivates a highly charged sexual atmosphere, simultaneously strictly monitoring women's right to end pregnancies that may result from consensual sex or assault.[68] The military also restricts the rights of US service members to obtain abortions in DoD facilities.[69] President Clinton lifted the military ban on abortions President Reagan first instituted in 1988, but Republican-controlled Congress reinstituted it in 1995. The idea is that a restriction on abortions discourages sex between service members and unintentional pregnancies.[70] It is, then, problematic for advocates and feminists to expect that an institution that promotes the premise that men and women cannot decide what happens to their bodies, might be able to respond sensitively and appropriately to sexual violence.

So, we may not expect anything different from the military or even some advocacy networks working with the DoD, but I contend that we must trace the ways in which responses to sexual violence are in fact deployed as means to manage and control lives, to better understand the military's role in democracy and to recognize that it is important not just *that* but *how* we respond to sexual violence. The increasing impetus for military-civilian collaboration is theoretically important for challenging the public/private issues discussed here. From the point of view of some of the advocates, the task forces have provided opportunities for the military and civilians to find points of mutual respect, communication, and accountability.[71] But an analysis of the texts reveal that there are boundaries around and limits to what can be discussed; further, the insistence on separate rules allows the military to, in a sense, resolve violence as it sees fit, without being held accountable to the general public, much less to the survivors of violence themselves. As a consequence, I claim that if the military reifies the public/private divide through its responses to sexual violence, then we must question whether the military itself is antithetical to the kind of democratic project that radically challenges this binary and opens up new possibilities for how people experience their lives.

DISSENT

My third claim is that the responses discussed thus far sharply limit the very ability to have conversations about the military's relationship to sexual violence and also privilege institutionalized responses and mechanisms over the type of dissent that is necessary to radically challenge the conditions in which sexual violence becomes so prevalent. Despite the DoD's insistence on separation from the civilian world, its official statements echo the way many advocates approach sexual violence. It makes sense that most advocates would advise the DoD to respond as they would, as they tend to seek to leverage democratic channels to address sexual violence. For example, the freedoms of association and expression allow speak outs, consciousness-raising workshops, and Take Back the Night rallies to raise awareness about sexual violence; accountable judiciaries, police forces, and legislatures enable legislators, lawyers and police to create laws and mandates to protect victims; and, the rule of law ensures that all perpetrators will experience due process and a trial for assaulting victims. Surely, advocates might reason, these principles can be applied to the military with some success, even with its undemocratic structure. In fact, since the DoD's 2005 decision to better coordinate its responses to sexual violence, it has, in conjunction with civilian advocates, promised to focus on key issues such as training standards for victim responders, better reporting methods, acknowledgment of victims' fear of punishment and retribution for reporting crimes, a need for preventative techniques, and increased collaboration with civilian services. Like advocates, the DoD apparently focuses on behavioral patterns, gender-sensitive education and training, reliance on infrastructural support, and the immediate safety and confidentiality of victims and their families.[72]

But is it the case that collaboration and this array of responses is the most appropriate for challenging sexual violence within the military? Even if the DoD does eventually start to better integrate the 'civilian' approach, despite evidence that it does not seek to do so in actual sexual violence cases, I ask: will increased evaluation, assessment, and movement towards certain goals, such as victim advocates at every military installation and systematized training on sexual violence prevention, make a palpable difference in the intimate relationship between the military and sexual violence? On the one hand, we might want military responses to sexual violence to be in line with civilian responses, so that the military is more public and transparent and so as to challenge the secrecy of the military sphere. On the other hand, perhaps doing so will have its own set of consequences for the possibility of dissent.

Because they impact sociopolitical recognition and perpetuate the private/public divide, I suggest that the military's responses actually keep intact the structures and practices that enable sexual violence to occur at such a pervasive, ongoing rate within the military. I challenge, for instance, the merit of the introductory remarks for the task force's report on relationship violence:

> As the nation's largest employer, the DoD sponsors the largest 'employer based' domestic violence prevention and intervention program in the country. This provides the DoD with a unique opportunity to contribute substantively to the nation's overall effort in this area. The DoD has already made a significant commitment of manpower and financial resources to address the problem of domestic violence, but, like civilian communities, the DoD can and must continue to improve its response to this national problem.[73]

The military is hardly the best environment for struggles against sexual violence, so we should challenge any advocates supporting the notion that DoD is an excellent site for crafting and implementing a sustained response to sexual violence.

It is the case that the DoD creates more and more policies and endless training seminars, surveys, memos, assessments, and promises. When media or advocates point to the rise in official statistics of sexual violence crimes committed by the military, the DoD responds that the reporting mechanisms must be working; at the same time, the military comments that the persistence of sexual violence is due to the lack of awareness by victims, offenders, and military command about the resources available. The assumption is that procedures, in and of themselves, will somehow prevent or address sexual violence cases. For example, the task forces seem to accord with the emphasis on 'awareness-building,' a key component of the anti-sexual violence movement. The idea is that more education, training, and consciousness about the existence of sexual violence will help to prevent sexual violence. Recommendation 27A, in particular, suggests a curriculum with an emphasis on the following areas:

> implications of sexual harassment and assault for military readiness; personal safety, prevention, and risk reduction; human sexuality and mature and healthy interaction; factors contributing to sexual harassment and assault (e.g., gender-motivated assault, toleration/bystander phenomenon, etc.); military leadership strategies for preventing and/or responding to sexual harassment or assault; awareness of contemporary youth culture and attitudes; resources available to both victims and the chain of command; confidentiality options available to victims of sexual assault.[74]

Increased literacy and awareness about the pervasiveness of sexual violence and the resources available is indeed an important element of assisting victims and trying to prevent assault. But, awareness-building could also presume that if violence continues, it is simply because victims did not know to consult the resources, that knowing one's options will actually help the situation of sexual violence, and/or that responders and military command, simply because they have checklists and procedures of how to respond, will handle the matter in a way in which victims feel heard, protected, and valued.

Consider when the military easily dismissed more partner murders at Fort Bragg, between December 2007 and the summer of 2008. Once again, the DoD and civilian advocates commented about whether enough people living on bases knew about the domestic violence services and options offered. Even as Fort Bragg's local Fayetteville Observer was inundated with calls from army wives with their own testimonials of relationship violence, some civilian and military members continued to insist that these victims must not have known about the resources available to them.[75] Even the recommendation to change military culture as a result and part of awareness-building is not about changing militarization but about somehow controlling and managing factors within the given context of militarization. Recommendation 27A in the military academies' report and the suggestions in the reports on relationship violence and sexual assault against US soldiers are framed in terms of the responsibility of military command and military leadership in order to reinforce the importance and efficacy of military hierarchy. The resulting idea from the recommendations is that the military does not need to substantially change in order to effectively address sexual violence; rather, we need to leverage the institutions and mechanisms already in place in the civilian world and make them work in the military context.

The lived experience of democracy, as noted by quality of democracy scholars, is not measured by the proliferation of bureaucratic, procedural, and institutional mechanisms but is understood through multiple narratives and discourses about alternative ways of being and interacting. Dissent, in particular, requires an active engagement with what violence is, and, accordingly, a commitment to unmask where violence exists. As such, I contend that one of the effects of the approach advocated within the task forces is the insulation of the military from a more thorough and radical critique of its existence and violence. We are left to rely upon mechanisms and with the hope that more documents and procedures will somehow tackle the problem of sexual violence in the military. If we can instead respond to sexual violence in ways that reveal the limits of institutionalized responses that work through given power hierarchies and relationships, we could potentially open the way for politically courageous dissent that imagines different types of power relationships.

The DoD's responses to sexual violence are not about truth-seeking or about the political courage of naming and calling attention to sexual violence. This is why the military has either labeled as irrelevant, anomalous, or problematic or actively refused to acknowledge those who raise attention about sexual violence in the military, particularly when they are not interested in collaborating with or supporting the DoD's claims about sexual violence.[76] The DoD needs to have control over the narrative of military sexual violence, but the voices and stories of sexual assault victims and survivors have been a central component to dissident action and discourses about the military, the wars, and the Bush administration. While dissident activists may very well be appropriating such stories for their own political claims about the viability of Bush's foreign policy, they are not only attempting to engage in sociopolitical recognition of marginalized experiences but also in creating space to even discuss these experiences.

For example, the recent Winter Soldier: Iraq and Afghanistan testimonial hearings from March 13–16, 2008, included testimony on military sexual assault against local civilians and US service members. Tanya Austin, a US Army Veteran, points to statistics on military sexual violence and the low rates of military criminal investigation;[77] she then discussed her own assault and subsequent discharge, noting, "[t]he Department of Defense's definition of morale booster for male soldiers: female soldiers-take as needed, dispose when finished and continue serving with honor."[78] At an anti-war rally on March 18, 2006, in Eugene, Oregon, one mother discussed how her daughter's choice to go AWOL drew heavily on her daughter's fears of attack, rape, molestation, and harassment from male military service members.[79] Counter-recruiters often discuss the potential for sexual harassment as a strategy of alerting potential recruits about violence in the military.[80] Other activists and journalists attempt to subvert the very idea of military as honorable, by pointing to the military policy of allowing honors burials for veterans convicted of rape.[81] And, organizations, such as Color of Change (www.colorofchange.org), have stepped in to help military families bring to light the cases of female soldiers killed due to circumstances that point to sexual violence.

Sexual violence will not be eliminated in the context of the military. Military responses simply perpetuate (and hide) the problem. Thus, I challenge how and why we even hold the military responsible and accountable for responding to sexual violence because we must first understand the relationship between militarization, sexual violence, and democracy. Perhaps we should ask not what the military can do about sexual violence but rather what the military would be without it—without the exotic playthings on foreign military bases, displays of virility and prowess, big guns and sexual metaphors, and sexual violence as a tool of suppression and discipline. This kind of political questioning is not about institutional mechanisms but about challenging the militarization and inherent masculinism of US democracy.

CONCLUSIONS

I intend for the discussion thus far to be a point of departure for further interrogation of the relationship between the military, sexual violence, and democracy, particularly since I am left with more questions than concrete answers about the military's intentions, the struggles of the advocates collaborating with the military, and the far-reaching effects of the military's responses. Taken together, the claims about sociopolitical recognition, the public/private divide, and dissent illustrate how bound up these indicators are with each other. For example, a lack of recognition of certain victims' experiences has much to do with trying to legitimize the military's public role and consequently trying to suppress and discourage dissent against militarization in the United States and abroad.

In effect, the military's responses fail to challenge sexual violence but rather aim to ensure the military's centrality, importance, and self-understanding. From the military's point of view, its credibility is crucial. The military is a tenuous edifice, caught in the contradictions of obeying honor codes yet training in mass murder, of carrying out an enduring, indeterminable 'war on terror' yet facing a crisis of support and morale, and of being central to national security yet caught in historical and contemporary conflicts that have fundamentally rendered US national security policy ineffective and counterproductive. As such, how far can the military really go in challenging sexual violence if it is simultaneously trying to secure its place in US democracy? And, as long as certain political actors believe and invest in militarization as necessary to US democracy's survival and endurance, how could we address military sexual violence in ways that re-imagine democracy and critique militarization?

If we are to answer these questions, it is important to understand how sexual violence has attained a symbolic political currency. Transnational advocates and feminist domestic movements have worked tirelessly to put sexual violence on the agendas of countries' legislatures and armed forces, the United Nations, and international law. The unintended consequence of this feat is to create a concept, 'sexual violence,' or its variations, such as 'rape as a war crime,' or 'violence against women,' that is now a part of normative language, along with racism, apartheid, colonialism, genocide, ethnic cleansing, etc. And norms can be appropriated; they have a reso-nance that allows political actors to deflect attention from but presume a common language about the issue. We too often suppose that we all know what we are talking about when we say, "we must stop sexual violence," that we have the same codes of intelligibility when we listen to the testimo-nies, and that by responding to sexual violence, we are by default resisting it. To take ownership over naming and attending to sexual violence can open the way for cementing one's own political necessity (whether it is the military, advocacy groups, lawyers, policymakers, or academics).

Theorist Susan Marcus argues, "the horror of rape is not that it steals something away from us but that it makes us into things to be taken."[82] Sexual violence is often theorized as an assault on what it means to be a woman yet also inherent to what a woman should expect: she is at once reduced to her body and always already rapeable. It is possible that we are failing to challenge this assumption, whether we collaborate with or resist the military. It is also possible that our power struggles to name what counts as sexual violence (for example, unwanted sexual intercourse between a man and a woman? coerced abortions?) and who counts as a victim (for example, women and girls snatched in the middle of the night by sex traffickers? sex workers abused by their clients?) might reflect less about the violence itself and more about the political agenda of the advocate. And, because democ-racy is an ongoing process with painful, difficult choices, it is possible to use the powerful sign of sexual violence to compromise particular political projects of democracy, such as transformation, redistribution, and solidarity, for the hope of preventing just one case of sexual violence, for the chance of bringing a measure of justice to just one survivor of sexual violence on a military base. But, what is at stake in making these types of strategic choices? The task now as we continue to theorize sexual violence is to continue to understand how political actors, including feminist theorists and activists, intentionally or unintentionally might interfere with attempts to rigorously challenge the very existence and meaning of such violence.

NOTES

1. To understand the military's responses to sexual violence, I consulted the websites, press releases, publications, transcripts, and reports issued by the Defense Department, the Defense Technical Information Center, and the Military Analysis Network of the Federation of American Scientists, by governmental and civilian sexual violence advocacy groups working with and making recommendations to the military, such as the Battered Women's Justice Project, the National Domestic Violence Hotline, the Department of Justice's Office for the Victims of Crime, the Miles Foundation, the National Center for Domestic and Sexual Violence, and by national newspapers and magazines, such as the New York Times. Future studies involving archival research and interviews are in order, but for the purposes of this chapter, I limit my research to the aforementioned documents.

2. Martha Finnemore and Kathryn Sikkink, "International Norm Dynamics and Political Change," *International Organization* 52, 4 (1998): 887–917; Margaret Keck and Kathryn Sikkink, *Activists Beyond Borders: Advocacy Networks in International Politics* (Ithaca, NY: Cornell University Press, 1998); Jacqui True and Michael Mintrom, "Transnational Networks and Policy Diffusion: The Case of Gender Mainstreaming," *International Studies Quarterly* 45, 1 (2001): 27–57.

3. Meghana Nayak and Jennifer Suchland, eds., "Introduction: Gender Violence and Hegemonic Projects," *International Feminist Journal of Politics Special Issue* 8, 4 (2006): 467–485.

4. Sheila Jeffreys, "Double Jeopardy: Women, the US military and the war in Iraq," *Women's Studies International Forum* 30, 1 (January–February 2007): 16–25.

5. Jane Jaquette, "Women and Democracy: Regional Differences and Contrasting Views," *Journal of Democracy* 12, 3 (2001): 111–125; Amy G. Mazur, *Theorizing Feminist Policy* (New York: Oxford University Press, 2002); Sue Tolleson-Rinehart and Susan J. Carroll, "'Far From Ideal': The Gender Politics of Political Science." *American Political Science Review* 100, 4 (2006): 507–513. See also Volume 5, Issue 3 (2003) of *International Feminist Journal of Politics* and the "Critical Perspectives on Gender and Politics" section of *Politics and Gender*, particularly Volume 2, Issue 2 (2006).

6. Kinhide Mushakoji, "Engendering the Japanese 'Double Standard' Patriarchal Democracy: The Case of the 'Comfort Women' and Military Sexual Slavery." in *Gender, Globalization and Democratization*, eds. Rita Mae Kelly et al. (Oxford, UK: Rowman and Littlefield Publishers, 2001), 205–222; Deborah Posel, "The scandal of manhood: 'Baby rape' and the politicization of sexual violence in post-apartheid South Africa," *Culture, Health and Sexuality* 7, 3 (2005): 239–252; Hannah Britton, "Organizing against Gender Violence in South Africa," *Journal of Southern African Studies* 32, 1 (2006): 145–163; Jessica Greenberg, "'Goodbye Serbian Kennedy': Zoran Dindić and the New Democratic Masculinity in Serbia," *East European Politics and Societies* 20, 1 (2006): 126–151.

7. Elizabeth Jelin and Eric Hershberg, eds., *Constructing Democracy: Human Rights, Citizenship, and Society in Latin America* (Boulder, CO: Westview Press, 1996); Guillermo O'Donnell, Jorge Vargas Cullell, and Osvaldo M. Iazzetta, eds., *The Quality of Democracy: Theory and Applications* (Notre Dame, IN: University of Notre Dame, 2004).

8. Michelle J. Anderson, "Rape in South Africa," Georgetown Journal of Gender and the Law 1, 1 (2000): 789–821; Sheila Meintjes, Anu Pillay, and

Meredeth Turshen, *The Aftermath: Women in Post-Conflict Transformation* (London: Zed Books, 2001).

9. Aihwa Ong, "Cultural Citizenship as Subject Making: Immigrants Negotiate Racial and Cultural Boundaries in the United States." in *Race, Identity, and Citizenship: A Reader*, eds. Rodolfo D. Torres, Louis F. Mirón, Jonathan Xavier Inda (Malden, MA: Blackwell, 1999), 262–294, 263.

10. Carole Pateman, *The Sexual Contract* (Palo Alto, CA: Stanford University Press, 1988); Charles Mills, *The Racial Contract* (Ithaca, NY: Cornell University, 1997).

11. Diana Coole, "Cartographic Convulsions: Public and Private Reconsidered," *Political Theory* 28, 3 (2000): 337–354.

12. Chris Beasley and Carol Bacchi, "Citizen bodies: embodying citizens—a feminist analysis." *International Feminist Journal of Politics* 2, 3 (2000): 337–358, 349.

13. Coole, op. cit.

14. James C. Scott, *Domination and the Arts of Resistance: Hidden Transcripts* (New Haven, CT: Yale University Press, 1990); Holloway Sparks, "Dissident Citizenship: Democratic Theory, Political Courage, and Activist Women," *Hypatia* 12, 4 (1997): 74–110.

15. Jane Monica Drexler, "Politics Improper: Iris Marion Young, Hannah Arendt, and the Power of Performativity," *Hypatia* 22, 4 (Fall 2007): 1–15.

16. Partha Chatterjee and Pradeep Jeganathan, eds. *Community, Gender and Violence. Subaltern Studies XI* (New York: Columbia University Press, 2000).

17. Nivedita Menon, *Recovering Subversion: Feminist Politics Beyond the Law* (Champaign, IL: University of Illinois Press, 2004).

18. Menon, op. cit., 155–156.

19. Renée Heberle, "Deconstructive Strategies and the Movement Against Sexual Violence," *Hypatia* 11, 4 (1996): 63–76.

20. Cynthia Enloe, *The Morning After: Sexual Politics at the End of the Cold War* (Berkeley, CA: University of California Press, 1993); idem., *Maneuvers: The International Politics of Militarizing Women's Lives* (Berkeley, CA: University of California Press, 2000); Cynthia Cockburn and Dubravka Zarkov, eds. *The Postwar Moment: Militaries, Masculinities and International Peacekeeping* (London: Lawrence and Wishart, 2002).

21. The Miles Foundation, "A Considerable Sacrifice: The Costs of Sexual Violence in the U.S. Armed Forces," The Baldy Center for Law and Social Policy Military Culture and Gender Conference, The Baldy Center for Law and Social Policy, University of Buffalo, September 15–16, 2005. http://www.law.buffalo.edu/baldycenter/pdfs/MilCult05Hansen.pdf, pp. 3–4 (accessed July 24, 2008).

22. Catherine Lutz, "Living room terrorists," *Women's Review of Books* 21, 5 (Feb. 2004): 17–18, 17.

23. Defense Task Force on Domestic Violence, "Initial Report," February 28, 2001, http://stinet.dtic.mil/cgi-bin/GetTRDoc?AD=A389984&Location=U2&doc=GetTRDoc.pdf (accessed July 5, 2008).

24. National Victim Assistance Academy, Chapter 3, "Specific Justice Systems and Victims' Rights" Supplement, National Victim Assistance Academy Textbook, http://www.ojp.usdoj.gov/ovc/assist/nvaa2002/toc.html (accessed March 2, 2008).

25. US Government Accountability Office, "Military Personnel: Progress Made in Implementing Recommendations to Reduce Domestic Violence, but Further Management Action Needed," May 24, 2006, http://www.gao.gov/new.items/d06540.pdf (accessed July 10, 2008).

26. Gerald L. Hoewing and Delilah Rumburg, "Report of The Defense Task Force on Sexual Harassment and Violence at the Military Service Academies," June 30, 2005, http://www.defenselink.mil/home/pdf/High%5fGPO%5fRRC%5ftx.pdf (accessed December 20, 2008).
27. Ibid., 8.
28. Defense Department Care for Victims of Sexual Assault Task Force, "Task Force Report on Care for Victims of Sexual Assault," April 2004. http://www.hooah4health.com/prevention/injurytrauma/docs/d20040513SAT-FReport.pdf (accessed June 5, 2008).
29. Please see the website of the US Department of Defense Sexual Assault Prevention and Response at http://www.sapr.mil/.
30. The Miles Foundation, op. cit., 4.
31. Bradley Graham, "Military Faulted on Assault Cases: Panel Calls Policies, Programs on Sexual Misconduct 'Incomplete,'" The Washington Post, May 14, 2004, http://www.washingtonpost.com/wp-dyn/articles/A25567–2004May13.html (accessed June 20, 2008).
32. Kristen Houser, "Analysis and Implications of the Omission of Offenders in the DoD Care for Victims of Sexual Assault Task Force Report," *Violence Against Women* 13, 9 (2007): 961–970.
33. The National Domestic Violence Hotline, "Public Awareness Campaign: Take a Stand Against Domestic Violence," http://www.ndvh.org/military/index.html (accessed March 1, 2008).
34. National Victim Assistance Academy, op. cit.
35. Defense Task Force on Domestic Violence, op. cit., 1.
36. Catherine Lutz and Jon Elliston, "Domestic Terror," *The Nation*, October 14, 2002, http://www.thenation.com/doc/20021014/lutz (accessed March 3, 2008).
37. Charles Henning et al. "The FY2007 National Defense Authorization Act: Selected Military Personnel Policy Issues," CRS Report for Congress, July 21, 2006, http://fas.org/sgp/crs/natsec/RL33571.pdf, p. 4 (accessed March 10, 2008).
38. National Center on Domestic and Sexual Violence, "House Panel Focuses on Prevention of Sexual Assault in the Military," The Source on Women's Issues in Congress 10, 18 (2004): 1–4. http://www.ncdsv.org/images/HousePanel-FocusesPreventionSexual.pdf (accessed December 7, 2008).
39. Defense Department Care for Victims of Sexual Assault Task Force, op. cit., 33.
40. Ibid., 34.
41. Hoewing and Rumburg, op. cit.; Defense Department Care for Victims of Sexual Assault Task Force, op. cit., 43–44.
42. Enloe, 1993, 2000, op. cit.; Cockburn and Zarkov, op. cit.
43. Lutz and Elliston, op. cit.
44. US Army Surgeon General. "Fort Bragg Epidemiological Consultation Report," Washington, DC: Department of the Army, October 18, 2002.
45. Ibid.
46. Lutz, op. cit., 17.
47. Ibid.
48. Col. Ann. Wright, "Sexual Assault in the Military: A DoD Cover-Up?" Truth-Dig, August 1, 2008, http://www.truthdig.com/report/item/20080801_sexual_assault_in_the_military_a_dod_cover_up/?ln (accessed July 14, 2008).
49. Ryan Lens, "Accused Soldier Diagnosed with Mental Problems," Military Families Against the War Website, January 10, 2007, http://www.mfaw.org.uk/index.php?option=com_content&task=view&id=83&Itemid=28 (accessed January 20, 2008).

50. Organizations involved with these families include Truthout, Military Families Against The War, Military Families Speak Out, ColorofChange.com, Courage to Resist, and The Service Women's Action Network.

51. Helen Benedict, "The private war of women soldiers," Salon.com, March 7, 2007, http://www.salon.com/news/feature/2007/03/07/women_in_military/index.html (accessed March 10, 2008); Sara Corbett, "The Women's War," The New York Times Magazine, March 18, 2007, http://www.nytimes.com/2007/03/18/magazine/18cover.html (accessed June 10, 2008).

52. Hoewing and Rumburg, op. cit., 8.

53. Loretta Frederick and Connie Sponsler, "Domestic Violence in the Military: Who Commits It, What the Victims Experience, and How the Military Responds." Presentation at the Women's Human Rights Speaker Series, Advocates for Human Rights, Minneapolis, MN, February 12, 2008. Audio file of presentation available at http://www.stopvaw.org/Expert_s_Corner.html#Domestic_Violence_in_the_U_S_Military_Who_Commits_It_What_the_Victims_Experience_and_How_the_Military_Responds (accessed March 12, 2008).

54. Defense Department Care for Victims of Sexual Assault Task Force, op. cit., 61–62.

55. Hoewing and Rumburg, op. cit., 9.

56. Ibid., 39.

57. The Miles Foundation, op. cit., 4.

58. Lutz and Elliston, op. cit.

59. Carol Cohn, "Sex and Death in the Rational World of Defense Intellectuals," *Signs* 12, 4 (1987): 687–718.

60. Defense Department Care for Victims of Sexual Assault Report, op. cit., 39.

61. Ibid., 49.

62. Ibid., 48.

63. Defense Task Force on Domestic Violence, op. cit., 53–54.

64. The full report can be found at: http://www.sapr.mil/contents/references/2007%20Annual%20Report.pdf (accessed July 10, 2008).

65. Frederick and Sponsler, op. cit.

66. Ibid.

67. Daniel Pulliam, "Defense Officials Release Set of Sexual Assault Policies," GovernmentExecutive.com, January 4, 2005, http://www.govexec.com/dailyfed/0105/010405p1.htm (accessed July 2, 2008).

68. The Miles Foundation, op. cit.

69. National Center on Domestic and Sexual Violence, op. cit.

70. Tina Susman, "Critics Want Military Abortion Rules Changed," Newsday, August 12, 2004, http://www.stopfamilyviolence.org/ocean/host.php?folder=28&page=24 (accessed December 29, 2008).

71. Lynn Levey, "The Defense Task Force on Domestic Violence: Interview with Debby Tucker," The National Center for State Courts, Summer 2003, http://www.ncsconline.org/COPs/FamVio/FVForumSum2003/TheDefenseTF2.htm (accessed June 14, 2008).

72. The memos and supplementary documentation can be found on the Defense Department's website, particularly http://www.defenselink.mil/releases/release.aspx?releaseid=8104

73. Defense Task Force on Domestic Violence, op. cit., 1.

74. Hoewing and Rumburg, op. cit., 37–38.

75. Chuck Fager, "Reflection: Domestic Violence Murders at Ft. Bragg," Quaker House: Working for Peace and GI Rights, August 2002, http://www.quakerhouse.org/DV-Military.htm (accessed July 4, 2008).

76. See Steve Vogel, "War stories echo another winter," Washington Post, March 15, 2008, http://www.afterdowningstreet.org/node/31821 (accessed July 10, 2008); Wright, op. cit.
77. http://www.stopmilitaryrape.org
78. Transcript from Democracy Now. "Half a Decade of War: Five Years After Iraq Invasion, Soldiers Testify at Winter Soldier Hearings," March 19, 2008, http://www.democracynow.org/2008/3/19/half_a_decade_of_war_five (accessed May 15, 2008).
79. Sara Rich, "A Moment of Silence is Not Enough," truthout, March 20, 2006, http://www.truthout.org/article/video-military-sexual-violence-command-rape (accessed July 4, 2008).
80. Douglas Belkin, "For Youth, advice on military, and dissent," Boston Globe, June 11, 2006, http://www.boston.com/news/local/articles/2006/06/11/for_youth_advice_on_military_and_dissent/ (accessed June 20, 2008).
81. Anne K. Ream, "Does a rapist deserve a military burial?" Los Angeles Times, January 23, 2008, http://www.latimes.com/news/opinion/commentary/la-oe-ream23jan23,0,3805998.story (accessed July 5, 2008).
82. Sharon Marcus, "Fighting Bodies, Fighting Words," in *Feminist Theorize the Political*, eds. Judith Butler and Joan W. Scott (New York: Routledge, 1992), 385–403, 30.

8 Feminism, International Law, and the Spectacular Violence of the 'Other'
Decolonizing the Laws of War

Elizabeth Philipose

Blood! Blood! . . . Birth! Ecstasy of becoming! Three-quarters engulfed in the confusions of the day, I feel myself redden with blood. The arteries of all the world, convulsed, torn away, uprooted, have turned toward me and fed me.[1]

SPECTACULAR VIOLENCE ACROSS BORDERS

In her comparative analysis of violence against women in India and the United States, Uma Narayan argues for the importance of attending to the epistemology of "border-crossings" and the historically and politically specific contexts in which violence against women is manifested.[2] In particular, Narayan focuses on the wide circulation of the reductionist story that "women in India are burned everyday," a reference that mistakenly conflates the incidence of contemporary so-called 'dowry-deaths' with what is wrongly assumed to be an ancient and hegemonic Hindu tradition of suttee. She asks feminists to consider the function and effects of the circulation of these stories of 'spectacular violence' against women, and the dehumanizing and decontextualizing effects that ensue from attributing to a complex, dynamic and diverse peoples the practice of burning-women-since-the-beginning-of-time. Narayan offers multiple insights that enable us to understand that 'dowry deaths' are incidents of domestic violence that have increased in response to economic globalization and a growing demand amongst middle-class Indians for wealth, economic mobility, and consumer goods. As such, they are thoroughly secular, capitalist, and contemporary manifestations of violence against women. By contextualizing the incidence of dowry deaths in a structural analysis of economic globalization and patriarchal power, frameworks that are not foreign or Other, she humanizes Indians and offers an analysis of the structural power that makes domestic violence possible. In doing so, her analysis connects Us to Them and enables us to see the violence of the Other as something quite familiar, comprehensible, and continuous with a range of domestic violence issues.

A MODEL FOR ANALYSIS

Narayan's essay points to persistent distortions as issues of violence against women across borders and are translated into different contexts. This is the case whenever 'spectacular violence' against women comes to the attention of global audiences and even as they come to the attention of global women's movements, human rights organizations, and international legal institutions charged with the task of prosecuting violations against human rights and humanitarian law. This persistent pattern in a contemporary, neocolonial era reflects a colonial pattern in that the narrative of violence against women recurs throughout Euro-colonial imaginaries as evidence of the inferiority and backwardness of Native men and women, and as a racializing trope. Suttee, for instance, was of great interest to British administrators in India during the 1800s as a matter of both revulsion and admiration: "almost every European commentator of the sixteenth and seventeenth centuries stops to savour that picture of Oriental barbarity and female helplessness and devotion."[3]

In a parallel way, rape narratives have played a large role in colonial ventures, as critiques and challenges to imperialism when invoked by nationalists, and as preludes to intervention and suppression of Native and/ or minority populations when invoked by colonialists. In fact, "in colonialist as well as nationalist writings, racial and sexual violence are yoked together by images of rape, which in different forms, becomes an abiding and recurrent metaphor for colonial relations."[4] Jenny Sharpe suggests that talk about sexual violence and rape in mid-1800s British India emerges in response to a need to draw strong racial distinctions and reconsolidate British rule after the Indian Mutiny in 1857 when the 'mild Hindoo' was transformed into a threatening aggressor in the British imaginary.[5] She states: "The stereotype of the dark rapist speaks more strongly to the failure of the civilizing mission, which is why the rape stories tend to emerge at moments of political instability. When articulated through images of violence against women, a resistance to British rule does not look like the struggle for emancipation, but rather an uncivilized eruption that must be contained."[6] Rape stories served to activate and justify a renewed and stronger "will to civilize" and the moral imperative of modern colonialism to bring the colonized into civil society. Throughout colonial history, both colonizing and Native women signify hierarchies of race, and stories of rape and sexual violence are triggers for intervention, occupation and other kinds of legalist civilizing missions. Rape stories play a function in the meting out of 'extra-judicial justice' as well, as many victims of lynchings in the United States were accused of raping white women and brutalized for their presumably perverse and violent sexualities. These are all variations on the colonial 'rescue narrative.' Either the Native woman is taken up as a helpless victim of her own people in need of rescue by the superior white men, or white women, presumably endangered by the presence of racialized men, is the catalyst for intervention by white men. In any case, rescue narratives revolve around the presumed weakness of women, whether Native or European, and the moral superiority of white men, proven through their ability to rescue women from rape and exploitation committed by those deemed uncivilized.

This project investigates the discursive terrain that constructs the 'spectacular violence' of rape and sexual violence in armed conflict and war in international human rights and humanitarian law discussions. Especially since the conflicts in the region once known as Yugoslavia in the 1990s, a global consciousness that women are targeted in war and by militarist cultures has emerged and the establishment of several international legal institutions has enshrined that recognition. The Statutes for the ad hoc International Criminal Tribunal for the Former Yugoslavia (ICTY) and the International Criminal Tribunal for Rwanda (ICTR) enumerate forms of violence against women over which the tribunals have jurisdiction, as do the Statute for the Permanent International Criminal Court (ICC) and subsequent ad hoc tribunals and ICC cases for Sierre Leone, Lebanon, Cambodia, East Timor, and Iraq.

At the same time that there is a global consciousness about women's status and victimization in war and armed conflict, a superficial glance at the regions and peoples who are most often held accountable for their violent crimes against women indicates that it is non-Euro-descended peoples, or people of color. For instance, the cases under investigation by the ICC include the Democratic Republic of the Congo, Uganda, Central African Republic, and Darfur Sudan. The exception of the ad hoc tribunal for the former Yugoslavia draws our attention to the ways that 'race' is a social construction enacted to serve particular political ends—in this instance, drawing a post-communist region into a capitalist global order. While the whole story cannot be told on the basis of a superficial glance, the discourse of 'sexual violence against women in war' is suspect as an instance of a consciousness about the spectacular violence committed by peoples who are 'uncivilized,' where sexuality is the racializing factor, constructing primitive, culture-bound and static Others in need of being civilized.

In the post-Cold War period, the implementation of law to protect civilians in militarized zones has been selective. There is a range of violence committed that is rarely noted by mass media, publicized by UN and human rights officials, or prosecuted through international law. A brief sample of these muted stories includes rape, sexual harassment and murder committed by US male soldiers against US female soldiers;[7] US soldiers' treatment of women in Iraq under the occupation;[8] Western peacekeeping missions that are often accompanied by violence and violations against women;[9] or French soldiers who sought out Tutsi women in Rwanda after the genocide to violate them sexually.[10] There are various ways to explain why these occurrences do not become part of the international legal conversation about protecting civilians in war zones. In relation to the example of French soldiers in Rwanda, the argument might refer to the fact that the International Criminal Tribunal for Rwanda has been established to primarily hear crimes committed in the course of the genocide of Tutsi civilians by Hutu militias. Other arguments might suggest that what happens between US soldiers is subject to internal military tribunals, the crimes committed by French soldiers are subject to French military law, and as such, there is no legal vacuum in which an international criminal tribunal might become relevant. Or, more compellingly, it might be explained by "the banal fact that powerful states are never held accountable to such institutions, that only the weak and defeated can be convicted of war crimes and crimes against humanity."[11]

This 'banal fact,' as described by Talal Asad, redirects our attention from the urgent sense that law must be used to stop crimes against women wherever and whenever they occur, to more structural concerns about the purpose and function of concepts such as war crimes and crimes against humanity in maintaining a global hierarchy between races and nations, and the function of international legal systems as they have come to be constituted in the radically unequal global system since at least the 1600s.[12] In the cases of sexual violence against women in war, the well-being and security of women is used as the grounds for maintaining global hierarchies and 'the global color line.'[13]

At stake in this analysis are several related issues: firstly, the persistently uneven application of international laws governing violence which holds those who are constructed as non-European and/or racialized accountable while granting relative immunity to Euro–American perpetrators; secondly, the narrative framing of the perpetrators and the crimes themselves through implicit and explicit colonial tropes; thirdly, the imperial and racial purposes served by the circulation of 'rape stories' from armed conflict zones; and finally, the governance and administration of the sexuality of those deemed inferior. My argument, indebted to the astute insights of Anne Orford, suggests that at the heart of international law is a civilizing mission that aims to incorporate and assimilate peoples and nations to what is presumed to be, or is projected as, a Euro–American standard of civilization that carries with it racial, sexual, religious, and gendered connotations.[14]

In the course of pursuing the prosecution of rape and sexual violence, international laws governing war in the post-Cold War period rely upon the politicization of women's bodies as members of ethnic, racial, or national groups and as victims requiring protection in war zones. The bodies of particular women are rendered spaces to be protected through the mechanisms of international law and managed through a range of post-war stabilization practices. These practices often involve new territorial divisions along ethnic designations that are patrolled by peacekeeping forces, and the institution of new techniques of managing populations; from refugee relocations, to legislating minority group representation in government, to documenting births, deaths and border crossings according to ethnicity. As a mechanism of post-war stabilization, international war crimes tribunals prosecute crimes of sexual violence in and through ethnic and national designations of populations, and in effect, contain and regulate sexual relations and sexuality, thereby racializing populations on the grounds of their sexual conduct and echoing the colonial practices upon which international law is founded.

Further, the documentation generated through investigations and prosecutions of individuals accused of sexual violence amass a grand case archive of the bestiality of the Other that stands alone as incomparable, unprecedented, and unimaginable violence, given that the violence of the powerful is not catalogued in a similar fashion. Taken together, my suggestion is that the assumptions and implementation of international law as it is presently constituted function as a contemporary mechanism of a colonial order that has not been decolonized and nor excised of its racial grammars that establish an ongoing division between 'Us' and 'Them.' Put another way, the current manifestation of international legal regimes serves a neocolonial global order predicated on the maintenance of a racial social order. For feminist and social justice advocates, it is crucial to investigate the historical and foundational assumptions of international law. Yet, most scholarship and analysis of international legal cases of sexual violence against women in war has not engaged such analyses. This chapter seeks to contribute to a broadened and contextualized feminist analysis of international laws prohibiting violence against women.

The next section discusses the colonial origins of international law, the development of the concept of sovereignty in relation to European expansion, and the deployment of 'civilization' as the measure of capacity for self-rule. The following section focuses on the concern with sexuality within and by European nations and the function of sexuality within the context of European rule in the colonies. The chapter then turns to a discussion of recent international criminal tribunal trials that have focused on the prosecution of sexual violence, rape as a weapon of war, rape as genocide, and rape as a crime against humanity. The last section reflects on the possibilities for a feminist decolonization of international law.

INTERNATIONAL LAW AND THE DISCOVERY OF THE NEW WORLD

The regime of international law that exists today was constructed by European powers to serve their interests as they sought to colonize much of the world's territory and population. Following from his assertion that European public law is reflective of an emergent planetary consciousness that was made possible, initially, by circumnavigation, Carl Schmitt dates the inception of international law to 1492 and the 'discovery of the new world.'[15] Schmitt's concept of the nomos of the Earth refers to the community of political entities united by common rules, and the order of the Earth itself, as established through international law. As a spatial, political, and juridical concept, the nomos distinguished between European territory that was to be protected and united, and non-European territory that existed for the exploration and discovery by Europe itself. The ideas of civilization and humanity were considered in exclusively European terms, as reflective of European habits and traditions and ways of being which were considered to be the spiritual and political telos of everyone who fit the category of human, ultimately. As Schmitt states:

> From the 16th to the 20th century, European international law considered Christian nations to be the creators and representatives of an order applicable to the whole earth. The term 'European' meant the normal status that set the standard for the non-European part of the earth. Civilization was synonymous with European civilization. In this sense, Europe was still the center of the earth.[16]

A planetary consciousness simultaneously brought with it the problem of creating order; hence international law, derived from European interests and traditions, was developed as the set of ordering principles for the globe. The core of international lawmaking from its inception was to establish the right of land appropriation, either through the legal categories of conquest, war, colonialism, or discovery, and to resolve arising disputes between European nations and their imperial and territorial interests. Until the late nineteenth century and the Hague Peace Conferences of 1899 and 1910, European civilization and territory were the spatial and political foundations from which international law evolved.

The Hague Conferences resulted in the Hague Conventions of 1899, an elaborate codification of international humanitarian law that outlined the parameters of the range of legitimate action in war, and legitimate purposes for war. These conferences were seen to be important events in the consolidation of European solidarity and a shared commitment to grapple with the problem of violence between the armies of civilized nations, assumed to be European states. Laws governing the treatment of prisoners of war, the use of torture, allowable weaponry, the distinctions between combat and noncombat zones, and between combatants and civilians were codified in the Hague Convention of 1899.[17] Yet, the Hague Convention came at the end of a twenty-year period of massive and violent invasions of African nations, during which time most of Africa was transformed into colonies dominated by Europe.[18] The codification of humanitarian law in a time of colonial expansion and the 'scramble for Africa' excluded colonial violence from its jurisdiction. Natives and Africans were not understood as civilized peoples or nation. They were 'savages,' and though several commentators advocated for the application of humanitarian law to colonial wars, they did not waver from the idea that natives were savages. Where colonial states used violence against natives, it was seen as 'law maintenance' rather than armed conflict, 'pacification' rather than massacres: Europe's civilizing mission was taken as self-evident even by its critics.[19] As such, because colonial violence did not have the status of war or armed conflict, humanitarian law afforded no protection to Native populations and no limits on colonial violence.

During this same period, a transnational consciousness of whiteness united disparate and diverse regions of the world, and nineteenth century imperial rule was marked by the global ascendance of whiteness and the self-conscious alliance between Euro-descended peoples throughout dominion countries. In their recent book *Drawing the Global Colour Line: White Men's Countries and the International Challenge of Racial Equality*, historians Marilyn Lake and Henry Reynolds chart "the emergence of the transnational community of white men in the globalised world of the late nineteenth century."[20] Drawing on the insights of WEB Dubois' 1910 essay *The Souls of Black Folk*, Lake and Reynolds argue that a global solidarity between peoples in dominion countries developed in defense of colonialism against strengthening independence and anti-colonial movements. When Natal was granted sovereign rights in 1896, for instance, "the colony joined the exclusive club of self-governing settler colonies— Canada, Newfoundland, the Australian colonies, New Zealand and the Cape of Good Hope. White men were deemed to have both the capacity and the right to self-government . . . "[21] The authors argue that the global ascendancy of the politics of whiteness recast previously held notions about the multiplicity of nations, races, and religions into binary terms of white/non-white, thus constructing an alliance of peoples in diverse lands as part of the same international society, in contradistinction to the rest of the world within and outside of sovereign states who were deemed to be non-white. In this way, Europe was decentered and at the same time, Euro-descended nations developed a self-consciousness about their identity as 'white'; they evolved as united through shared culture, tradition and commitment to expanding and maintaining European rule over the peoples of the world. These shared identities and commitments informed the development of international law.

THE FOUNDATION OF SOVEREIGNTY

From its origins, then, the making of international law is a colonial enterprise, and colonialism, as Brett Bowden and others argue, is a thoroughly juridical enterprise.[22] The conventional international relations story locates the origins of international law in 1648 with the Treaty of Westphalia, suggesting that the primary characteristic of international law was about increasing inclusion and equality within Europe. However, if we accept

Schmitt's story of the origins of international law as that which comes into being with the 'discovery of the New World,' then the development of international law is "a story of the violent exclusion of others outside of Europe, first on the basis of religious, then cultural, difference."[23] In this way, Schmitt offers an important shift in the conventional perception of the origins of international law and the form and function of law itself.

Anthony Anghie's analysis of the development of sovereign statehood tells a parallel story about international law.[24] Non-European peoples (either colonized or yet to be colonized) were not accorded sovereignty, and as Anghie demonstrates, the entire concept of sovereignty itself depended upon the exclusion of non-Europeans from self-determination, and the inclusion of them as subject peoples. Anghie shows that two types of sovereignty were created: one is the sovereignty inherent to European powers that was thought to reflect their essential civilized nature; and the other is a second-tier and contingent sovereignty granted to non-European states after decolonization and the decline of the European imperial order. Second-tier sovereignty required that newly decolonized states retain or adopt idealized European 'standards of civilization' to prove themselves worthy of a truncated version of self-rule. In contemporary global politics, standards of civilization are at work when states are characterized as failed, despotic, rogue, rights-violating, quasi, criminal, or corrupt, suggesting that their sovereignty is contingent and not inherent to their character or essential nature as it is assumed to be in European culture.

GENDER, SEXUALITY AND SOVEREIGNTY

Anghie calls international law "the grand project that has justified colonialism as a means of redeeming the backward, aberrant, violent, oppressed, undeveloped people of the non-European world by incorporating them into the universal civilization of Europe."[25] Within the universe of colonial logic, measuring backwardness is predicated on gendered and sexualized concepts of what it means to be human, self-determining, sovereign and civilized. An aspect of being civilized in the eyes of colonial law and modernist thought revolves around sexuality and the self-regulating capacity to be sexually appropriate. In her reading of Grotius' Laws of War and Peace, Helen Kinsella demonstrates that nations and men are distinguished according to a social hierarchy of reason, judgment, comportment, and containment of sexual appetite that indexes both barbarity and the capacity of men to be self-governing.[26] In turn, the modern conception of sexuality is a Euro-colonial construct that is central to national and racial preoccupations about lineage, inheritance, and blood.[27] Historical and contingent racial projects are conceived of as biological projects in the European imaginary; or as George Frederickson puts it, racism "is when differences that otherwise might be considered ethnocultural are regarded as innate, indelible and unchangeable."[28] The modern concept of race is a biological category that suggests an innate set of characteristics and human potentiality that is passed through blood. As such, family reproduction and kinship became integral to racial thinking, and gender and sexuality are central considerations. Women's sexuality and reproduction need to be governed so that lineage can be protected, and male sexuality comes to be identified as a site of potential racial violence and a threat to order, civilization, or the nation. This is informed by the patriarchal assumption that lineage is passed through the male alone; and through a preoccupation with heterosexuality. Lineage, white supremacy, and the purity of the race are at stake in the reigning symbolic order.[29]

In colonial literature and artistic representations, women's bodies are often metaphors for 'undiscovered' lands, capturing both "the promise and fear of the colonial land"[30] the conquered land, and the emptiness of the land.[31] Nationalist and independence movements also drew on women's bodies as a metaphor for the symbolic rape of the nation by imperialists, and throughout colonial and postcolonial history, contradictory images of women appear. Sometimes black and brown women are victims, desirable and passive. Sometimes they are Amazonian, deviant, insatiable, licentious, libidinally excessive, sexually uncontrolled, lesbian, and brutal,[32] what Anne McLintock has characterized as "porno-tropics for the European imagination—a fantastic magic lantern of the mind onto which Europe projected its forbidden sexual desires and fears."[33] Those forbidden desires were dangerous to civilization and to European rule if both Natives and Europeans were not contained and regulated. Fear of miscegenation, cultural or racial pollution, and loss of whiteness meant that regulating sexuality was the means for purifying lineage, maintaining racial difference,[34] soothing demographic anxieties, expanding imperial races, challenging imperial rivalries, and maintaining imperial rule over colonized peoples.[35] Throughout these narratives, women's bodies and femininity are politicized by imperial and national preoccupations with consolidating power through the management of population, and hence, are spaces to be regulated and contained by sovereign and masculine rule.

Within the colonial configuration of modern Western versions of gender, masculinity is a raced, classed, and sexualized category, encompassing the attributes of the ideal human as white, Euro-descended, Christian, propertied, heterosexual, and male. In this sense, to be male and seen as undeveloped is to be feminized as an unfit male, terms that both signal the abject and object, and the assumptions of deviant sexuality, impotency, and pollution. To be female in its colonial connotations conjures a passive/dangerous, victimized-by-culture, object-of-rescue, in need of civilization.[36] These gendered and sexualized configurations are biological categories caught up in the obsession with blood, lineage, and purity. They constitute the distinction between Human and inferior alien species, or non-Human, or second-tier human, all of whom lack personality, agency, and individual uniqueness worthy of preservation. In its colonial connotations, hetero-sexuality is a commodity of the ideal Human in need of continuously being proven, protected, and coded as unambiguous. Establishing the masculin-ity, whiteness and heterosexuality of colonial agents demands the produc-tion of themselves as the ideal Human through the gendered and racialized oppositional terms of Self and Other.[37]

As European empires declined and more non-European peoples became independent, sovereignty came to be measured by the ability of non-Euro-peans to best approximate European civilization. Their sovereignty is not the right of self-determination; rather, it is the surrender of freedom to be self-governing and self-determining, and a surrender of their uniqueness and identity to become more like Europeans. This includes the suppression of traditional practices and indigenous knowledges; establishing central-ized government; promoting secular nationalism; asserting the monopoly over the use of violence as a prerogative of the state; enshrining private property rights; establishing the gendered household division of labor and masculine rule; and the public regulation of sexuality.[38] In these ways, to be sovereign meant that nations were obliged to organize themselves around the idealized culturally and historically specific traditions of specific Euro-pean populations, thereby confirming the claims that their ways were infe-rior and weak in comparison to European cultural formations that were, by nature, universally valid. Whereas the Westphalian story suggests that sovereignty is a guarantee of diversity and self-definition in the interstate system, seen through a colonial history lens, it becomes clear that homoge-neity and the denial of non-European cultural value are more prevalent and definitional of the system.

This move in the development of the concept of sovereignty, of splitting between European and non-European versions, revolves around the idea that international society or a society of states must reflect shared common values and traditions. In Anghie's analysis, the concept of "society, rather than sovereignty, is the central concept used to construct the system of international law."[39] He continues:

> Society, then, provides the matrix of ideas, the analytical resources which, allied with sovereignty, could establish a positivist international legal order. This is an important shift: for implicit in the idea of society is membership; only those states accepted into society and which agree upon principles regulating their behaviour can be regarded as belong-ing to society. The concepts of society, furthermore, enabled the for-mulation and elaboration of the various cultural distinctions that were crucial to the constitution of sovereignty doctrine.[40]

Thus, on one hand, international law had at its core a civilizing mission that would draw people deemed backwards into modernity. On the other hand, non-Europeans could not ultimately be redeemed; they were not incorporated into 'civilization' as equals, and neither were they civilized, that is, Europeanized, by their incorporation. Instead, the civilizing project of international law sustained the ongoing dichotomy between the civilized and backwards. Incorporation into international law meant that the uncivilized were under correct and appropriate tutelage and protectorship so that they could be managed more effectively. This management was seen to be beneficial for all parties: Europeans could fulfill their universalist mandates of taming the world, and subject peoples would benefit from the guidance of their masters, a need they would never outgrow given modern racisms' assumption of the eternal immaturity and hereditary backwardness of subject peoples.[41]

Anghie rewrites the conventional wisdom that suggests that Europeans forged sovereignty rights which were then universalized to non-Europeans in the decolonization period. Instead, he shows that the sovereignty of the non-European is contingent upon acquiring European traits, and dependent upon non-European states' alliance with Europe, and now, with the United States. Bowden's analysis of 'standards of civilization' directly counters the international relations idea that sovereignty is the guarantee of diversity in the international system, instead showing that cultural, religious, political, economic, and other types of conformity are prerequisites to being recognized as legitimate members of international society. The political culture of international law is about protecting transnational whiteness, and containing and maintaining control over non-Europeans or those who do not meet the standards of whiteness. These are insights that counter a core idea in the field of international relations that retains the mythology that sovereignty is the guarantee of equality between states. These are insights that answer the question of why it is that some states appear to be more sovereign than others. Finally, these insights answer the question of why international legal sanctions are rarely applied against imperial states, especially in relation to legislating war and armed conflict.

LEGITIMACY, SOVEREIGNTY AND THE USE OF VIOLENCE

As sovereignty is historically derived from the imperial need to distinguish between legitimate and illegitimate uses of violence, sovereignty is constituted as the foundations of legitimacy for the use of violence. The laws of war are notable as much for what they sanction and legitimate and make possible, as they are for what violence they prohibit.[42] They are attempts to establish the legitimate monopoly on the use of violence by soldiers acting at the behest of sovereign, and therefore, legitimate actors. This is done in tandem with identifying and punishing those who wield, or who intend to wield, non-authoritative violence. The dichotomy of legitimate and illegitimate uses of violence is paralleled by the colonial dichotomy of the civilized and the backwards,[43] and both formulations rest upon the construction of sovereignty as the marker of the legitimate monopoly over the use of violence.[44] In turn, the constitution of sovereignty in the history of international law making is linked to European imperial needs, modernity and the racial grammars of European empire.

In fact, the racial grammar of international law structures claims of sovereignty and the legitimate right to use violence between sovereign nations for defensive purposes and against those who are barbarous, savage, and not self-determining. For instance, in his discussion of James Lorimer, a nineteenth century jurist who celebrated the science of races as a great contribution to international politics, Bowden refers to Hugo Grotius' claim that "a band of robbers is not a state," and therefore, the conquest of Algeria by France was not regarded as a violation of international law.[45] Further, the distinction between legitimate war and terrorism revolves around the acquisition of sovereign statehood and recognition by the prevailing society of states. As such, sovereignty is a feature of masculinity and whiteness, and the central concept in the racial grammar of international law. This is not necessarily a permanent feature of the international law system, but it is a relatively enduring feature that has yet to be unraveled from its colonial and imperial precepts and commitment to ensuring that Euro-descended states retain the monopoly over the legitimate use of violence.

Bowden suggests that the end of the Cold War saw the comeback of certain ideas, including the idea that there is a linear progression of human history with the end point in liberal democratic capitalism; and the idea that the world can be divided into societies of varying degrees of civilization. Replacing 'standards of civilization' are 'standards of human rights,' 'standards of modernity,' 'standards of economic development,' or 'standards of democracy,' in what Bowden refers to as shifting 'standards of civilization' in globalization.[46] The laws of war and the turn to war crimes tribunals after the Cold War reflect a renewed interest and opportunity to impose a 'standard of civilization' centralizing adherence to humanitarian and human rights laws as the key measurement of fitness for society membership. The standard of civilization in the case of international tribunals in armed conflict zones is the 'standard of war-making.' It is significant that the first tribunal after the end of the Cold War was for the former Yugoslavia, the former Communist federated republic that was now, perhaps, open for business to U.S. and European Union interests.[47]

SEXUAL VIOLENCE, INTER-ETHNIC SEX, AND STANDARDS OF CIVILIZATION

Further, the racial grammar of international law codes legitimacy as the claim of white, Euro-derived or Euro-allied, masculine heterosexual chivalrous agents to defend the honor and dignity of women and to rescue them from the forces of tyranny and barbarism.[48] The laws of war are part of the larger civilizing mission of international law, designed to incorporate and assimilate the barbarous misogynist Other into the imperial order of modernity, chivalry, and lawfulness.

International law deems those who are sexually inappropriate justiciable, that is, subject to incorporation into modernity and civilization through legal prosecution.[49] International prosecution of rape and sexual assault in war, as a crime against humanity, a tool of genocide, or a war crime, has been criticized on a number of grounds for not following through on their promise of gender justice. Criticisms range from the absence of adequate witness protection programs to the reliance on arcane Geneva Convention provisions that protect the 'honor and dignity of women' but that do not recognize crimes against women as 'grave breaches,' on par with torture, for instance.[50]

As international law has been historically constituted, however, the laws of war also operate within the colonial and racialized frameworks I have been discussing, and for this reason, international legal attention to what happens to women in war should raise suspicions. The post-Cold War opportunity to construct a war zone as a place of sexual deviance reflects a colonial impulse that mobilizes international law to justify a range of interventions: armed intervention, foreign occupation, incarceration, criminal trials, the use of torture against those who are constituted as sexual deviants, including mass or genocidal rapists, and economic restructuring.[51] The attention paid to sexual violence against women in war is part of a civilizing impulse of international law, one that aims to incorporate the barbarous, violent, nationalist Other into the presumably civilized, genteel, and chivalrous modern.[52] As Kinsella argues, the rape of women in war is presumed to be the actions of the barbarous, whereas the hallmark of enlightened nations is their judgment, reason, moderation, and their ability to restrain their appetites. Through her reading of Grotius and the Geneva Conventions, it becomes clear that prosecuting sexual violence against women in war is not about the protection of women, but about creating and regulating a particular hierarchy of relations among nations that maintains the distinction between those who are presumed to be civilized and those that are presumed to be barbarous.[53]

The International Criminal Tribunal for the Former Yugoslavia (ICTY) case of the Prosecutor v. Dragoljub Kunarac, Radomir Kovac, and Zoran Vukovic (hereafter "Kunarac,") is characterized as a landmark decision in the prosecution of mass rape as a crime against humanity.[54] The crimes were committed in and around the city of Foca in 1992, when the Bosnian Muslim-majority city was taken by Serb forces and Bosnian Muslims were expelled, killed, or taken to detention centers in the area. The statistics suggest a massive expulsion, from approximately twenty-two thousand Bosnian Muslims pre-war to a postwar population of ten. The defendants in the case were found to be involved in various aspects of the occupation, including removing women and girls from detention centers to local houses and apartments; participating in rapes and offering the women to others to be raped; subjecting some of the women to constant rapes over a period of several months; enslaving women to perform household duties; and selling women to other soldiers. The Trial Chamber found that women were disappeared, murdered, sexually violated, terrorized, and enslaved over the course of several months and that responsibility for the violence was with the defendants in the case.

The ICTY found the men to be guilty of committing war crimes and crimes against humanity. This is the first case to be heard that has a singular focus on violations against women. It is also the first case to successfully prosecute rape as a crime against humanity. Together with the International Criminal Tribunal for Rwanda (ICTR) case against Jean-Paul Akayesu that found rape to be an act of genocide, these cases elevate the crime of rape and violence against women to the status of the most egregious violations of humanitarian law.[55] For many feminist advocates, elevating violence against women to the status of the worst violence a person can commit against another according to international law elevates the value accorded to women as women, a welcome advance in humanitarian law.[56]

Doris Buss points out that the decisions in this case are complex, convoluted, and innovative, and indeed, the decisions draw from various instruments of the laws of war to determine the exact nature of different charges of rape and sexual violence, and to be precise about the relevant humanitarian law.[57] One of the important developments in the case against Kunarac is that an Appeals Chamber decision was made about the relevance of a woman's consent to the charges against Kunarac and the legal definition of a rape. In appealing the decision in the Prosecutor v. Kunarac, the defense argued that the detained women consented to sexual relations with the accused and that rape charges are unwarranted.

In domestic prosecutions in many countries, a woman's non-consent has to be proven in order for a charge of rape to be legitimate, and the case revolves around her words, conduct, deeds, and believability to determine whether there has been a rape. Within the jurisdiction of international criminal tribunals, consent is a rather contradictory and ambiguous issue. On one hand, a context of war is, by definition, a context of coercion, and if a woman is being forcibly held in a detention center, on what grounds could she give her consent to have sexual relations? On the other hand, a context of war is not only a context of coercion, that is, it is possible to imagine that many kinds of relationships occur within a territory and time period known as war that may not constitute coercive relationships. Certainly, as Engle notes, in the multiethnic community of Bosnia–Herzegovina, there were many interethnic relationships and marriages prior and during the wars.[58] Further, even in a context of coercion, a woman could consent to sexual relationships in exchange for security or freedom or some other potential and relative benefit. This logic follows from one of the animating precepts of a wide range of feminist analysis that seeks to understand that women are agentic and that they act, although not always in a context of their choosing. However, in the Kunarac case, the Appeals Chamber determined that within his overall pattern and conduct that included the enslavement of women, psychological control, cruel treatment and forced labor, women's consent for sexual relations could not have been given and thus, is not a mitigating factor in the case against him. Further, the decision found that the circumstances of Foča were inherently coercive and therefore, the issue of consent is meaningless in such circumstances.

In the convolutions and complexities of this case, there are alarming and unintended implications to consider. The ICTY operates within very specific jurisdictional considerations of time and space, definitions of combatants and noncombatants, ethnic group identities, and the broader parameters of humanitarian law. The full name of the Tribunal, established by Security Council Resolution 827, May 25, 1993, spells out some of these jurisdictional parameters: International Criminal Tribunal for the Prosecution of Persons Responsible for Serious Violations of International Humanitarian Law Committed in the Territory of the Former Yugoslavia since 1991.[59] This title establishes the temporal and spatial jurisdiction of the ICTY, delimiting its attention to serious crimes committed after 1991 and on the soil of Yugoslavia. Further jurisdictional parameters are established within the cases and background documents. Kunarac falls under the larger rubric of the ICTY that avers that the major conflicts were between Serbs, Muslims, and Croats, and that a large proportion of ethnic cleansing was committed by Serbs in Muslim-dominated territories in Bosnia–Herzegovina and Croatia. While the ICTY does not restrict its focus to the crimes of Serbs,[60] the idea that there are three relevant ethnic groups is not challenged and the priority belligerents in the ICTY cases come to be known under the law through their ethnic designations.[61] To determine whether an act of violence falls under the jurisdiction of ICTY provisions on crimes against humanity, the perpetrators and victims or combatants and civilians could not be of the same ethnicity. Because the wars in Yugoslavia were defined as wars between ethnicities, violence committed by a person identified as Serbian against a person identified as Serbian would not be justiciable under ICTY regulations. Thus, an act of sexual violence committed by a Serbian soldier against a Serbian civilian woman (or many Serbian civilian women) would not be a justiciable crime under the international criminal tribunal for the former Yugoslavia, no matter how brutal the violence might be. However, any manner of sexual relations, coerced or consensual, committed by a Serbian soldier against or with a Bosnian Muslim civilian woman during the time of the wars would be considered a crime under the criminal tribunal's jurisdiction. Effectively, the focus on ethnic, racial, and national identities to determine the nature of a crime means that international laws of war against sexual violence transmogrify into the criminalization of interracial or inter-ethnic sex.

Though these are surely unintended effects of ICTY rulings, they are the consequences of committing to a racial taxonomy for the adjudication of sexualized crimes. The ICTY reifies ethnic distinctions, reduces people to their ethnicities and characterizes the violence as caused by ethnic differences, rather than wars that made use of ethnic differences to engender terror. In doing so, the international criminal tribunal works on the logic of the war makers, thus aiming to mitigate the problem of international conflict through precisely the same frameworks that make such wars possible.

Further implications of the decision on consent include the denial of women's sexual and political agency within the conflicts. As Engle suggests, the international criminalization of rape has had the effect of characterizing women as powerless victims who are incapable of defending themselves or others, or of taking sides and participating in the war. In the cases before the ICTY, for instance, all Bosnian Muslim women are essentialized as powerless victims because they came to be understood as the primary and constant victims of the wars. Through the framework of international criminal law, we lose the possibility of understanding women's agency, especially in the context of war.

Further, in determining that consent is irrelevant in the context of Foča, the ruling "essentially makes consensual sexual relationships legally impossible," and all sexual relations between Serb combatants and Bosnian Muslim women acts of torture.[62] As such, inter-ethnic sexual relations within a certain time and space are criminalized, men are characterized as rapists, women are rendered victims, and both are in need of regulation. Although these rulings are determined in reference to a precise set of events within a proscribed time and place, the decisions of international criminal tribunals set precedents that are then used by other international trials and domestic law makers in developing their rape legislation.[63] Further, as an institution connected to the broader international machinery designed for post-conflict rehabilitation, the meanings that are made through these trials resonate beyond the original cases. Finally, in the situation of Yugoslavia, the ICTY rulings that prohibit interracial sex parallel post-conflict peace-building exercises that ethnically cleansed regions through legal means. That is, the rulings parallel the racial thinking that informed the Dayton Accords Peace Agreements that divided Yugoslavian territory into ethnically homogenous zones, often following the lines that were violently drawn in the wars.[64]

The Kunarac case brings to light some of the more pernicious and vexing consequences of such rulings on consent, and in some ways, similar concerns are relevant to the case of Jean-Paul Akayesu in the ICTR. The ICTR was convened to hear charges against people who had participated in the genocide in Rwanda in 1994, and more precisely, to hear charges against the Hutu leadership and the Interahamwe militia, who had participated in and contributed to the genocide against Tutsi civilians. Jean-Paul Akayesu was the bourgmestre, the most powerful figure in the commune of Taba in the prefecture of Gitarama at the time of the genocide in Rwanda. Between

April and June 1994, hundreds of civilians sought refuge at the bureau communal, the majority of which were Tutsis, many of whom were women and girls. The ICTR Trial Chamber found that many of those who sought refuge became the victims of murder, torture, sexual violence, and rape under the leadership of Akayesu. He was charged with individual criminal responsibility for his failure to prevent violence and to arrest perpetrators of violence in his prefecture and commune, complicity with the murder of Tutsis, and inciting violence against them.

The Trial Chamber found that Akayesu's role and actions constituted genocidal violence, and he was charged with nine counts of complicity and incitement to genocide, crimes against humanity, and command responsibility for encouraging rape and sexual violence for the purpose of committing genocide. Genocide is a complex and comprehensive crime that includes the intent, planning, and/or commission of acts that are designed to destroy a specific group targeted on the grounds of national, ethnic, racial, or religious identity and affiliation. The ICTR found that sexual violence that included mutilation, sterilization, forced birth control, sex segregation, prohibition of marriages, and psychological damage, had the intent and effect of preventing births within the Tutsi population. These are among some of the reasons that the Trial Chamber found that rape and sexual violence constituted extreme mental and physical suffering, and was an element of the violence deployed for genocidal purposes under Akayesu's leadership. The decision is considered to be a breakthrough ruling in humanitarian law.

In a manner not unlike ICTY rulings, the ICTR and the Akayesu case reify ethnic differences and reduce persons to their ethnic affiliation in the prosecution of genocidal and sexual violence. In the Akayesu case, all Tutsi women were characterized as victims and though consent was not an explicit part of the ruling, the entire context is characterized as coercive. The implication is that any sexual acts committed between the Interahamwe men and Tutsi women are suspect. The jurisdiction of the ICTR limits its focus to Interahamwe violence against the Tutsi population, and this delimits the scope and focus of the tribunal to violence between ethnically defined and distinctive groups of people, namely Hutus and the Tutsis. In doing so, it is outside the jurisdiction of the ICTR to hear charges of systematic violence committed against Hutu women. Further, it is outside ICTR jurisdiction to issue charges against French and Belgian soldiers who allegedly committed rape and sexual violence against Rwandese women during their peacekeeping missions in Rwanda.[65] This is the case even though the violence was committed since the time of the establishment of the ICTR, that it potentially constitutes international criminal activity, and that it falls under humanitarian provisions governing violence against civilians.

Whether it is in the context of 'ethnic cleansing' or 'genocide,' the tribunals rely upon a biological or lineage-based foundation for determining the identity of victims and their relevance to the tribunals. This is the case even as the Trial Chamber notes that the determination of ethnic identities in Rwanda revolve around "objective" criteria, including patrilineal lines of heredity and government-issued identity cards, and subjective criteria that includes Rwandese own sense of belonging that has come to be culturally embedded.[66] Hence, several of the rulings revolve around the aspect of genocide legislation that condemns measures to prevent births within a group, including violence that has long-lasting mental or psychological impacts on a woman's future desire to procreate, presumably under circumstances where she is sexually autonomous. The ICTR also suggests that Tutsi women are victims who cannot be understood as political or sexual agents, who could not act on behalf of themselves or others, and who could not themselves be participants in the violence. The construction of women as victims, their sexuality as their weakness and their function as reproducers is affirmed by international tribunal decisions.[67] In the process, Hutu men are constituted as vicious and violent rapists.

Many of these results are the inadvertent, unanticipated, and unintended implications of the Akayesu and Kunarac trials. Yet, they are also the playing out of racialist thinking, that is that there are biological or indelible differences between peoples that cause conflicts and they must be managed through the mechanisms of law and criminalization. This is the case even when the Trial Chamber acknowledges that there is a larger context that could explain war and violence. For instance, the ICTR Trial Chamber in the Akayesu case noted that there had been propaganda campaigns prior to the genocide "to make the economic, social and political conflict look more like an ethnic conflict."[68] Yet, in the language of humanitarian law and the jurisdictional limitations of the ICTR, to hear charges against Akayesu means that his crimes have to be understood within the frameworks of ethnic conflict, and further, that his crimes exceed domestic legislation and fall within international legal frameworks governing genocide. Genocide legislation relies upon the ability to know victims in particular, but perpetrators too, through their ethnic, racial, national, or religious identity. Though these are social acquired identity markers, they become essentialized and biologized through the trial process. As such, the option to subject Rwandese to administrative and legal mechanisms that contain and regulate their interactions, particularly in relation to sexuality, becomes a logical outcome of racialized law.

The subjects of the laws of war are not just any gendered bodies. These are bodies that are racialized through colonial/global structures of power, and racialized again as victims and agents of exceptionally deviant and perverted violent sexuality through the colonial tropes and racial grammars of international laws governing war. International law racializes these bodies to be brought into modernity as subject peoples or second-tier sovereign subjects, triggering a regime of governance and management that revolves around sexual deviance and crime. The attempt to adjudicate sexual violence as genocide or as crimes against humanity through essentialized ethnic designations results in prohibitions on sexual relations between people who are not of the same ethnicity. In effect, the rulings result in anti-miscegenation laws and thus, take their place amongst the iconic administrative mechanisms of racial governance.

BIZARRE REPRESENTATIONS OF THE OTHER

The ICTY Trial Chamber deliberations in the Kunarac case involve three-hundred pages of evidence and testimony about women's experiences in and around the detention centers of Foča. Yet, several acts of alleged violence could not be adjudicated because they did not meet the conditions of the rules of evidence and relevance. Buss notes "the result is bizarre," suggesting that international criminal trials have an air of unreality about them that does not match the emotional content of the experiences that are recounted, nor their implicit demand that something retributive be done.[69] A similar sentiment can be expressed about the Akayesu case; it includes pages and pages of testimony about horrific experiences told in emotionless and dry tones, much of which conformed to the rules of evidence and jurisdictional relevance, and much of which did not.

The following excerpts from the Trial Chamber I Decision summarize the testimony of several witnesses, by way of establishing the grounds for prosecuting crimes of sexual violence. These testimonies are part of what led to the Trial Chamber decision to prosecute Akayesu for rape and sexual violence, genocide, and crimes against humanity. I include them here as examples of the way that narratives of sexual violence in war are documented in international criminal procedures.

> Allegations of sexual violence first came to the attention of the Chamber through the testimony of Witness J, a Tutsi woman, who stated that her six year-old daughter had been raped by three Interahamwe when they came to kill her father. On examination by the Chamber, Witness J also testified that she had heard that young girls were raped at the bureau communal. Subsequently, Witness H, a Tutsi woman, testified that she herself was raped in a sorghum field and that, just outside the compound of the bureau communal, she personally saw other Tutsi women being raped and knew of at least three such cases of rape by Interahamwe. Witness H testified initially that the Accused, as well as commune police officers, were present while this was happening and did nothing to prevent the rapes. However, on examination by the Chamber as to whether Akayesu was aware that the rapes were going on, she responded that she didn't know, but that it happened at the bureau communal and he knew that the women were there. Witness H stated that some of the rapes occurred in the bush area nearby but that some of them occurred 'on site.' On examination by the Chamber,

she said that the Accused was present during one of the rapes, but she could not confirm that he saw what was happening. While Witness H expressed the view that the Interahamwe acted with impunity and should have been prevented by the commune police and the Accused from committing abuses, she testified that no orders were given to the Interahamwe to rape. She also testified that she herself was beaten but not raped at the bureau communal.[70]

Following the amendment of the Indictment, Witness JJ, a Tutsi woman, testified about the events which took place in Taba after the plane crash. She said that she was driven away from her home, which was destroyed by her Hutu neighbours who attacked her and her family after a man came to the hill near where she lived and said that the bourgmestre had sent him so that no Tutsi would remain on the hill that night. Witness JJ saw her Tutsi neighbours killed and she fled, seeking refuge in a nearby forest with her baby on her back and her younger sister, who had been wounded in the attack by a blow with an axe and two machete cuts. As she was being chased everywhere she went, Witness JJ said she went to the bureau communal. There she found more than sixty refugees down the road and on the field nearby. She testified that most of the refugees were women and children.[71]

These segments of witness testimony are representative of the Trial Chamber narrative in its deliberations about the charges against Akayesu. Women tell of multiple and overlapping horrors. They are raped by their neighbors and friends after their fathers are killed in front of them, while their daughters are raped in front of them, after fleeing all night or spending the night in the rain or after walking over the body of their sister, or between discovering their house is destroyed and their husband has been killed.

Whether testimonies of this nature result in prosecutions or if they are dismissed for lack of relevance, something remains bizarre in the way these stories are told. In the process of court transcription, the form that the testimonies take stands quite apart from the content of the women's experiences. The content is horrific, yet the narrative form and the rules of relevance demand a focus on the facts without prejudice or emotion. Although it serves humanitarian law, there is a way that such documentation creates distance between those who experience the violence and those who hear and read about it. The court observes but cannot fully comprehend the unfathomable behavior of peoples whose ethnic and blood loyalties move them to violence. The trial becomes an experimental laboratory, delving into the motivations and interests and actions of people involved with the aim to uncover the violent, sexual, and irrational secrets of the Other. The clinical formality of an international criminal trial with its focus on the empirical facts of a case has the uncanny effect of revealing the behaviors, motivations and intentions of perpetrators in ways that creates distance between observer and observed, between us and Others. The unspoken motivation of the trial is to expose and scrutinize the violence that is already assumed to be the behaviors of agents who are depraved and irrational by the fact of establishing an international criminal tribunal in the first instance. The juxtaposition of the rationalized and unemotional trial procedure that purports to deal with facts without prejudice, with the exposure of horrendous acts of violence, brings into stark relief the otherness of those enacting the violence in contrast to the purveyors of international law.

Take, for instance, the ICTY case of Prosecutor v. Dragan Nikolic that found Nikolic guilty of crimes against humanity, torture, rape as a crime against humanity, and other grave breaches.[72] Under the section called "factors related to individual responsibility," the Sentencing Judgment included a subsection outlining the "depravity of the crimes," wherein beatings, murder, torture, and sexual violence were described as especially brutal and sadistic because "he played with the emotions of inmates and tortured them with his words."[73] The Trial Chamber noted a "chilling aspect" of his behavior is that Nikolic enjoyed the violence, and as such, "the depravity speaks for itself."[74] In the decision, the trial chamber comments, necessarily, on the political intent behind the violence committed by Nikolic to establish the jurisdiction of international law in the charges against him. However, the trial chamber is further moved to comment on Nikolic's personality as elements that compound the severity of the violence committed, thereby shifting the focus from Nikolic as an agent of the state and nation to the deep personality and psyche of Nikolic as a peculiarly depraved individual. In doing so, violations of the laws of war are spectacularized, suggesting that only genuinely depraved individuals would participate in such violations, or only his depravity could explain the violence.

What the laws of war count on is the participation in war of "social ideal types": responsible commanders, chivalrous officers, reliable non-commissioned officers, and disciplined foot soldiers.[75] This, however, is a contradictory and rather unlikely scenario that idealizes what it means to train for and engage in war. Armed forces are formally or informally trained in ways that cultivate a collective and individual willingness to commit violence against those designated as enemy, often through the repetition of racist and sexualized imagery and the cultivation of fear and hatred of the enemy. It is a leap of the imagination to think that chivalry, discipline, reliability, and responsibility are the leading concerns of armed forces in the midst of waging war. Yet, the ideal types of the laws of war are cast as the silent signifiers of European/Western militaries and their commitment to honoring the laws, in implicit contrast with those who are held accountable for illegitimate violence in war through war crimes tribunals.

When we consider that there are masses of testimonies similar to the ones outlined previously, refracted through court transcription and with emotional content excised, we should remember that an archive of case law and precedent-setting trials is consolidated on the basis of narratives about the spectacular violence of the Other through international criminal trials.

Further, that such an archive is developed solely through the investigation of violence committed by populations who are duly constituted as marginal, second-tier and Other to those presumed to respect international law creates a distorted and partial story about the purveyors of violence. The wars that become subject to international criminal trials are characterized as exceptionally brutal and vicious and excessive in their use of violence. Yet, the determination of what constitutes excessive violence, genocide, or a crime against humanity, is the interpretive privilege of the states and institutions of populations who historically have been understood as the inherent keepers of international law. In the terms of international law, it is the Other who commits the worst acts known to humanity. As such, the 'savage' or colonial 'other' of the laws of war is intrinsic to the logic of the laws themselves as the constitutive outsider that legitimates war crimes tribunals and international law.

CONCLUSION

Most feminist debates about the potential for gender justice through war crimes tribunals tend to be isolated from broader studies of violence against women and debates about legal remedies for violence against women. War is taken as a zone of exception where law is suspended, legitimacy has failed, and anything goes. Feminist hope for tribunals to achieve gender justice is in part derived from a sense that war zones must be transformed into places of lawfulness, where combatants honor the conventions and treaties designed to protect non-combatants and civilians from militarized violence. There is an investment (albeit skeptical) in legal mechanisms and a faith (albeit ambiguous) that justice can or must be achieved through the proper implementation of law, and the concept of legal legitimacy remains compelling. There are culturally persuasive narratives that contribute to the rhetorical power of naming violence and violators as 'war crimes' and 'war criminals,' designations that have come to represent the worst kinds of people and violence that can, or cannot, ever be imagined. The notion of criminalizing those who commit violence against women, especially in situations that appear to be utterly lawless, through the rhetorically persuasive mechanisms of the international justice system, offers an authoritative and active option to countering violence.

In international politics, however, war zones are actually already zones of lawfulness. They are law-saturated zones made possible by the logic of the sovereign state system that centralizes the legitimate right to wage war in the pursuit of sovereign interests. They are made possible by the UN Charter that grants states the right to wage war in defense of their individual interests, and that grants the UN Security Council the right to determine when collective military action will be taken against others. Lawful war zones are made possible by the Hague and Geneva Conventions and the multiple treaties that outline and delimit the parameters of legitimate war making.

As such, there is something puzzling about the discourse of humanitarian law and its animating precepts that declare that sorting legal violence from illegal violence, within a context that is inherently violent, is possible, necessary, and reasonable. Humanitarian law assumes that war and violence are inevitable parts of human existence, for which we must be in constant preparation. The sovereign state system is forged and maintained in conditions of violence, conquest, racism, and patriarchal authority that depend upon the logic of domination to function in its present constitution. Debates about violence against women in war have tended to exceptionalize such violence, yet when the sovereign state system is considered through the lens of colonial history, the historically specific and structural manifestations of ubiquitous violence are apparent.

Further, most feminist debates about the potential for gender justice through war crimes tribunals tend to be isolated from broader debates about the colonial foundations of international law. In doing so, feminist analyses sustain assumptions about the racial and national hierarchies central to international legal systems and meanings. While those hierarchies are coded and/or disappeared through liberal and legal universalisms, the concept of humanity itself is forged in a Euro-colonial context that continuously seeks to maintain Euro-derived whiteness as the definition of humanity.[76] Through the lens of colonial history, it becomes clear that as it has come to be constituted, the contemporary practice of naming of war crimes and spectacular violence is both a racialized and a racializing enterprise that reflects gendered and sexualized assumptions about the perverse sexuality of the Other.

This chapter suggests that structurally, international law maintains a commitment to its colonial precepts and racial grammars in contemporary international criminal tribunals governing the use of violence in war. Racial grammars themselves are structural and highly malleable; once in place, new populations can be subject to racialization and old racisms are deployed to serve new political ends, depending on the political needs of the moment. For this reason, it is important to investigate processes of racialization and the various ways that people come to be understood as the racial Other, rather than assume the fixity of racial categories.[77] International law developed to serve the interests of Euro-colonial states and nations as they sought to dominate the majority of the world's population. Sovereignty enshrines the right and capacity for full self-determination as intrinsic to the logic of Euro-descended states and an expression of masculinity and whiteness, while making it a contingent characteristic of non-Euro-descended peoples. The right to wage war and to use violence that exceeds contemporary humanitarian law is monopolized by Euro–American states, and international institutions continue to implement these rights by only holding those who are racialized as Other accountable for their crimes. The process of criminalization, itself a racializing process, further reifies the Other as an exceptionally deviant and sexually perverted agent, echoing the nineteenth century idea that they are illegitimate warriors and unfit to determine when the use of violence serves their interests. The monopoly on the use of violence is retained by Euro–American states through the consistent omission of criminalizing their violence, even when it exceeds humanitarian law parameters.

Further, criminalizing sexual violence through the racial taxonomy of international law results in legal decisions that suggest sexuality in general must be governed and authorized by agents of international law. The governance of sexuality is a core mission of European political traditions since at least the seventeenth century, and is central to racial administration. Women's bodies are the fulcrum around which decisions to intervene, colonize and restructure societies revolve, and men are either seen to be vicious aggressors, or the rightful protectors of women's virtue. In these various ways, international law iterates the colonial, racial, and sexual notion that women are not agentic, the world is made up of 'Us' and 'Them' or white and non-white, and produces that division in contemporary implementation of the law. In doing so, the body of case law generated through international criminal tribunals reiterates colonial commitments to retaining Euro–American authority over global affairs, especially in terms of the right to wage war, and is thus, key to neocolonial rule. Extending Bowden's argument about colonial rule, neocolonialism is also a juridical enterprise; international law is in the service of neocolonial interests in the contemporary era. To ensure that feminist work does not inadvertently support the work of empire by deploying racial and colonial hierarchies in the pursuit of gender justice, it is important to integrate an understanding of the colonial foundations and contemporary imperialist functions of international law in our analysis and advocacy. Given the ubiquity of war, militarist cultures and violence against women, it is crucial to resist the temptation to exceptionalize sexual violence against women as the work of the barbarous Other in wartime.

The insight from Narayan with which this chapter begins, that feminists need to account for the political function of border-crossing stories of violence against women if, in fact, the goal is to eradicate violence against women in solidarity with women, signals the need for careful attention to the historical development and contemporary context of geopolitics. Her argument further suggests that our own subjectivities are a necessary site of decolonization as they have come to be constituted through subterranean assumptions and racial grammars about the agents of spectacular violence, the legitimacy of (Euro–American) legal systems and the differential ability to be self-determining. In similar ways, Jacqui Alexander[78] suggests that a crucial center of imperial power, and the place from which feminists and other people of conscience might begin to unravel the dehumanization of both bequeathed and contemporaneous structures of domination, is within ourselves. As individuals who have come to be through the long histories of colonization and western imperialism, as subjects of capital and corporatization and the academy, we are the micro-embodiments of the palimpsest of here and now and then and there; with "psychic residues of the imperial project;"[79] subjectivities forged in circumstances that imply that divisions, hierarchies, exploitation, and the use of violence are just the way things are, and the way that things have always been. The wounds of imperialism sting our psyches; we are a collective body in pain.

Violence is an expression of humanity. Humans commit violence against each other, and if one amongst us is capable of violence, we all are capable of violence. This is not to suggest that violence is a natural condition of humanity. Rather, it is to say that violence is something that human beings commit, and all that human beings do is reflective of the collective capacities of humanity. If we begin to see that We are Them and They are Us, we move closer to an understanding of the conditions which make such violence possible, and the conditions that might unravel our violent and colonial engagements with each other. In doing so, contemporary feminism moves beyond establishing its relevance to the world in which we live, to become relevant to the emergence of possible new paradigms of human relations that abandon systemic commitments to domination. Shifting out of the paradigm rooted in violence and domination means abandoning attempts to solve problems through the same paradigms that created them, thereby ushering in a new planetary consciousness that brings with it concrete possibilities for peaceful coexistence.

ACKNOWLEDGEMENT

Much gratitude to Renée J. Heberle and Victoria Grace for their astute editorial guidance, Doris Buss for generously offering important clarifications of the law, and Mary Hawkesworth for her kind and continuous support.

NOTES

1. Frantz Fanon, *Black Skin, White Masks* (New York: Grove Press, 1967), 125.
2. Uma Narayan, "Cross-Cultural Connections, Border-Crossings, and 'Death by Culture,'" in *Dislocating Cultures: Identities, Traditions, and Third World Feminism* (New York: Routledge, 1997), 81–117.
3. Ania Loomba, *Colonialism/Postcolonialism* (New York: Routledge, 1998), 153.
4. Ibid.,164.
5. Jenny Sharpe, *Allegories of Empire: The Figure of Woman in the Colonial Text* (Minneapolis, MN: University of Minnesota Press, 1993).
6. Ibid., 7.
7. Helen Benedict, "The Private War of Women Soldiers," Salon.com, March 7, 2007, http://www.salon.com/news/feature/2007/03/07/women_in_military/

(accessed May 30, 2008); Marjorie Cohn, "Military Hides Cause of Women Soldiers' Deaths," Truthout.org, January 30, 2006, http://www.truthout.org/article/military-hides-cause-women-soldiers-deaths (accessed May 30, 2008); Jane Harman, "Rapists in the Ranks," Los Angeles Times, Opinion. March 31, 2008, http://www.latimes.com/news/opinion/commentary/la-oe-harman31mar31,0,5399612.story (accessed May 30, 2008).

8. Lila Rajiva, "Iraqi Women and Torture, Part I: Rapes and Rumors of Rapes," *Dissident Voice*, July 27, 2004, http://www.dissidentvoice.org/July2004/Rajiva0727.htm (accessed May 30, 2008); "Iraqi Women and Torture, Part I: Violence and Virtual Violence," *Dissident Voice*, August 4, 2004, http://www.dissidentvoice.org/Aug04/Rajiva0804.htm (accessed May 30, 2008); "Iraqi Women and Torture, Part II: Theater That Educates, News That Propagandizes," *Dissident Voice*, July 30, 2004, http://www.dissidentvoice.org/July2004/Rajiva0730.htm (accessed June 1, 2008).

9. Human Rights Watch, Human Rights News, "MONUC: A Case for Peacekeeping Reform," testimony of Anneke Van Woudenberg before the US House Committee on International Relations, Subcommittee on Africa, Global Human Rights and International Operations, March 1, 2004, http://www.hrw.org/english/docs/2005/03/01/congo10222.htm (accessed May 30, 2008); Sandra Whitworth, Men, Militarism & UN Peacekeeping: A Gendered Analysis (Boulder, CO: Lynne Rienner, 2004).

10. James Munyaneza and Felly Kimenyi, "Rwanda: Here It Is," *The New Times* (Kigali), November 17, 2007, http://allafrica.com/stories/200711170017.html (accessed May 30, 2008).

11. Talal Asad, *On Suicide Bombing* (New York: Columbia University Press, 2007), 22.

12. See Helen M. Kinsella, "Gendering Grotius: Sex and Sex Difference in the Laws of War," *Political Theory* 34 (2006): 161–191, for her discussion of the purpose of law, and humanitarian law in particular, for the maintenance of a Christian social order in the 1600s, and the traces of the hierarchy of nations that runs through subsequent humanitarian provisions of the Geneva Conventions.

13. Marilyn Lake and Henry Reynolds, *Drawing the Global Colour Line: White Men's Countries and the International Challenge of Racial Equality* (Cambridge, UK: Cambridge University Press, 2007).

14. Anne Orford, "Feminism, Imperialism and the Mission of International Law," *Nordic Journal of International Law* 71 (2002): 275–296; "Muscular Humanitarianism: Reading the Narratives of the New Interventionism," *European Journal of International Law* 10, 4 (1999): 679–711.

15. Carl Schmitt, *The Nomos of the Earth in the International Law of the Jus Publicum Europaeum* (New York: Telos Press Publishing, 2003).

16. Ibid., 86.

17. Michael W. Reisman and Chris T Antoniou, eds., *The Laws of War: A Comprehensive Collection of Primary Documents on International Laws Governing Armed Conflict* (New York: Vintage Press, 1974), 38–283.

18. Frederic Mégret, "From 'Savages' to 'Unlawful Combatants': A Postcolonial Look at International Humanitarian Law's Other," in *International Law and Its Others*, ed., Anne Orford (Cambridge, UK: Cambridge University Press, 2006), 265–317.

19. Ibid.

20. Lake and Reynolds, op. cit., 12.

21. Ibid., 123.

22. Anthony Anghie, *Imperialism, Sovereignty and the Making of International Law* (Cambridge, UK: Cambridge University Press, 2004); Brett Bowden,

"The Colonial Origins of International Law, European Expansion and the Classical Standard of Civilization," *Journal of the History of International Law* 7, 1 (April 2005): 1–23.

23. Teemu Ruskola, "Canton is not Boston: The Invention of American Imperial Sovereignty". *American Quarterly* 57, 3 (September 2005): 863.

24. Anghie, op. cit.

25. Ibid., 3.

26. Kinsella, op. cit.

27. Ann Laura Stoler, *Carnal Knowledge and Imperial Power: Race and the Intimate in Colonial Rule* (Berkeley, CA: University of California Press, 2002); Ann Laura Stoler, *Race and the Education of Desire: Foucault's History of Sexuality and the Colonial Order of Things* (Durham, NC: Duke University Press, 1997); Loomba, op. cit., 151–183; Michel Foucault, *The History of Sexuality: An Introduction, Volume 1* (New York: Vintage Books, 1990), 135–159.

28. George Frederickson, *Racism: A Short History* (Princeton, NJ: Princeton University Press, 2002), 5.

29. Kalpana Sheshadri-Crooks, *Desiring Whiteness: A Lacanian Analysis of Race* (New York: Routledge, 2000).

30. Loomba, op. cit., 151.

31. Ibid., 152.

32. Ibid., 154.

33. Anne McLintock, *Imperial Leather: Race, Gender and Sexuality in the Colonial Contest* (New York: Routledge, 1995), 22.

34. Stoler, 1997, op. cit.; Loomba, op. cit., 159.

35. Stoler, ibid.; McLintock, op. cit.; Anna Davin, "Imperialism and Motherhood," in *An Introduction to Women's Studies: Gender in a Transnational World*, 2nd edition, eds. Inderpal Grewal and Caren Kaplan (New York: McGraw-Hill, 2006), 60–66.

36. Orford, 2002, op. cit.; Narayan, op. cit.

37. Orford, ibid.; Liz Philipose, "The Politics of Pain and the End of Empire," *International Feminist Journal of Politics* 9, 1 (2007): 60–81.

38. Stoler, 1997, op. cit.; Stoler, 2002, op. cit.; McLintock, op. cit.; Loomba, op. cit.; Fanon, op. cit.; David Theo Goldberg, *Racist Culture: Philosophy and the Politics of Meaning* (Oxford, UK: Blackwell Press, 1993); Edward Said, *Orientalism* (New York: Vintage Press, 1979).

39. Anghie, op. cit., 48.

40. Ibid.

41. Goldberg, op. cit.

42. Liz Philipose, "The Laws of War and Women's Human Rights," *Hypatia* 11, 4 (Fall 1996): 46–62.

43. Kinsella, op. cit., notes that the distinction between the civilized and the barbaric is derived from Euro-Christian concepts, and thus predates modern forms of racism and modern European colonialism. This connects with Frederickson who traces the emergence of racism, "mainly, if not exclusively, a product of the West," to the fourteenth and fifteenth centuries, "originally articulated in the idioms of religion more than in those of natural science" (Frederickson, op. cit., 6). While there are historically specific distinctions to be made for each manifestation of racism, Frederickson argues that there is a historical trajectory in the development of racist thought that links Christian concepts with subsequent scientific forms of racism.

44. Liz Philipose, "Prosecuting Violence, Performing Sovereignty: The Trial of Dusko Tadic," *International Journal for the Semiotics of Law* 15 (2002): 159–184.

45. Brett Bowden, "In the Name of Progress and Peace: The 'Standard of Civilization' and the Universalizing Project," *Alternatives* 29 (2004): 51.
46. Brett Bowden, "Globalisation and the Shifting 'Standard of Civilization' in International Society," refereed paper presented to the Australasian Political Studies Association, Australia National University, 2002, arts.anu.edu.au/sss/apsa/Papers/bowden.pdf (accessed May 30, 2008).
47. As Yugoslavian states sought autonomy from the federated republic, the region was targeted as a new market for cheap labor and foreign investment and as a second-tier in the hierarchical system of economic globalization. The Dayton Peace Accords that partitioned the state into ethnic enclaves, "ethnic cleansing by other means", included provisions that put the IMF in charge of the BH and Croatian central banks and promises for economic liberalization. See David Campbell, National Deconstruction: Violence, Identity and Justice in Bosnia (Minneapolis, MN: University of Minnesota Press, 1998), 178. The evil of Slobodan Milosevic, from the perspective of the United States in particular, was that he was a nationalist who aimed to keep his markets closed, protect industry, and to shift from a dollar dependency to the Euro. See Michel Chossudovsky, "Dismantling Former Yugoslavia, Recolonising Bosnia," 1996, http://www.nadir.org/nadir/initiativ/agp/free/chossudovsky/dismanteling.htm (accessed June 1, 2008); "NATO's War of Aggression Against Yugoslavia: An Overview," 1999, http://www.nadir.org/nadir/initiativ/agp/free/chossudovsky/overview.htm (accessed June 1, 2008).
48. Orford, 1999, op. cit.; Orford, 2002, op. cit.; Ratna Kapur, "The Tragedy of Victimization Rhetoric: Resurrecting the Native Subject in International/Postcolonial Feminist Legal Politics," *Harvard Human Rights Law Journal* 15 (2002): 1–37.
49. See Kinsella, op. cit., for her discussion of the assumptions of international law that rely on gendered and heterosexual concepts of power and the regulation of sex and sex difference, from household arrangements that situate women as the subjects of men, to prohibitions against the rape of women in war.
50. Karen Engle, "Feminism and its (Dis)contents: Criminalizing Wartime Rape in Bosnia and Herzegovina," *American Journal of International Law* 99 (2005): 778–804; Doris Buss, "Women at the Borders: Rape and Nationalism in International Law," Feminist Legal Studies 6, 2 (1998): 171–203; Philipose, 1996, op. cit.; Rhonda Copelon, "Surfacing Gender: Reconceptualizing Crimes Against Women in Time of War," in *Mass Rape: The War Against Women in Bosnia-Herzegovina*, ed. Alexandra Stiglmayer (Lincoln, NE: University of Nebraska Press, 1994), 1–34.
51. Buss, ibid.; Chossudovsky, 1996, op. cit.; Chossudovsky, 1999, op. cit.
52. Buss, ibid.; Orford, 1999, op. cit.
53. Kinsella, op. cit.
54. International Criminal Tribunal for the former Yugoslavia, Trial and Appeals Chambers, "Kunarac et al." (IT-96–23&23/1) "Foča," http://www.un.org/icty/cases-e/index-e.htm (accessed June 1, 2008).
55. International Criminal Tribunal for Rwanda, Trial and Appeals Chamber Decisions, "The Prosecutor versus Jean-Paul Akayesu," Case No.ICTR-96–4-T, http://69.94.11.53/default.htm (accessed June 1, 2008).
56. Copelon, op. cit.
57. Doris Buss, "Prosecuting Mass Rape: Prosecutor v. Dragaojub Kunarac, Radomir Kovac and Zoran Vukovic," *Feminist Legal Studies* 10 (2002): 91–99.
58. Engle, op. cit.
59. United Nations Security Council, Resolution 827 (1993) (S/RES/827 (1993)), http://www.un.org/icty/legaldoc-e/basic/statut/S-RES-827_93.htm (accessed May 30, 2008).

60. Karen Engle offers a discussion of the disputes amongst advocates about whether the focus should be on 'genocidal rape' and thereby restricted to prosecuting the violence committed by Serb forces; or whether all rapes committed in the region should be under the jurisdiction of the ICTY. A third set of debates questioned why wartime rape would be seen as distinct and more injurious than 'everyday rape'. See Engle, op. cit.

61. The Celebici case charged Bosnian Muslim defendants with committing rape and sexual violence against Serbian women; and the Furundzija case prosecuted crimes committed by Croatian defendants. Together with the Kunarac decision, these cases comprise ICTY jurisprudence on rape and sexual violence. See ICTY, "Furundžija" (IT-95-17/1) "Lašva Valley"; and "Mucić et al." (IT-96-21) "Čelebici," http://www.un.org/icty/cases-e/index-e.htm. (accessed June 1, 2008).

62. Engle, op. cit., 804.

63. Ruth Miller describes the potential adoption of the Kunarac decision in Turkish rape law, arguing that the effects of doing so are potentially problematic for the sexual autonomy of both men and women. See Ruth A. Miller, "Rape and the Exception in Turkish and International Law," *Washington and Lee Law Review* 64, 4 (2007): 1349–1362.

64. Campbell, op. cit.; Philipose, 2002, op. cit.

65. Munyaneza, op. cit.

66. International Criminal Tribunal for Rwanda, "The Prosecutor versus Jean-Paul Akayesu", Case No.ICTR-96-4-T, Chamber I Judgment, 2 September 1998: paragraphs 168–173, http://69.94.11.53/default.htm (accessed June 1, 2008).

67. Buss, 2002, op. cit.; Engle, op. cit.

68. ICTR, op. cit., paragraph 99 (my emphasis).

69. Buss, 2002, op. cit., 98.

70. ICTR, op. cit. paragraph 416.

71. ICTR, ibid., paragraph 418.

72. ICTY, Prosecutor V Dragan Nikolic, Case IT-94-2-S, Sentencing Judgment, 18 December 2003.

73. Ibid.

74. Ibid.

75. Mégrét, op. cit., 313.

76. Goldberg, op. cit.

77. See my argument about racial structures of perception in Liz Philipose, "The Politics of Pain and the Uses of Torture," *Signs* 34, 4 (Summer 2007): 1047–1071.

78. Jacqui M. Alexander, *Pedagogies of Crossing: Meditations on Feminism, Sexual Politics, Memory and the Sacred* (Durham NC: Duke University Press, 2005).

79. Ibid., 115.

Contributors

Melanie Boyd is a postdoctoral lecturer in Women's, Gender, and Sexuality Studies at Yale University. Her research focuses on the construction and distribution of agency within feminist testimonial politics. She is currently completing a project on shifting rhetorics of victimhood within US and Canadian narratives of father–daughter incest, entitled *Unsettling Intimacy: Feminist Victimhood in the Aftermath of Sentimentality*.

Ann J. Cahill is Associate Professor of Philosophy at Elon University. She is the author of *Rethinking Rape* (2001, Cornell University Press), and the co-editor of *Continental Feminism Reader* (2003, Routledge) and *Critical Evaluations in Cultural Theory: de Beauvoir, Kristeva, Cixous, and Irigaray* (2008, Routledge). She is currently working on a full-length work, tentatively titled *Feeling Bodies: Ethics, Materiality, and the Problem of Objectification*, that explores the concept of sexual objectification.

Nicola Gavey is Associate Professor of Psychology at the University of Auckland, New Zealand, where she teaches in the areas of gender and sexuality. Her research has focused on a critical examination of the continuities between rape, sexual coercion, and more normative forms of gendered heterosexual practice. She has published numerous journal articles and book chapters. Her 2005 book, *Just Sex? The Cultural Scaffolding of Rape* received a 2006 Distinguished Publication Award from the Association for Women in Psychology.

Victoria Grace is Professor of Sociology and Gender Studies at the University of Canterbury, New Zealand. She is the author of *Baudrillard's Challenge: A Feminist Reading* (Routledge, 2000), co-editor of *Baudrillard West of the Dateline* (Dunmore Press, 2003), and is currently writing a book *Victims, Gender and Jouissance* (forthcoming, Routledge). She has published widely on a number of substantive topics in the broad field of critical science studies of health and medicine, and has an interest in psychosomatics and psychoanalysis.

Renée J. Heberle is Associate Professor of Political Science and co-director of the Program in Law and Social Thought at the University of Toledo. She works in the areas of political philosophy, feminist theory and politics, and law and society. Her particular research agenda focuses on state, civil, and private forms of violence, philosophical and practical approaches. She is the author of several essays, editor of and contributor to *Feminist Interpretations of Theodor Adorno* and co-editor of *Imagining Law: On Drucilla Cornell.*

Ann V. Murphy is Assistant Professor of Philosophy at Fordham University in New York City. Her background is in twentieth century French philosophy, phenomenology, political philosophy and feminist theory. Her current research focuses on violence, vulnerability, and embodiment.

Meghana Nayak is Assistant Professor of Political Science and teaches in the Women's and Gender Studies Department at Pace University–New York City. She received her PhD in Political Science and Graduate Minor in Feminist Studies from the University of Minnesota (2003). Her teaching and research interests include feminist security studies, international law and human rights, and the gendered politics of religion and violence. She is co-editor, with Jennifer Suchland, of the special issue, "Gender Violence and Hegemonic Projects," in the *International Feminist Journal of Politics* (2006), and co-author, with Eric Selbin, of *Doing International Relations from the Margins* (forthcoming, Zed Books).

Elizabeth Philipose is Associate Professor of Women's Studies at California State University, Long Beach. She received her PhD in Political Science from York University, Toronto. Her teaching and research interests are in critical race and feminist theory, colonial history, international law, militarist cultures, and the role of emotions in global politics. Her articles have appeared in *Hypatia, Signs, International Feminist Journal of Politics,* and in edited collections on feminism and war.

Index

Printed in the USA/Agawam, MA
October 13, 2011

561857.017